London Yearly Meeting o. Society of Friends

Extracts from the Minutes and Epistles

of the Yearly Meeting of the Religious Society of Friends held in London, from its first institution to the present time, relating to Christian doctrine, practice and discipline. Fourth Edition

London Yearly Meeting o. Society of Friends

Extracts from the Minutes and Epistles
of the Yearly Meeting of the Religious Society of Friends held in London, from its first institution to the present time, relating to Christian doctrine, practice and discipline. Fourth Edition

ISBN/EAN: 9783337266547

Printed in Europe, USA, Canada, Australia, Japan

Cover: Foto ©Lupo / pixelio.de

More available books at **www.hansebooks.com**

EXTRACTS FROM

THE MINUTES AND EPISTLES

OF

THE YEARLY MEETING

OF THE

RELIGIOUS SOCIETY OF FRIENDS,

HELD IN LONDON,

FROM ITS FIRST INSTITUTION TO THE PRESENT TIME,

RELATING TO

CHRISTIAN DOCTRINE,

PRACTICE, AND DISCIPLINE.

Fourth Edition.

LONDON:
FRIENDS' BOOK DEPOSITORY, 86, HOUNDSDITCH.

1861.

PREFACE.

To bear witness by practice, as well as by profession, to righteousness and true holiness, as necessary fruits of faith in our Lord and Saviour, is one of the great duties of the Christian Church. This important truth our religious Society has, from an early period of its history, earnestly endeavoured to uphold ; evidence of which will be found in the ensuing pages, consisting of statements of Christian doctrine and counsel, as well as of regulations for the maintenance of good order, adopted from time to time by the Yearly Meeting, as the representative body of the Society.

From the year 1672, down to 1781, the minutes of the Yearly Meeting, in relation to these subjects, were preserved and circulated in manuscript — each Monthly or Quarterly Meeting being expected to make provision for the supply of copies for the use of its own members. In the year 1781, the Meeting for Sufferings, by direction of the Yearly Meeting, prepared a digest of the regulations and advices issued up to that period. This was afterwards carefully revised, and "compared with the original records," by a large committee appointed by the Yearly Meeting to unite with the Meeting for Sufferings in the service ; and, having been submitted to the Yearly Meeting of 1782, was soon afterwards published, as approved by that meeting, under the title of "Extracts from the Minutes and Advices of the Yearly Meeting of Friends held in London from its first institution."

The first edition had been in circulation about eighteen years, when the Yearly Meeting recommended the Quarterly Meetings to send representatives to London to join the Meeting for Sufferings in revising the whole, and preparing a new edition. In proceeding with this work, "it was found expedient to omit several advices which stood in the first edition; chiefly because there were others under the same head of equal or superior pertinency; or because, in a few instances, it seemed eligible to exchange them for others issued since the printing of the Book of Extracts; and there was a considerable abridgment of some of those which remained." Some change was also made in the general arrangement of the contents. The volume, thus revised, was adopted by the Yearly Meeting of 1801, and published in 1802.

A third and enlarged edition, after undergoing a similar course of revision, was issued by direction of the Yearly Meeting in the year 1834, under the title of "Rules of Discipline of the religious Society of Friends, with Advices, being Extracts from the Minutes and Epistles of their Yearly Meeting, held in London from its first institution." A supplement to this volume appeared in 1849.

This edition being nearly exhausted, and various alterations having been made in some of our disciplinary regulations within the last few years, another edition became necessary, the preparation of which was, as on previous occasions, referred by the Yearly Meeting of 1860 to the Meeting for Sufferings, in conjunction with representatives from the several Quarterly or General Meetings. The results of the care and patient attention bestowed upon this important service were presented to our last Yearly Meeting, and, with a few alterations then agreed to, form the contents of the present volume.

As on former occasions, considerable omissions have been made, and new matter has been added. Under the conviction that all sound Christian practice must be based upon the unchangeable truth of the Gospel of our Holy Redeemer, it has been thought right to commence the work with a chapter on "Christian Doctrine," consisting of extracts from documents issued at different periods on behalf of the Society. The other materials are comprised in two chapters, bearing the titles of "Christian Practice," and "Christian Discipline." These have been subdivided into sections, according to the various subjects to which they relate. This arrangement of the work renders it more convenient for reference, and, at the same time, tends to increase its usefulness, by presenting in a clearer and more intelligible form than heretofore the important subjects on which it treats.

The variety and excellence of the matter offered to the reader invite an attentive and serious perusal. There will be found instruction for the inexperienced, as well as that which may confirm the faith of the more advanced Christian. The inquirer after truth may here see that the maintenance of Christian discipline is altogether compatible with the just claims of Christian liberty; and that, without the intervention of a human priesthood, and without any provision either for the appointment or for the payment of a stated ministry, the regular performance of public worship, and the free exercise of spiritual gifts, may be secured in a manner which long experience has proved to be in harmony with the apostolic injunction, "Let all things be done decently and in order."

To the members of our own Society we commend the ensuing pages, in the earnest desire that the blessing of the Lord may rest upon their publication. May it ever be borne in mind that rules, however wisely devised or carefully digested, if acted on with a mere rigid adherence to the letter, will tend only to formalism. It is a marked feature of this volume, that whilst exhibiting the *form* of our discipline, it bears abundant testimony to the *spirit* in which it should be conducted—to that wisdom, patience, forbearance and love, which ought ever to prevail in the hearts of those engaged in its administration.

MEETING FOR SUFFERINGS, LONDON,
Eleventh Month 15th, 1861.

NOTICE TO THE READER.

In this compilation are included documents of various dates. The figures appended to the extracts indicate the respective years in which they were issued. Where two or more dates are appended to one paragraph, it is intended to show either that some change has been made in the original at the time of the second or other later date, or that two or more paragraphs, issued at different times, have been combined. The letters P. E. added to the date denote that the paragraph was taken from a printed epistle of the Yearly Meeting; whilst all paragraphs to which these letters are not affixed were taken either from special addresses, or from minutes issued by that meeting.

CONTENTS.

	PAGE
CHAP. I.—CHRISTIAN DOCTRINE	1
CHAP. II.—CHRISTIAN PRACTICE	
SECTION I.—MEETINGS FOR PUBLIC WORSHIP	22
II.—PRIVATE RETIREMENT AND PRAYER	28
III.—ON READING THE HOLY SCRIPTURES	31
IV.—ON GIFTS AND SERVICES FOR THE RELIGIOUS BENEFIT OF OTHERS	37
V.—GENERAL CHRISTIAN COUNSEL	42
VI.—EXHORTATIONS TO CHRISTIAN SIMPLICITY, MODERATION, AND SELF-DENIAL	47
VII.—EXHORTATIONS TO LOVE AND UNITY	55
VIII.—EXHORTATIONS TO LIBERALITY AND BENEVOLENCE	61
IX.—ADVICE IN RELATION TO THE MINISTRY	63
X.—COUNSEL TO PARENTS AND HEADS OF FAMILIES	66
XI.—COUNSEL TO EMPLOYERS	76
XII.—COUNSEL TO THE YOUNG	77
XIII.—ADVICE IN RELATION TO MARRIAGE	83
XIV.—ADVICE IN RELATION TO THE AFFAIRS OF THIS LIFE	86
XV.—ADVICE TO EMIGRANTS	96
XVI.—AMUSEMENTS AND RECREATIONS	97
XVII.—ON BOOKS AND READING	101
XVIII.—ON THE RIGHT OCCUPATION OF THE FIRST DAY OF THE WEEK	103
XIX.—ECCLESIASTICAL DEMANDS	104
XX.—ON WAR	108
XXI.—SLAVERY AND THE SLAVE-TRADE	113

		PAGE
XXII.—Oaths		118
XXIII.—Advice in Relation to Civil Government		120
XXIV.—National Fasts and Rejoicings		125
XXV.—Burials and Mourning Habits		127

CHAP. III.—CHRISTIAN DISCIPLINE.

Historical Sketch		129
Section I.—Yearly Meeting		139
II.—Quarterly Meetings		142
III.—Monthly Meetings		143
IV.—Preparative Meetings		155
V.—Women's Meetings		156
VI.—Australian Meetings for Discipline		158
VII.—General Counsel in Relation to Meetings for Discipline		160
VIII.—Advices		165
IX.—Queries		167
X.—Oversight		171
XI.—Ministers and Elders, and their Meetings		178
XII.—Meeting for Sufferings		184
XIII.—National Stock		189
XIV.—Care of the Poor		191
XV.—Marriage Regulations		193
XVI.—Regulations for Recording Births and Deaths		208
XVII.—Removals		213
XVIII.—Arbitration		217
XIX.—Appeals		221
XX.—Trust Property		232
Conclusion		237

CHAPTER I.

CHRISTIAN DOCTRINE.

FROM AN EPISTLE ADDRESSED BY GEORGE FOX AND OTHERS, TO THE GOVERNOR OF BARBADOES, 1671.

We do own and believe in God, the only wise, omnipotent, and everlasting God, who is the Creator of all things both in heaven and in the earth, and the Preserver of all that He hath made; who is God over all, blessed for ever; to whom be all honour and glory, dominion, praise and thanksgiving, both now and for evermore! And we do own and believe in Jesus Christ, his beloved and only begotten Son, in whom He is well pleased; who was conceived by the Holy Ghost, and born of the Virgin Mary; in whom we have redemption through his blood, even the forgiveness of sins; who is the express image of the invisible God, the first-born of every creature, by whom were all things created that are in heaven and that are in earth, visible and invisible, whether they be thrones, or dominions, or principalities, or powers; all things were created by Him. And we do own and believe that He was made a sacrifice for sin, who knew no sin, neither was guile found in his mouth; and that He was crucified for us in the flesh, without the gates of Jerusalem; and that He was buried, and rose again the third day by the power of his Father, for our justification; and we do believe that He ascended up into heaven, and now sitteth at the right hand of God. This Jesus, who was the foundation of the holy prophets and apostles, is our foundation; and we do believe that there is no other foundation to be laid but that which is laid, even Christ Jesus; who, we believe, tasted death for every man, and shed his blood for all men, and is the propitiation for our sins, and not for ours only, but also for the sins of the whole world: according as John the Baptist testified of Him, when he said, "Behold the Lamb of God, which taketh away the sin of the world," John i. 29. We believe that He alone is our Redeemer and Saviour, even the Captain of our salvation, (who saves us from sin, as well as from hell and the wrath to come, and destroys the devil and his works) who is the Seed of the woman that bruises the serpent's head, to wit, Christ Jesus, the Alpha and Omega, the First and the Last. That He is (as the Scriptures of truth say of Him) our wisdom and righteousness, justification and redemption; neither is there salvation in any other, for there is no other name under heaven given among men, whereby we may be saved. It is He alone who is the Shepherd and Bishop of our souls: He it is who is our Prophet, whom Moses long since testified of, saying, "A prophet shall the Lord your God raise up unto you of your brethren, like unto me; him shall ye hear in all things whatsoever he shall say unto you: and it shall come to pass, that every soul which will not hear that prophet shall be destroyed from among the people," Acts iii. 22, 23. He it is that is now come "and hath given us an understanding, that we may know Him that is true." And He rules in our hearts by his law of love and of life, and makes us free from the law of sin and death. And we have no life but by Him; for He is the quickening Spirit, the second Adam, the Lord from Heaven, by whose blood we are cleansed, and our consciences sprinkled from dead works, to serve the living God. And He is our Mediator, that makes peace and reconciliation between God offended and us offending; He being the Oath of God, the new covenant of light, life, grace, and peace; the Author and Finisher of our faith. Now this Lord Jesus Christ, the heavenly man, the Emmanuel, God with us, we all own and believe in; Him whom the high-priest raged against, and said He had spoken blasphemy; whom the priests and the elders of the Jews took counsel together against, and put to death; the same whom Judas betrayed for thirty pieces of silver, which the priests gave him as a reward for his treason; who also gave large money to the soldiers to broach an horrible lie, namely, that his disciples came and stole Him away by night whilst they slept. And after He was risen from the dead, the history of the acts of the apostles sets forth how the chief priests and elders persecuted the disciples of this Jesus, for preaching Christ and his resurrection. This, we say, is that Lord Jesus Christ, whom we own to be our life and salvation.

And as concerning the Holy Scriptures, we do believe that they were given forth by the Holy Spirit of God, through the holy men of God, who (as the Scripture itself declares, 2 Pet. i. 21,) "spake as they were moved by the Holy Ghost." We believe they are to be read, believed, and fulfilled (He that fulfils them is Christ;) and they are "profitable for doctrine, for reproof, for correction, for instruction in righteousness, that the man. of God may be perfect, throughly furnished unto all good works," 2 Tim. iii. 16, 17; and are able to make wise "unto salvation, through faith which is in Christ Jesus." We call the Holy Scriptures, as Christ and the apostles called them, and holy men of God called them—the words of God.

We do declare, that we do esteem it a duty incumbent on us to pray with and for, to teach, instruct, and admonish, those in and belonging to our families. Now Negroes (and) Indians make up a very great part of the families in this island, for whom an account will be required by Him who comes to judge both quick and dead, at the great day of judgment, when every one shall be rewarded according to the deeds done in the body, whether they be good or whether they be evil: at that day, I say, of the resurrection both of the good and of the bad, of the just and the unjust, "when the Lord Jesus shall be revealed from heaven with his mighty angels, in flaming fire, taking vengeance on them that know not God, and obey not the Gospel of our Lord Jesus Christ: who shall be punished with everlasting destruction from the presence of the Lord, and from the glory of his power; when He shall come to be glorified in his saints, and to be admired in all them that believe in that day," 2 Thess. i. 7–10. See also 2 Pet. iii. 3, &c.

FROM THE GENERAL EPISTLE, 1683.

May all keep and walk in Christ Jesus, the Sanctuary; for in Him are peace and safety, who destroys the destroyer, the enmity, and adversary. For Christ is your Sanctuary in this day of storm and tempest, in whom you have rest and peace. And, therefore, whatever storms or tempests do or should arise within or without, Christ your Sanctuary is over them all, who has all power in heaven and earth given unto Him; and none is able to pluck his lambs and sheep out of his Father's or his hand, who is the true Shepherd; neither are any able to hurt the hair of your head, except it be permitted by his power for your trial. And therefore rejoice in his power, the Lamb of God who hath the victory over all, both within and without; He by whom all things were made, and is over all; the first and the last; the Amen.

FROM A DECLARATION OF CHRISTIAN DOCTRINE GIVEN FORTH ON BEHALF OF THE SOCIETY, 1693.

We sincerely profess faith in God by his only begotten Son, Jesus Christ, as being our Light and Life, our only way to the Father, and also our only Mediator and Advocate with the Father.

That God created all things; He made the worlds, by his Son Jesus Christ, He being that powerful and living Word of God, by whom all things were made; and that the Father, the Word, and the Holy Spirit are one, in divine being inseparable; one true, living, and eternal God, blessed for ever.

Yet that this Word, or Son of God, in the fulness of time, took flesh, became perfect man according to the flesh, descended and came of the seed of Abraham and David; but was miraculously conceived by the Holy Ghost, and born of the Virgin Mary: and also further, declared powerfully to be the Son of God, according to the spirit of sanctification, by the resurrection from the dead.

That in the Word (or Son of God) was life, and the same life was the light of men; and that He was that true light which enlightens every man coming into the world; and therefore that men are to believe in the light, that they may become the children of the light. Hereby we believe in Christ the Son of God, as He is the light and life within us; and wherein we must needs have sincere respect and honour to (and belief in) Christ, as in his own unapproachable and incomprehensible glory and fulness; as He is the fountain of life and light, and giver thereof unto us; Christ, as in Himself, and as in us, being not divided. And that as man, Christ died for our sins, rose again, and was received up into glory, in the heavens. He having, in his dying for all, been that one great universal offering and sacrifice for peace, atonement, and reconciliation between God and man; and He is the propitiation not for our sins only, but for the sins of the whole world.

That Jesus Christ, who sitteth at the right hand of the throne of the Majesty in the heavens, yet is He our King, High Priest, and Prophet; in his church, a Minister of the sanctuary, and of the true tabernacle which the Lord pitched, and not man. He is Intercessor and Advocate with the Father in heaven, and there appearing in the presence of God for us, being touched with the feeling of our infirmities, sufferings, and sorrows. And also by his Spirit in our hearts, He maketh intercession according to the will of God, crying, Abba, Father.

That the Gospel of the grace of God should be preached in the name of the Father, Son, and Holy Ghost, being one in power, wisdom, and goodness, and indivisible (or not to be divided,) in the great work of man's salvation.

We sincerely confess (and believe in) Jesus Christ, both as He is true God, and perfect man, and that He is the author of our living faith in the power and goodness of God, as manifested in his Son Jesus Christ, and by his own blessed Spirit (or divine unction) revealed in us, whereby we inwardly feel and taste of his goodness, life, and virtue; so as our souls live and prosper by and in Him: and the inward sense of this divine power of Christ, and faith in the same, and the inward experience, are absolutely necessary to make a true, sincere, and perfect Christian in spirit and life.

That divine honour and worship is due to the Son of God; and that He is, in true faith, to be prayed unto, and the name of the Lord Jesus Christ called upon (as the primitive Christians did), because of the glorious union or oneness of the Father and the Son, and that we cannot acceptably offer up prayers and praises to God, nor receive a gracious answer or blessing from God, but in and through his dear Son.

That Christ's body that was crucified was not the Godhead, yet by the power of God was raised from the dead; and that the same Christ that was therein crucified, ascended into heaven and glory, is not questioned by us. His flesh saw no corruption, it did not corrupt; but yet doubtless his body was changed into a more glorious and heavenly condition than it was in when subject to divers sufferings on earth; but how and what manner of change it met withal after it was raised from the dead, so as to become such a glorious body as it is declared to be, is too wonderful for mortals to conceive. The Scripture is silent therein, as to the manner thereof, and we are not curious to inquire or dispute it; nor do we esteem it necessary to make ourselves wise above what is written, as to the manner or condition of Christ's glorious body, as in heaven; no more than to enquire how Christ appeared in divers manners or forms; or how He came in among his disciples, the doors being shut; or how He vanished out of their sight, after He was risen. However, we have cause to believe his body, as in heaven, is changed into a most glorious condition, far transcending what it was in on earth, otherwise how should our low body be changed, so as to be made like unto his glorious body; for when He was on earth, and attended with sufferings, He was said to be like unto us in all things, sin only excepted; which may not be so said of Him as now in a state of glory; otherwise where would be the change both in Him and in us.

Concerning the resurrection of the dead, and the great day of judgment yet to come, beyond the grave, or after death, and Christ's coming without us, to judge the quick and the dead; what the Holy Scriptures plainly declare and testify in these matters, we have been always ready to embrace.

1. For the doctrine of the resurrection: "If in this life only we have hope in Christ, we are of all men most miserable," 1 Cor. xv. 19. We sincerely believe not only a resurrection in Christ from the fallen sinful state here, but a rising and ascending into glory with Him hereafter; that when He at last appears, we may appear with Him in glory. Col. iii. 4; 1 John iii. 2. But that all the wicked who live in rebellion against the light of grace, and die finally impenitent, shall come forth to the resurrection of condemnation. And that the soul or spirit of every man and woman shall be reserved in its own distinct and proper being, and every seed (yea every soul) shall have its proper body, as God is pleased to give it, 1 Cor. xv. A natural body

is sown, a spiritual body is raised; that being first which is natural, and afterward that which is spiritual. And though it is said, this corruptible shall put on incorruption, and this mortal shall put on immortality; the change shall be such as (will accord with the declaration) "flesh and blood cannot inherit the kingdom of God, neither doth corruption inherit incorruption," 1 Cor. xv. 50. We shall be raised out of all corruption and corruptibility, out of all mortality; and the children of God and of the resurrection shall be equal to the angels of God in heaven. As the celestial bodies do far excel terrestrial, so we expect our spiritual bodies in the resurrection shall far excel what our bodies now are. Howbeit we esteem it very unnecessary to dispute or question how the dead are raised, or with what body they come: but rather submit that to the wisdom and pleasure of Almighty God.

2. For the doctrine of eternal judgment: God hath committed all judgment unto his Son Jesus Christ; and He is Judge both of quick and dead, and of the states and ends of all mankind. John v. 22, 27; Acts x. 42; 2 Tim. iv. 1; 1 Pet. iv. 5.

That there shall be hereafter a great harvest, which is the end of the world, a great day of judgment, and the judgment of that great day, the Holy Scripture is clear. Matt. x. 15; xiii. 39, 40, 41; Jude 6. "When the Son of Man shall come in his glory, and all the holy angels with him, then shall he sit upon the throne of his glory; and before him shall be gathered all nations," &c. Matt. xxv. 31, 32, to the end, compared with Luke ix. 26, and 1 Cor. xv. 52; 1 Thess. iv. 16, and 2 Thess. i. 7, 8, to the end; Rev. xx. 12, 13, 14, 15.

FROM THE GENERAL EPISTLE, 1736.

And, dear friends, in order that as we have received Christ, so we may walk in Him, in all holiness and godliness of conversation, we earnestly exhort that ye hold fast the profession of the faith of our Lord Jesus Christ, without wavering; both in respect to his outward coming in the flesh, his sufferings, death, resurrection, ascension, mediation, and intercession at the right hand of the Father; and to the inward manifestation of his grace and Holy Spirit in our hearts, powerfully working in the soul of man, to the subduing of every evil affection and lust, and to the purifying of our consciences from dead works to serve the living God; and that, through the virtue and efficacy of this most holy faith, ye may become strong in the Lord, and in the power of his might.

DECLARATORY MINUTE OF THE YEARLY MEETING, 1829.

We feel ourselves called upon, at this time, to avow our belief in the inspiration and divine authority of the Old and New Testament.

We further believe, that the promise made after the transgression of our first parents, in the consequence of whose fall all the posterity of Adam are involved, that the seed of the woman shall bruise the head of the serpent, and the declaration unto Abraham, "In thy seed shall all the nations of the earth be blessed," had a direct reference to the coming in the flesh of the Lord Jesus Christ. To Him, also, did the prophet Isaiah bear testimony, when he declared, "Unto us a child is born, unto us a son is given: and the government shall be upon his shoulder: and his name shall be called Wonderful, Counsellor, the mighty God, the everlasting Father, the Prince of Peace. Of the increase of his government and peace there shall be no end." And again, the same prophet spoke of Him when he said, "Surely he hath borne our griefs, and carried our sorrows: yet we did esteem him stricken, smitten of God and afflicted; but he was wounded for our transgressions, he was bruised for our iniquities: the chastisement of our peace was upon him; and with his stripes we are healed." The same blessed Redeemer is emphatically denominated by the prophet Jeremiah, "THE LORD OUR RIGHTEOUSNESS."

At that period, and in that miraculous manner, which God in his perfect wisdom saw fit, the promised Messiah appeared personally upon earth, when "He took not on him the nature of angels; but he took on him the seed of Abraham." He "was in all points tempted like as we are, yet without sin." Having finished the work which was given Him to do, He gave himself for us an offering and a sacrifice to God. He tasted death for every man. "He is the propitiation for our sins: and not for ours only, but also for the sins of the whole world." "We have redemption through his blood, even the forgiveness of sins." He passed into the heavens; and being the brightness of the glory of God, "and the express image of his person, and upholding all things by the word of his power, when he had by himself purged our sins, sat down on the right hand of the Majesty on high;" and ever liveth to make intercession for us.

It is by the Lord Jesus Christ that the world will be judged in righteousness. He is "the mediator of the new covenant;" "the image of the invisible God, the first-born of every creature: for by him were all things created, that are in heaven, and that are in earth, visible and invisible, whether they be thrones, or dominions, or principalities, or powers: all things were created by him, and for him: and he is before all things, and by him all things consist." "In him dwelleth all the fulness of the Godhead bodily:" and to Him did the Evangelist bear testimony when he said, "In the beginning was the Word, and the Word was with God, and the Word was God. The same was in the beginning with God. All things were made by him; and without him was not anything made that was made. In him was life; and the life was the light of men." He "was the true light, which lighteth every man that cometh into the world."

Our blessed Lord himself spoke of his perpetual dominion and power in his church, when He said, "My sheep hear my voice, and I know them, and they follow me: and I give unto them eternal life:" and, when describing the spiritual food which He bestoweth on the true believers, He declared, "I am the bread of life: he that cometh to me shall never hunger, and he that believeth on me shall never thirst." He spoke also of his saving grace, bestowed on those who come in faith unto Him, when He said, "Whosoever drinketh of the water that I shall give him shall never thirst; but the water that I shall give him shall be in him a well of water, springing up into everlasting life."

Our religious Society, from its earliest establishment to the present day, has received these most important doctrines of Holy Scripture in their plain and obvious acceptation; and it is the earnest desire of this meeting, that all who profess our name, may so live, and so walk before God, as that they may know these sarced truths to be blesed to them individually. We desire that, as the mere profession of sound Christian doctrine will not avail to the salvation of the soul, all may attain to a living efficacious faith, which, through the power of the Holy Ghost, bringeth forth fruit unto holiness; the end whereof is everlasting life through Jesus Christ our Lord. "Blessing, and honour, and glory, and power, be unto Him that sitteth upon the throne, and unto the Lamb for ever and ever."

FROM THE GENERAL EPISTLE, 1830.

We cannot meditate on a subject more fraught with instruction and comfort, than the coming of the Son of God in the flesh, and the many blessings which through Him have been conferred on the human race,—the coming of Him, who, being born of a virgin, "was made in the likeness of men:" "who being in the form of God, thought it not robbery to be equal with God; but made himself of no reputation, and took upon him the form of a servant." He "was delivered for our offences, and was raised again for our justification." He ascended on high, He led captivity captive, He "received gifts for men, yea, for the rebellious also, that the Lord God might dwell among them." He "sitteth on the right hand of God," making intercession for us. He is made unto us of God, "wisdom and righteousness, and sanctification and redemption;" and unto Him we must look as our mediator and advocate with the Father. He emphatically describes Himself as "the good Shepherd." He is our Lawgiver; and solemn indeed is the declaration, that we must all appear before his judgment-seat, to receive our reward, according to the deeds done in the body, whether they be good or bad.

We beseech all whom we are addressing, to contemplate these solemn truths with due reverence; yet frequently to meditate thereon, seeking for the assistance of the grace of God to direct their understandings aright. As this is done with humble and believing hearts, the conviction will increase, and ultimately become settled, that it is a great mercy to know individually that we have not a High Priest who cannot be touched with a feeling of our infirmities, but who was in all points tempted like as we are, yet without sin.

But, blessed be God, He has not only provided the means of reconciliation unto Himself, through the sacrifice of Christ; He hath also, through the same compassionate Saviour, granted unto us the gift of the Holy Spirit. By this, the patriarchs, and the holy men of old who lived under the law, walked acceptably before God. Its more plenteous effusion, and its powerful and life-giving effects, were distinctly foretold by the ancient prophets. Christ himself declared, that it was expedient that He should go away, that He might send the Comforter, the Spirit of Truth, who should guide into all truth; in allusion to whose coming He also said, "I will not leave you comfortless, I will come to you." To be guided by his Spirit is the practical application of the Christian religion. It is the light of Christ which enlightens the darkness of the heart of man; and, by following this light, we are enabled to enjoy and maintain communion with Him. The children of God are led by the Spirit of God; and this is the appointed means of bringing us into that state of "holiness, without which no man shall see the Lord." It is not a doctrine of mysticism, but one of practical piety. The great office of the Holy Spirit, we firmly believe to be, to convince of sin, to bring the soul to a state of deep and sincere repentance, and to effect the work of sanctification. A holy and constant watchfulness is required, to preserve the mind alive to the guidance of this divine Teacher; who, if diligently sought after and waited for, will be found to be a swift witness for God in the soul, producing that tenderness of spirit, and that quickness of understanding in the fear of the Lord, which are essential to our growth in grace. It is through Him "whom God hath set forth to be a propitiation, through faith in his blood," that we obtain pardon for sin; and it is through the power of his Spirit working mightily in us, that we come eventually to experience freedom from sin.

FROM THE GENERAL EPISTLE, 1836.

Often as our religious Society has declared its belief in the divine authority of the Holy Scriptures, and upheld the sacred volume as the only divinely authorised record of the doctrines of true religion, we believe it right at this time to revive some important declarations of Scripture itself on the subject. It is expressly declared by the Apostle Peter, that "the prophecy came not in old time by the will of man: but holy men of God spake as they were moved by the Holy Ghost." The Apostle John declares respecting the gospel which he wrote, "These are written, that ye might believe that Jesus is the Christ, the Son of God; and that believing ye might have life through his name." Very pertinent and comprehensive is the language which the Apostle Paul addressed to Timothy: "From a child thou hast known the holy scriptures, which are able to make thee wise unto salvation through faith which is in Christ Jesus. All scripture is given by inspiration of God, and is profitable for doctrine, for reproof, for correction, for instruction in righteousness: that the man of God may be perfect, throughly furnished unto all good works." Again, the Apostle says, "Whatsoever things were written aforetime were written for our learning, that we through patience and comfort of the scriptures might have hope." Finally, our blessed Lord, in reference to those divine writings of which the grand object, in accordance with his own declaration, was to testify of Himself, emphatically declares "the scripture cannot be broken."

Although most of these passages relate to the Old Testament, our Society has always freely acknowledged that the principles developed in them are equally applicable to the writings of the Evangelists and Apostles. In conformity with these principles it has ever been, and still is, the belief of the Society of Friends, that the Holy Scriptures of the Old and New Testament were given by inspiration of God; that therefore the declarations contained in them rest on the authority of God himself; and there can be no appeal from them to any other authority whatsoever: that they are able to make us wise unto salvation through faith which is in Christ Jesus; being the appointed means of making known to us the blessed truths of Christianity: that they are the only divinely authorized record of the doctrines which we are bound as Christians to believe, and of the moral principles which are to regulate our actions: that no doctrine which is not contained in them can be required of any one to be believed as an article of faith: that whatsoever any man says or does which is contrary to the Scriptures, though under profession of the immediate guidance of the Spirit, must be reckoned and accounted a mere delusion.

We trust, however, that none of our members will content themselves with merely entertaining a sound view on this subject; but that they will remember that the Holy Scriptures are given to us that they may be diligently used, and that we may obtain a right understanding of them in the fear of the Lord. Let us never forget that their main purpose is, under the influence of the Holy Spirit, to bring us to our Lord Jesus Christ; that by a living operative faith in Him, we may obtain reconciliation with the Father, and be made partakers of everlasting life.

As the Holy Spirit influences our hearts, and enlightens our understandings, we are brought to a lively apprehension of the character and offices of the Messiah; and Christ, received by faith into the soul and ruling there by his Spirit, becomes our sure and only hope of glory. We have always held, that the reliance of the penitent soul for the forgiveness of sins and for acceptance with our heavenly Father, must ever be placed on the sole ground of the free mercy of God in Christ Jesus. "For all have sinned, and come short of the glory of God; being justified freely by his grace through the redemption which is in Christ Jesus; whom God hath set forth to be a propitiation through faith in his blood, to declare his righteousness for the remission of sins that are past, through the forbearance of God:"—"that he might be just, and the justifier of him which believeth in Jesus."

We think it right plainly to declare, that we have never acknowledged any principle of spiritual light, life, or holiness, inherent by nature in the mind of man. Like our early Friends, we believe in no principle whatsoever of spiritual light, life, or holiness, except the influence of the Holy Spirit of God, bestowed on mankind in various measures and degrees through Jesus Christ our Lord. We are deeply solicitous that the precious doctrine of the Holy Ghost, as plainly unfolded by our Lord Jesus Christ and his Apostles, may be maintained amongst us in all its fulness.

FROM AN ADDRESS ISSUED BY THE YEARLY MEETING, ENTITLED "A TESTIMONY TO THE AUTHORITY OF CHRIST IN HIS CHURCH," 1841.

The Holy Scriptures clearly record for our instruction the setting up, and the continuance through successive generations, under the immediate direction of the Most High, of an outward priesthood, of ceremonial laws and ordinances, of tithes, of feasts and sacrifices, of types and figures, which, however, were all to be fulfilled in Christ, and which were abolished by that one offering of Himself, by which He hath perfected for ever all them that are sanctified.

He is come in the flesh: He hath made reconciliation for iniquity, and hath appeared to put away sin by the sacrifice of Himself: He is the propitiation for the sins of the whole world: He is our unchangeable and only High Priest, who ever liveth to make intercession for us, and through Him by one Spirit we have access unto the Father. The Mosaic institutions, and all the rituals of a ceremonial law, are terminated. The Levitical priesthood has ceased, being superseded by Christ, who has ascended into heaven, and now sitteth at the right hand of the Father. No outward provision similar in nature or character was established by Him. He conferred no power on man to provide a line of successors to his apostles.

It is the prerogative of Christ to call and qualify by the Holy Spirit his servants to minister in word and doctrine, and to preach repentance toward God and faith toward our Lord Jesus Christ. In the earliest period of the Christian church his Spirit was, agreeably to ancient prophecy, poured upon servants and upon handmaidens, and we believe that He continues to call, from the young and from the old, from the unlearned and from the poor, from the wise and from the rich, from women as well as from men, those whom He commissions to declare unto others the way of salvation. And seeing that this gift of the Holy Spirit cometh from God only, the ministry ought not, in our apprehension, to be performed at stated times of human appointment, neither ought there to be any previous preparation by the minister, of matter to be communicated by him to an audience, when met for the purpose of performing the solemn duty of worship unto God. But it should be exercised in that ability which He giveth on the occasion, and which He graciously renews from time to time, as it seemeth Him good.

The servants of Christ who labour in the ministry, are to be highly esteemed for their work's sake, and when they leave their outward avocations, at his call, to preach the Gospel, their outward wants should be cheerfully supplied, if needful; yet we consider the gift of the ministry to be of so pure and sacred a nature, that no payment should be made for its exercise, and that it ought never to be undertaken for pecuniary remuneration. As the gift is free, the exercise of it ought to be free also, in accordance with the precept of our Lord, "Freely ye have received, freely give." We think that all payments to ministers of the Gospel for their services, are calculated, in their effects, to obstruct the faithful ministration of the word—to hinder the honest declaration of the whole counsel of God, in the authority of Him who is given to be Head over all things to his church.

In accordance with the views already stated, we consider that no provision of man's arrangement ought to be resorted to for qualifying those who feel themselves called to minister unto others. We believe it to be the duty of the ministers of the Gospel, to be diligent, in the fear of God, in reading the Holy Scriptures: neither do we undervalue human learning. But to subject any such to a course of teaching, as a necessary preparation for the ministry, is, in our apprehension, to interfere with that work of the Holy Spirit which our Lord carries forward in the hearts of those whom He calls to preach his Gospel unto others, or to minister to the conditions of the people.

Our Lord leadeth not only his ministers in the path of duty, but He giveth to all his believing children, as they are individually concerned to look unto Him, rightly to occupy with those talents which He entrusts to them for the good of others. And we believe that He will, as the eye is single unto Him for spiritual light and guidance, open their understandings more clearly and experimentally to see that, as all the types and shadows and ordinances of the Law were fulfilled in Him, and as He established no outward priesthood, so He established no new ordinances to be administered or to be observed in his church. His baptism is that of the Holy Ghost and of fire.

He himself is the bread of life. It is He who giveth the meat which endureth unto everlasting life. He maketh all his faithful followers members of that royal priesthood and holy nation of which the Apostle Peter writes; and as they are concerned to order their households in the fear of God, He enables them to instruct their families in the truths of his blessed Gospel, and to train them up in the way of holiness.

FROM THE GENERAL EPISTLES, 1842, 1843.

Great is the blessedness of that life which is hid with Christ in God. We therefore earnestly covet that every one may be willing patiently to submit to the turning of the Lord's hand upon him. Then shall we be brought to experience, as we follow on to know the Lord, that Christ is indeed our light and our life; that, according to his own declaration, He is the bread which came down from heaven, and if a man eat of this bread, he shall live for ever;—words of consolation to the hungry soul. Thus feeding on Him, the living substance, we shall clearly see that all the types and ceremonies of a former dispensation were the shadow of those good things which are already come; and we shall truly feel that "the kingdom of God is not in word, but in power;" "not meat and drink; but righteousness, and peace, and joy in the Holy Ghost."

The religion of Jesus, in its full development, abrogates all the symbols and rituals of the Jewish church, and destroys those works of the carnal mind, by which, in the time of the apostacy, the priesthood of man was substituted for that of Christ, and outward forms took the place of the unchanging power and holiness of the Gospel. There is a great tendency to have recourse to sensible objects and outward observances in the service and worship of God; by which the mind is in imminent danger of resting in forms, rather than coming to the substance of the Gospel. Warm are our desires that our ancient testimony to the spiritual nature of the Christian religion and against all ceremonial usages may be preserved inviolate; and we strongly recommend our dear friends to be very watchful, that nothing be allowed to estrange them from a full appreciation of its value and importance.

Wherefore, beloved brethren, let it be the frequent engagement of your souls, in deep reverence and humility, to "consider the apostle and high priest of our profession, Christ Jesus." The promised Messiah, He to whom all preceding dispensations had pointed, and in whom they were ended and fulfilled, He who was with God, and was God, the Word who hath declared to man Him that is invisible, even He was made flesh and dwelt amongst men. Though He was rich, yet for our sakes He became poor; veiling in the form of a servant, the brightness of his glory, that, through Him, the kindness and love of God toward man might appear, in a manner every way suited to our wants and finite capacities. His righteous precepts were illustrated and confirmed by his own holy example. He went about doing good; for us He endured sorrow, hunger, thirst, weariness, pain; unutterable anguish of body and of soul even unto death; and was "in all points tempted like as we are, yet without sin." Thus humbling Himself that we might be exalted, He emphatically recognized the duties and the sufferings of humanity as among the means whereby, through the obedience of faith, we are to be disciplined for heaven; sanctifying them to us, by Himself performing and enduring them, and, as "the Forerunner," at once plainly marking and consecrating for his followers the path in which they must tread. But not only in these blessed relations must the Lord Jesus be ever precious to his people. Exalted to be a Prince and a Saviour, in Him has been revealed a Redeemer at once able to suffer and almighty to save; an High Priest, "touched with the feeling of our infirmities," who, having made reconciliation for our sins by the offering up of Himself once for all, "is gone into heaven," there to appear, our Mediator and Advocate, in the presence of God.

Beloved friends! how high and holy is our vocation in being called by the name, and invited to the service, of such a Saviour. There is not one amongst us, whatever be the advantages of his education, the amiableness of his disposition, or his advancement in refinement and intelligence,—there is not one of us to whom, in his natural state, the language of our adorable Redeemer may not be addressed, "Ye must be born again." These are words of universal and perpetual application; in them is set forth that work of the Holy Spirit in the conversion and sanctification of the heart, that *renewing* in the spirit of our minds, by which we may every one of us be made as "lively stones" in that spiritual house in which the Lord Himself delights to dwell.

FROM THE GENERAL EPISTLE, 1854.

It is they only who are washed, who are sanctified, who are justified, in the name of the Lord Jesus, and by the Spirit of our God, who can enjoy the unspeakable privilege of membership in the spiritual Israel. No rite, no outward membership in any church, can suffice to make us children of Abraham. There must be the circumcision of the heart, the putting off of "the old man which is corrupt, according to the deceitful lusts," and the putting on of "the new man which, after God, is created in righteousness and true holiness." The calling of the Christian is emphatically a "heavenly calling." "Therefore," says the Apostle, "the world knoweth us not, because it knew Him not." If we are conscious that the world loveth us, and that we love the world, how much reason is there to fear that we have not yet experienced that great and all-important change, whereby they who were "by nature the children of wrath," are brought nigh through the blood of Jesus, and made partakers of the adoption. They who are thus adopted into the Lord's family, who are sealed with the Holy Spirit of promise, and made heirs of God, and joint heirs with Christ, have their desires, their hopes and their affections set upon heavenly things, and are no longer conformed to this world. Strangers and pilgrims upon earth, their citizenship is in heaven.

FROM THE GENERAL EPISTLE, 1857.

How encouraging to the true penitent, how full of instruction to the advanced Christian, is the language of the Redeemer,

"I am the door; by me if any man enter in, he shall be saved." It is a distinguishing feature of the work of the Holy Spirit, that it bears an effectual witness to Christ, and brings to the enjoyment of his grace in those various relations in which He has been pleased to reveal Himself. Under the power of heart-searching conviction, it draws the believing soul, in contrition and humiliation, to the Saviour's feet. Here, through the acceptance of Him, in living faith, as the propitiation for sin, the reconciling love of God is shed abroad in the heart, and we are enabled to realize the inestimable privilege of access unto God; not in our own right, or for any works of righteousness that we have done, but for the sake of Christ alone. In thus witnessing of Him, and establishing the soul upon Him, the Holy Spirit becomes a Comforter indeed. Through his sanctifying power, the righteousness of God, through faith, is more and more manifested in the life and conversation, whilst all boasting is excluded. The promise of the New Covenant, in its most precious import, is fulfilled. The law of God becomes more and more plainly written upon the heart, whilst a yet clearer and clearer view is granted of the depth of that love which, in Christ Jesus, pardoneth iniquity, transgression, and sin. Fervently do we desire that our dear friends, everywhere, may press after an individual acquaintance with this heart-searching and heart-sanctifying knowledge of the Son of God. May none, under the heavy weight of conviction, stop short in the first stage of Christian experience; but, yielding without reserve to the further manifestations of light and truth, may they be brought from step to step, in faith and faithfulness, to the full enjoyment in their own souls of the covenant of life and peace.

FROM THE GENERAL EPISTLE, 1858.

He who loved his church, and gave Himself for it, yet lives and reigns and intercedes on its behalf. To Him John was commissioned to bear testimony, not only as the Lamb appointed for the sacrifice, but also, in his exaltation and glory, as the Dispenser of the promised Spirit. The voice in the wilderness that proclaimed, "Behold the Lamb of God which taketh away the sin of the world," declared also, "He shall baptize you with the Holy Ghost and with fire." "It hath pleased the Father that in Him should all fulness dwell." He is the anointed Priest and King; and all who, through living faith, become Christians indeed, receive an unction of the Spirit from Him, the Holy One. This is "the promise of the Father" under the new covenant; the seal of reconciliation to the humble believer in Jesus; the earnest and the foretaste of that full communion and perfect joy which are reserved for them that endure unto the end.

FROM THE GENERAL EPISTLE, 1861.

The gift of the Spirit is a special promise of the new covenant. The Saviour expressly declared, "I will pray the Father, and He shall give you another Comforter, that He may abide with you for ever." The light that shines into man's heart is not of man, and must ever be distinguished both from the conscience which it enlightens, and from the natural faculty of reason, which, when unsubjected to its holy influences, is, in the things of God, very foolishness. One with the Father and with the Son, the Holy Spirit works for the regeneration of fallen and rebellious man. Coming in the name and with the authority of the ascended Saviour, He remains to the church the most precious pledge of the power and continued care of its exalted King. Not merely as the enlightener of the conscience, and the reprover for sin, is the Spirit mercifully granted, but also, in an especial manner, to testify of and to glorify the Saviour; to apply, with sanctifying efficacy to the soul, his words and work when upon earth, and his mediation and intercession for us in heaven. Hidden and often very gradual as may be the work of the Spirit, it produces a real and most effectual change; and as obedience keeps pace with knowledge, the believer is privileged to receive more and more of the fulness which is in Christ. But let it never be forgotten that every increase of light and experience, how much soever connected with his usefulness to others, is also for the furtherance of the work in his own soul. He is taught by the Spirit to look unto Jesus; that "beholding as in a glass the glory of the Lord," he may be "changed into the same image from glory to glory, even as by the Spirit of the Lord." Can we enough meditate upon these heavenly truths, revealed for the very purpose that they may be understood and enjoyed? What encouragement do they afford us to seek to live as worshippers in the inner sanctuary, in nearness to God, in childlike faith, in loving obedience, walking in the Spirit!

Beloved friends, ye who in the riches of the Father's love have been partakers of the heavenly calling, may you receive with faith and thanksgiving, yet with a solemn sense of your responsibility, the words of the Apostle, "Ye have an unction from the Holy One." Let the anointing which ye have received of Him abide in you, we entreat you; cleansing, guiding, sanctifying; causing you in all things to grow up into Him who is the Head. The cross-bearing follower of Jesus, who sits in penitential love and holy hope at his feet, knows most of this precious anointing. In such the fruits of the Spirit are brought forth; not only conviction for sin, repentance and faith, but love, joy, peace, the sense of pardoning mercy, an humble reliance on sanctifying grace, the disposition of heart which finds its continual satisfaction in loving, serving and pleasing God; and, to crown all, the blessed hope of finally resting and worshipping with the general assembly and church of the first-born who are written in heaven. Oh! then, that neither the hurry of active life, nor the pressure of even necessary duty, may withdraw any from that retired, watchful frame, in which the soul, thirsting for the living God, still breathes the fervent petition, "Thy will be done."

CHAPTER II.

CHRISTIAN PRACTICE.

SECTION I.—MEETINGS FOR PUBLIC WORSHIP.

As it hath been our care and practice from the beginning, that an open testimony for the Lord should be borne, and a public standard for truth and righteousness upheld, in the power and spirit of God, by our open and known meetings; so it is our advice and judgment, that all Friends, gathered in the name of Jesus, keep up these public testimonies in their respective places; and do not decline, forsake, or remove their public assemblies, because of times of suffering; as worldly, fearful, and politic professors have done, because of informers and the like persecutors: for such practices are not consistent with the nobility of the truth, and therefore not to be owned in the church of Christ. 1675.

Let every one be watchful against an earthly spirit, for that will choke the good seed, and bring forth a slighting or neglecting of your testimony in your first-day and week-day meetings, and bring a decay of your strength and zeal for God, and his truth, and bring a weakness upon you, by reason whereof you will not be able to stand in an hour of temptation. 1689. P. E.

Advised that Friends, though meetings are sometimes held in silence, would not neglect their attendance; for the hungry soul will labour for bread, and the thirsty for the water of life; and the diligent hand will make rich in that treasure which is of an enduring substance. 1724. P. E.

In your religious meetings for the worship of God, both on the first and other days of the week, be diligent to wait on Him, whereby you may renew your strength, and witness Him your sufficient help; for surely many of us have cause thankfully to remember his early visitations in the assemblies of his people; where He broke in upon our hearts with his power and love, and did, in the needful time, administer help, comfort, and counsel;

whereby, in the renewings thereof, we have been upheld in a faithful testimony, and in the discharge of our duty to Him. 1725. P. E.

In all your meetings for the worship of Almighty God, let your deportment be such as may demonstrate, that you are in earnest in the great duty of waiting upon and worshipping God in spirit; that serious and tender-hearted inquirers may be encouraged to come and partake, in your assemblies, of that inward and spiritual consolation and refreshment, which the Lord is graciously pleased to impart to the souls of such as are humbled in his sight, and approach his holy presence with reverence and fear. 1744. P. E.

Although the labours of such as are called forth by the Spirit of Christ, and instructed thereby rightly to divide the word of truth, are highly serviceable in the church; yet the aim and design of every true gospel minister is to direct the minds of all to the divine teachings of the Holy Spirit, and to wait upon, and have their whole trust and expectation on the Lord alone. And as the religious strength and communion, both of preachers and hearers, consist in their united dependence on the power and Spirit of Christ, their guide and leader; so where any part of that dependence is broken off from Him, the Holy Head, and placed on any instrument or member of the body, it hath been sometimes experienced to become a weight or burden on such instrument, and a real impediment to its present service. Wherefore, brethren, we beseech you that, in all your assemblies for the worship of God, your eye be single unto Him, your expectation fixed on Him alone, and your faith standing in his power and Spirit: thus may you grow and be established therein, and be made one another's strength in the Lord.

And let the hearers be watchful over their own spirits, and not forwardly judge or censure the testimonies which may be delivered amongst them; for if they be not very careful and diligent in attending upon the Lord in meetings, they are liable to mistake in the judgment they may pass on the ministry. Now this being a matter of great moment, for the preservation of love and concord in the churches, and knowing the danger and ill consequences which attend a hasty and censorious judging of the ministry, we think it necessary to caution Friends, not to let their own spirits sway them, but to let the Spirit of God rule and reign in their hearts; for this will preserve all in sweetness and tenderness one towards another. 1731.—1753. P.E.

We tenderly exhort such as, through fear of neglecting their temporal concerns, or other considerations, are kept from a due attendance of meetings for worship, seriously to consider that gracious promise left upon record; "Seek ye first the kingdom of God, and his righteousness, and all these things shall be added unto you." Some of us have to testify, that our outward affairs have not suffered, by giving up our time, the few hours set apart for religious worship; but, on the contrary, our minds have been thereby greatly strengthened to come up with propriety in the duties we owe to God, to our families, and to all mankind. Let us call to remembrance the zeal of our honourable predecessors, who, when they had great reason to expect they should be driven into noisome and pestilential prisons, sent into banishment, or subjected to other grievous sufferings, for meeting together on no other account than to worship God according to their consciences; yet, in the strength of that holy faith and love which supported them in suffering, failed not constantly to keep up their meetings at the hazard of all, and expense of many of their lives, liberties, and properties. 1758. P. E.

"Where two or three," saith our Lord, "are gathered together in my name, there am I in the midst of them." In these words, He invites us not only to meet one with another, but in so doing, with Himself also. Shall the King of kings, and Lord of lords, condescend to offer his divine presence for our good, and shall we, his dependent creatures, set so light by his inestimable kindness, as, either wilfully or negligently, to let slip those precious seasons, wherein we might receive his blessed assistance so necessary to our help and salvation? Shall the poor, perishing gratifications of sense and self-love, or any inconveniences of a trivial nature, be suffered to prevent our dutiful attendance upon Him, in whom alone stands our everlasting interest? Shall a cloudy sky, a little wet, a little cold, a little ease to the flesh, a view to a little earthly gain, or any common incident, furnish an excuse for declining this duty, and thereby depriving ourselves of the blessed advantage, often vouchsafed to the faithful, of enjoying heavenly communion together in spirit, with the Lord of life and glory? 1765. P. E.

They who are obedient to this universal injunction of our Saviour, "Watch," are prepared for the due fulfilling of every duty; and eminently so, for that most essential one of worship. How many feel themselves languid, when assembled for this solemn purpose, for want of a previous preparation of heart! The mind, crowded with thoughts on outward things in approaching the place for public worship, and resuming them with avidity on its return, is not likely to fill up the interval to profit; and to such, their meeting together may prove a form as empty as any of those out of which, we believe, truth called our forefathers, and still calls us. 1800. P. E.

A punctual attendance at the hour appointed for public worship is a matter of no small importance. If we hurry away from our outward occupations to the meeting-house, thinking that, by the delay of a few minutes, we shall not be long behind our brethren, we are in great danger of having our thoughts employed on that in which we have been engaged, and of interrupting that holy silence, which, it is believed, would often prevail, if all the members of a meeting were assembled not only in one place, but at one time, with one and the same great object in view. 1821.

This meeting regarding the attendance of all our religious meetings as important in the training up of our youth in a life and conversation consistent with our Christian profession, thinks it right affectionately to express its concern, that Friends, on placing out their children in situations, may endeavour to make arrangements with their employers, for their enjoyment of this privilege. 1837.

Whilst we desire to cherish and to inculcate true Christian charity towards those from whom we differ, we would affectionately encourage all our members to confine themselves, in the public performance of this solemn duty, to a diligent attendance of our own meetings for worship; not seeking help in forms or modes of worship inconsistent with our principles. 1840. P. E.—1860. P. E.

We have been made afresh sensible at this time of the soundness and excellence of those views which our predecessors were led to take, on the important subject of public worship. May these views, and the practices which have resulted from them, ever be held and carried out amongst us, not in the deadness of the form, but in the life and power of godliness. Oh! that, in all our meetings for Divine worship, the hearts of those assembled may be truly exercised in reverent waiting upon the Lord; that, by the help of his Holy Spirit, those true sacrifices of brokenness and contrition, of prayer and reverent thanksgiving, may be prepared and offered, through our one Mediator, which are essential features of pure, evangelical worship, that stands neither in forms nor in the formal disuse of forms, and may be without words as well as with them, but *must* be " in spirit and in truth." May we ever bear in mind, that it is not the mere outward gathering together, but the inward gathering of our hearts unto the Lord, that makes a true meeting for worship. And how consoling is the remembrance that this worship is not dependent upon numbers: where two or three are gathered in the name of Christ, there is a church, and Christ the living Head in the midst of them. In his name, therefore, to use the language of George Fox, may you seek to keep all your meetings; " that you may feel Him in the midst of you exercising his offices. As He is a Prophet whom God has raised up to open to you, and as He is a Shepherd who has laid down his life for you, to feed you, so hear his voice; and as He is a Counsellor and a Commander, follow Him and his counsel; and as He is a Bishop to oversee you with his heavenly power and Spirit, and as He is a Priest who offered Himself for you, who is made higher than the Heavens, who sanctifies his people, his church, and presents them to God without blemish, spot or wrinkle, so know Him in all his offices, exercising them amongst you, and in you." 1855. P. E.

We have afresh rejoiced in the high privileges which abound in the Gospel. He who died for his people to save them from their sins, ever liveth to make intercession for them. Through his mediation, without the necessity for any inferior instrumentality, is the Father to be approached and reverently worshipped. The Lord Jesus has for ever fulfilled and ended the typical and sacrificial worship under the law, by the offering up of Himself upon the cross for us, once for all. He has opened the door of access into the inner sanctuary, and graciously appointed spiritual offerings for the service of his temple, suited to the several conditions of all who worship in spirit and in truth. The broken and the contrite heart, the confession of the soul prostrate before God, the prayer of the afflicted when he is overwhelmed, the earnest wrestling of the spirit, the outpouring of humble thanksgiving, the spiritual song and melody of the heart, the simple exercise of faith, the self-denying service of love;—these are among the sacrifices which He, our merciful and faithful High Priest, is Himself pleased to prepare by his Spirit in the hearts of them that receive Him, and to present with acceptance unto God.

May none yield to the idea that there can be worship in any prescribed system of observances apart from the ministrations of the Lord's Spirit, or conclude that there can be no true worship even where the immediate operations of his Spirit are enjoyed, without the accompaniment of outward teaching or services. And when assembled in our religious meetings, may none rest in a vacant stillness or indolent musing, or in thoughts wandering upon earthly things. May all seriously remember that the object of thus assembling is the worship of the infinite, all-seeing and ever-present God. And let it not be forgotten that the purpose of the immediate ministry of his Spirit is to bring us into deep searching of heart; to enlighten us to see our true state; to control and sanctify our thoughts and affections; and, beyond all, to take of the things of Christ, and apply them with power to the healing, strengthening and refreshment of the humble and believing soul. 1857. P. E.

You know, dear friends, that it is not to man, but unto the Lord alone, that we must look for the nourishment of the soul. Bearing in mind the words of our Holy Redeemer, "No man cometh unto the Father but by me," may it be your concern in all your assemblies to gather in the name of Jesus. That which is to be sought after is not silence merely, but worship,—even the worship of the Father in spirit and in truth. May the faith of our dear friends be increased in the immediate teaching of the Comforter, remembering the Saviour's declaration, "He shall take of mine and shall shew it unto you." But let not any think that because their meetings have been usually held in silence, therefore they are to go on from meeting to meeting, never expecting anything else. The true worshipper is he who is resigned to every intimation of the Divine will; not pre-judging the counsels of his Lord, nor allowing any habits or fears of his own to bring him under a bondage wherein the word of the Lord can neither have free course nor be glorified. A self-imposed silence in man's will may be scarcely less formal or hurtful than words wanting fitness or power.

May we ever be upon our guard against a superficial and unauthorized ministry; yet in the renewed persuasion that the preaching of the Gospel, under right authority, is a divinely appointed means for the conversion of sinners and the perfecting of the saints, and that true spirituality cannot prosper where the Spirit of the Lord is quenched, we are concerned to exhort our dear friends everywhere, humbly to wait for, and in all things to be obedient to, its precious operations, whether designed only for their individual profit, or gently constraining them to utter a word in season for the help or encouragement of others. 1860. P. E.

SECTION II.—PRIVATE RETIREMENT AND PRAYER.

FREQUENT waiting in stillness on the Lord, for the renewal of strength, keeps the mind at home in its proper place and duty, and out of all unprofitable association and converse, whether amongst those of our own, or other professions. Much hurt may accrue to the religious mind by long and frequent conversation on temporal matters, especially by interesting ourselves too much in them; for there is a leaven therein, which, being suffered to prevail, indisposes and benumbs the soul, and prevents its frequent ascendings in living aspirations towards the Fountain of eternal life. 1770. P. E.

In a well-ordered family, short opportunities of religious retirement frequently occur, in which the mind may be turned in secret aspiration to the Author of all our blessings; and which have often proved times of more than transient benefit. It is our present concern that no exception to this practice may be found amongst us; whether it take place on the reading of a portion of the sacred volume, or when we are assembled to partake of the provisions with which we are supplied for the sustenance of the body. May the experience of us all be such, that we can adopt the words of the Psalmist, "Evening, and morning, and at noon, will I pray." 1817. P. E.

In the sacred writings no duty is more clearly set forth than that of prayer. Prayer is the aspiration of the heart unto God: it is one of the first engagements of the awakened soul, and we believe that it becomes the clothing of the minds of those whose lives are regulated by the fear and love of their Creator. If, in moments of serious reflection, and when communing with our own hearts, we are sufficiently alive to our helpless condition, we shall often feel that we may pour forth our secret supplications unto the Lord. And as we believe that it is one of the greatest privileges a Christian can enjoy thus to draw nigh in spirit unto the Father of mercies, we earnestly desire that no one may deprive himself of so great a blessing. 1823. P. E.

We continue to believe that our disuse of set forms of prayers is founded on a correct view of the spiritual nature of the Gospel dispensation. At the same time we are persuaded, that all who have a just sense of the value of their immortal souls, and of their own great need of help from above, must rejoice with thankfulness, in knowing and in feeling that they may pray unto our Father who is in heaven. Oh! then that every one may, with a sincere and believing heart, and with reverential awe, approach the throne of grace; trusting in the mediation of Him through whom we "have access by one Spirit unto the Father." Let none be discouraged from the performance of this duty by a sense of their transgressions; but in humility and sincere repentance, let them implore the forgiveness of God, who, as they patiently wait before Him, will in his own time supply all their need. And if there be any, who, if they deal honestly with their own hearts, must acknowledge that they do not pray, may these deeply reflect upon the danger of their situation, and be alarmed at the great loss which they sustain; and avail themselves of the high privilege of drawing nigh unto God, and partaking of the assurance that He will draw nigh unto them. 1828. P. E.

May we all draw nigh unto God in prayer—ask the assistance

of his grace to help in time of need—and look unto Him as our merciful Father who is in heaven ; assuredly believing, that, as He is approached in reverence and faith, He will graciously answer our petitions, and supply all our need in and through Christ Jesus. As this sacred duty, so forcibly enjoined in Holy Scripture, is correctly understood and performed aright, parents will become so sensible of its great value to themselves, that they will feel the importance of turning thereto the attention of their beloved offspring; and, as they seek for wisdom and strength to act rightly herein, they will be assisted by Him, to whom they should desire that they and their children may be wholly dedicated. 1830. P. E.

Under the solemn conviction that, whatever be our circumstances in life, or our position in the church, prayer is, in the Divine appointment, essential to our spiritual health, we would earnestly press upon all to seek for opportunities in the course of each day for private retirement and waiting upon the Lord ; and tenderly to cherish those precious, but often gentle and easily resisted motions of the Lord's Spirit, which would contrite and humble our hearts, and draw them forth in fervent petitions for that spiritual food which can alone supply our daily, our continual need. May none amongst us be living in a state of unconcern, insensible to the righteous judgment of God upon all that is unholy; their sins, unrepented of and unforgiven, still resting on their souls : rather let them be encouraged to come in deep humiliation to the mercy-seat, there to plead for pardon and plenteous redemption, in the all-availing name of our crucified Redeemer. How precious for us all is the assurance "that we have a great High Priest, that is passed into the heavens, Jesus the Son of God ;" one who is "touched with the feeling of our infirmities ;" and in whose holy name we are invited to "come boldly unto the throne of grace, that we may obtain mercy, and find grace to help in time of need." 1854. P. E.

Impressed with the importance, to the spiritual life, of seasons of private retirement, we are engaged to encourage our friends frequently to avail themselves of this privilege, for reading the Holy Scriptures, for meditation, for deep searching of heart, and for seeking to draw nigh in prayer to God.

Fervent are our desires that we may be indeed a spiritually-minded people; cherishing that inward retiredness and spirit of prayer in which the voice of the Heavenly Shepherd may be distinctly heard, and ability received to follow Him, in the obedience of faith, in the path of duty. O for more constant dependence in our daily walk upon his guidance and grace! How precious the holy settlement, the quiet confidence of those who put their trust in the Lord!

The more we seek "to abide in Christ," the more fruitful shall we be in that field of offering into which He may call us, and the more shall we be enabled to glorify our Father in heaven. 1861.

SECTION III.—ON READING THE HOLY SCRIPTURES.

We recommend it as an incumbent duty on Friends, to cause their children to be frequent in reading the Holy Scriptures, and to observe to them the examples of such children as in Scripture are recorded to have early learned the fear of the Lord, and hearkened to his counsel; instructing them in the fear of the Lord, planting upon their spirits impressions of reverence towards God, from whom they have their daily support; showing them they ought not to offend Him, but love, serve, and honour Him, in whose hands all blessings are. 1709. P. E.

Let the Holy Scriptures be early taught our youth, and diligently searched, and seriously read by Friends, with due regard to the Holy Spirit from whence they came, and by which they are truly opened. 1720. P. E.

And, dear friends, inasmuch as the Holy Scriptures are the means of conveying and preserving to us an account of the things most surely to be believed concerning the coming of our Lord Jesus Christ in the flesh, and the fulfilling of the prophecies relating thereto, we therefore recommend to all friends, especially elders in the church, and masters of families, that they would, both by example and advice, impress on the minds of the younger a reverent esteem of those sacred writings, and advise them to a frequent reading and meditating therein;—and that you would, at proper times and seasons, when you find your minds rightly disposed thereunto, give the youth to understand, that the same good experience of the work of sanctification, through the operations of the Spirit of God, which the Holy Scriptures plentifully bear testimony to, is to be witnessed by believers in all generations, as well as by those in the first ages of Christianity; in which case, some account of your own experience may be helpful to them. And this we recommend as the most effectual means of begetting and establishing in their minds a firm belief of the Christian doctrine in general, as well as of the necessity of the aid and help of the operations of the Holy Spirit of God in the hearts of men in particular, contained in the Bible; and of preserving them from being defiled with the many pernicious notions and principles, contrary to sound doctrine, which are at this time industriously dispersed in the nation, to the reproach of the Christian profession in general. 1728. P. E.

We tenderly and earnestly advise and exhort all parents and masters of families, that they exert themselves in the wisdom of God, and in the strength of his love, to instruct their children and families in the doctrines and precepts of the Christian religion contained in the Holy Scriptures; and that they excite them to the diligent reading of those sacred writings, which plainly set forth the miraculous conception, birth, holy life, wonderful works, blessed example, meritorious death, and glorious resurrection, ascension, and mediation of our Lord and Saviour Jesus Christ; and to educate their children in the belief of those important truths, as well as in the belief of the inward manifestation and operation of the Spirit of God on their own minds, that they may reap the benefit and advantage thereof, for their own peace and everlasting happiness, which is infinitely preferable to all other considerations. We therefore exhort, in the most earnest manner, that all be very careful in this respect; a neglect herein being, in our judgment, very blameworthy. And further, where any deficiency of this sort appears, we recommend to Monthly and Quarterly Meetings, that they stir up those whom it may concern to their duty therein. 1732. P. E.

And, dear friends, as much as in you lies, encourage a frequent and diligent reading of the Holy Scriptures in your families. In them are contained the promises of eternal life and salvation. For as a steady trust and belief in the promises of God, and a frequent meditation in the law of the Lord, was the preservation of a remnant in old time, so it is even to th s day; and as a distrust and disbelief of the promises of God, and a neglect of his holy law, was the occasion of the complaints made against the Jews, the posterity of Abraham, even so we have reason to fear that the apparent decline in our time of true piety and godly zeal, in many places, is too much owing to a disregard of the doctrines of the Holy Scriptures, and the promises of the Holy Spirit in them recorded. Wherefore it greatly behoves every one, who would be united to Christ, and a member of his church, to believe in the promises of God and Christ, and wait to know the fulfilling of them in his own heart. It was by this the primitive believers became of " one heart, and of one soul." It was by one Spirit, namely, the Spirit promised by Christ, that they were " all baptized into one body." Having therefore, dearly beloved, such great and precious promises, and being encompassed with so great a cloud of witnesses, let us run with cheerfulness in the ways of the Lord; " looking unto Jesus, the author and finisher of our faith; who, for the joy that was set before him, endured the cross, despising the shame, and is set down at the right hand of the throne of God." 1740. P. E.

It has afforded us much satisfaction to believe, that the Christian practice of daily reading in families a portion of Holy Scripture, with a subsequent pause for retirement and reflection, is increasing amongst us. We conceive that it is both the duty and the interest of those who believe in the doctrines of the Gospel, and who possess the invaluable treasure of the sacred records, frequently to recur to them for instruction and consolation. We are desirous that this wholesome domestic regulation may be adopted every where. Heads of families, who have themselves experienced the benefit of religious instruction, will do well to consider whether, in this respect, they have not a duty to discharge to their servants and others of their household. Parents, looking sincerely for help to Him of whom these Scriptures testify, may not unfrequently, on such occasions, feel themselves enabled and engaged to open to the minds of their interesting charge, the great truths of Christian duty and Christian redemption. 1815. P. E.

The practice of frequent retirement in spirit greatly assists us on our way to the kingdom of heaven. If an impartial review of our conduct then takes place, and if the sincere and secret petition is raised for Almighty help, we are led from an undue attachment to the things of this life, and our hopes and dependence are increasingly placed upon our Holy Redeemer. The sacred truths of the Bible are often at such times brought to remembrance with consolation and strength. It is one among the many evidences of the divine authority of Holy Scripture, that, in the various ages of the Christian church, its invaluable contents have produced in true believers a harmonizing sense of their blessed effects. If, in humility and in reliance upon the Spirit which gave them forth, we are diligent in reading these sacred writings, we become increasingly sensible of their value. We are then prepared, from our own experience, to say that they are able to make us wise unto salvation through faith in Christ Jesus; we readily subscribe to the truth of the position, that, in order to the accomplishment of this great end, they need no human comment; and we are anxious that our fellow-men, in every region of the globe, may possess and may be able to read the volume of inspiration. 1825. P. E.

In addition to the practice of the family-reading of the Holy Scriptures, the importance of which we deeply feel, be encouraged often to read them in private: cherish a humble and sincere desire to receive them in their genuine import; and at the same time, dear friends, avoid all vain speculations upon unfulfilled prophecy. Forbear from presumptuously endeavouring to determine the mode of the future government of the world, or of the church of Christ. Seek an enlightened sense of the various delusions of our common enemy, to which we are all liable; ask of God that your meditations upon the sacred writings may be under the influence of the Holy Spirit. Their effect, when thus read, is to promote an increase of practical piety, and the right performance of all our civil and religious duties, and not to encourage vain and fruitless investigations. Remember, dear friends, that they are "profitable for doctrine, for reproof, for correction, for instruction in righteousness; that the man of God may be perfect, throughly furnished unto all good works." And whilst we fully acknowledge that "all Scripture is given by inspiration of God," a view supported by sound and undeniable rational evidence, let us ever bear in mind, that it is only "through faith which is in Christ Jesus" that they are able to make wise unto salvation. As this precious faith is sought for and prevails, the evidence of the Spirit of God in our hearts most satisfactorily confirms our belief in the divine authority of these inestimable writings, and increases our gratitude for the possession of them, and for the knowledge of that redemption which comes by the Lord Jesus. 1832. P. E.

While we are anxious that all our members should exercise a daily diligence in the perusal of the sacred volume, we would earnestly invite them to wait and pray for that divine immediate teaching, which can alone effectually illuminate its pages, and unfold their contents to the eye of the soul. "For what man knoweth the things of a man, save the spirit of man which is in him? even so the things of God knoweth no man, but the Spirit of God." As this is our humble endeavour, the various features of divine truth will be gradually unfolded to the seeking mind. We beseech you, dear friends, carefully to avoid all partial and exclusive views of religion; for these have ever been found to be the nurse of error. The truth as it is in Jesus forms a perfect whole; its parts are not to be contrasted, much less opposed to each other. They all consist in beautiful harmony; they must be gratefully accepted in their true completeness, and applied with all diligence to their practical purpose. That purpose is the renovation of our fallen nature, and the salvation of our never-dying souls. 1835. P. E.

We rejoice at the large degree in which our members, both older and younger, are imbued with the knowledge of the precious truths of Holy Scripture; believing that an intelligent acquaintance with their invaluable contents, under the discipline and teaching of the Holy Spirit, is a privilege which we cannot too highly prize. The powers of the understanding were given to be employed, not by any means exclusively upon worldly pursuits and engagements, but also upon objects of a far higher and an enduring nature, even the things of God and of his Kingdom, so far as He has been pleased to reveal them to us: yet it remains to be a truth of the greatest practical import, that "the things of God knoweth no man, but the Spirit of God." How instructive in relation to this subject is the prayer of the Apostle for the Ephesian converts, that the God of our Lord Jesus Christ, the Father of glory, might give unto them the spirit of wisdom and revelation in the knowledge of Him; the eyes of their understanding being enlightened that they might know what was the hope of their calling. How touching and impressive is the language of our Redeemer Himself: "I thank thee, O Father, Lord of heaven and earth, because thou hast hid these things from the wise and prudent, and hast revealed them unto babes." It is in simple child-like obedience to the manifestations of the Lord's will concerning us, that this will is opened, often very gradually, to the believing and watchful soul. In this heavenly training, the powers of the understanding are not laid aside as useless, but, through humility and the fear of the Lord, are strengthened and sanctified in the exercise of their highest functions. 1856. P. E.

Our minds have been brought into religious solicitude on behalf of our younger members, and especially such as may be in situations from home, in the desire that the care which, whether under the parental roof or in our several schools, may have been bestowed upon their religious instruction, may still be continued in this critical period of their life.

Deeply impressed with the claims which these have upon our sympathy and nurturing care, and the importance of endeavouring to imbue their minds with sound religious principles, we think it right to encourage well-concerned friends, in the exercise of a kind and Christian interest for this and every other portion of our society, to consider whether, without in anywise interfering with our meetings for worship, and entirely distinct from them, arrangements might not be made for meeting together for the serious perusal of the Holy Scriptures, which are able to make "wise unto salvation through faith which is in Christ Jesus." Such engagements, if rightly entered into, would, we believe, tend to promote, and not in any degree to supersede, the private perusal of the sacred volume.

When thus occupied, in an humble and teachable disposition, and in reverent dependence upon the enlightening influence of the Holy Spirit, opportunities would be afforded for the illustration of our religious principles, and for the mutual edification and establishment of our members in the faith and hope of the Gospel. 1861.

We would earnestly caution our members—though we trust that such a caution is needed by very few—against any attempts to undermine the authority of Holy Scripture. The more we are experimentally acquainted with the mind of Christ, the more shall we be taught the inestimable value of those records of which He is the central theme. Their inspiration will become not a matter of opinion merely, but of experience, as the great Inspirer of all Scripture opens and applies the precious truths which are there revealed.

We advert with much interest to the increased attention given by many of our members to the careful perusal of the Sacred Writings. May this be ever associated with a deepening sense that it is only through faith in Christ Jesus that they can make wise unto salvation. "The natural man receiveth not the things of the Spirit of God." The Comforter alone can open the understanding to the Truth as it is in Jesus, and to a right sense of its harmony and just proportions. And there are experiences of the inner life, which, though in perfect unison with Scripture, may not be there literally described. They can only be understood as they are unfolded to the soul waiting in simple dependence upon that Spirit who searcheth all things, yea, the deep things of God. 1861. P. E.

SECTION IV.—ON GIFTS AND SERVICES FOR THE RELIGIOUS BENEFIT OF OTHERS.

A LIBERTY was enjoyed during the purest ages of Christianity, for any person moved by the Holy Spirit of God to preach the doctrine of the glorious Gospel of our Lord and Saviour Jesus Christ freely; and of which they were not deprived, till great corruptions of doctrine and practice were found amongst the professors of Christianity, and the civil powers were prevailed upon to meddle with the consciences of the people, which of right are to be subject to God only. 1735. P. E.

The deplorable condition of the Heathen, and the degraded circumstances under which they are living, have been felt at this time, as well as in former years, to be truly affecting. And although no way appears to open for our adopting any specific measure, in order to communicate to them the knowledge of the truths of the Gospel, we earnestly recommend their benighted condition to the frequent remembrance and Christian sympathy of all our members. There are various means of diffusing a knowledge of Christianity among them, which in no degree compromise our religious principles. The Holy Scriptures abundantly testify how offensive in the Divine sight are the abominations of idolatry; and we desire that all may stand open to the intimations of the Heavenly Shepherd, and follow the leadings of his Spirit into such services as He may be pleased to appoint to them individually. We rejoice in the part which many of our members have taken in the general diffusion of the Holy Scriptures, and in promoting a Christian education of the poor in this and in other countries; and we desire that these very important objects may receive the continued attention and support of Friends.

We feel at this time a warm and affectionate solicitude that we may all strive, through the help of the Holy Spirit, to live up to that profession of the Christian religion, and to maintain those views of its simplicity, spirituality, and purity, which our Society has uniformly thought it right to uphold. And, as living faith in the doctrines of the Gospel, and a practical observance of the precepts and example of our blessed Lord, regulate our affections and conduct, we shall be enabled more correctly to perceive our individual places in the church. In the exercise of this faith and obedience, we shall become more weaned from the love of the world, and more filled with the love of God; and whether our lot be cast at home or abroad, in more civilized or in less enlightened countries, we shall be made instrumental in advancing that kingdom which is righteousness, and peace, and joy in the Holy Ghost. 1833. P. E.

"Where the Spirit of the Lord is, there is liberty." The freedom of gospel ministry, and the liberty of all the living members of the Christian church to exercise the gifts bestowed upon them by its Holy Head, have been among the most prominent testimonies of our religious Society. In the fear of God, our early friends protested against the exercise of authority over conscience in matters between man and his Creator, and against the assumption, by any one individual, to act as the sole agent for the people in their assemblies for divine worship. We believe that this arrangement, by which the conducting of services in a Christian congregation rests with the minister, and the hearers are precluded from the exercise of spiritual gifts in the public worship of God, is a departure from primitive Christianity. In regard to these things, beloved friends, accept the word of earnest exhortation:—Stand fast in the liberty wherewith Christ hath made us free. 1843. P. E.

It was the prayer of the Psalmist—may it be the prayer of us all—" So teach us to number our days, that we may apply our hearts unto wisdom." Whatever may be the duration of our earthly existence, no life is too long for the performance of the duties which He who measures it out, appoints for it. May you then, beloved friends, in the middle or more advanced stages of life, be faithful in your several stewardships. Beware, we entreat you, of the beguilements of ease and self-indulgence; of being absorbed by the cares of the world, or hindered by its entanglements. Honestly seek to be redeemed from the encumbrances of earth; dwell in retirement of spirit before the Lord, and in the habitual exercise of the faith and love of Christ. Whether it be in the family or in the shop, in the market, the bank, or the board-room—in those things which belong to your private or to your public duties, let the light of the Gospel shine through all. The parent, the master, the man of business, the citizen, the servant—each has a testimony to bear for Christ. Let all be willing to dwell under a sense of their responsibilities and of their needs. Let our prayers be fervent, in the name of Jesus, for ourselves and for others. May those upon whom it rightly devolves be diligent in feeding the Lord's flock, and in gathering souls to Christ. And may none, whatever their position, overlook the lesser openings of duty. A word of counsel, of reproof, or of encouragement, spoken in season, in ever so broken a manner, whether in the family and social circle, or more publicly, how good it is! How often does it reach the witness in the hearts of others! How often does the blessing of the Lord attend it! Let us bear in mind the christian duty of watching over one another for good. Each may be called to manifest his interest, by word or deed, on behalf of a brother or a sister; and thus to follow in the footsteps of our Divine Master, whose whole life was marked by sympathy for the sorrows and infirmities of man.

Walking before Him as a retired, self-sacrificing, spiritually-minded people, may He be more and more known to dwell amongst us, distributing of his gifts, and preparing a succession of faithful labourers. We would speak tenderly, yet plainly, of our jealousy lest any of our dear friends should be keeping back from that place in the Lord's house to which He is calling them. We hail with satisfaction the interest taken by many of them in works of benevolence. We rejoice in observing, among our beloved younger friends, many hopeful evidences of attachment to the cause of their Redeemer. The sacrifices of earlier years are blessed in their season. But larger experience, and new accessions of grace, call for still increasing devotedness. May there be a progressive advancement from strength to strength. May zeal for that which is good be ever tempered with heavenly wisdom. Let nothing take the place of that love which draws the soul to Christ, as its rest and home. May all keep the eye single unto Him; prepared, with subjected hearts, for every fresh manifestation of his counsel. Varied are the services of his household, but to each the language is applicable, "Be ye clean, that bear the vessels of the Lord." The work of the Lord is ever an humbling work, bringing low and keeping low. Many are its conflicts and humiliations, but unspeakable its joys. "Where I am," saith our Holy Redeemer, "there shall also my servant be: if any man serve me, him will my Father honour." 1859. P. E.

We desire that our views as to the spirituality of divine worship, the authority and qualification for the ministry of the gospel, and the mode of holding our meetings for worship, may continue to be faithfully maintained.

Christ, who is Head over all things to the church, and who hath promised to be in the midst of those gathered in his name, does also condescend to make use of his servants, by imparting to them spiritual gifts, to be exercised under the renewed anointing of the Holy Ghost, for the conversion of sinners, and for the edification, exhortation, and comfort of the assembled worshippers.

Whilst careful to uphold the gospel standard in the things of God, we desire to be preserved from limiting in any degree the fulness and the freeness of the operation of the Holy Spirit. Each living member of the Church of Christ has a place of service, and to such the manifestation of the Spirit is given to profit withal.

We thankfully acknowledge the goodness of the Lord in the diversities of gifts, intellectual as well as spiritual, which, in his care for the church, He is pleased to confer upon its several members. May we ever bear in mind that, however great their diversities, it is by the one Spirit they are given; however differing in the administrations, it is the same Lord; however diversified the operations, it is the same God which worketh all in all.

We desire to encourage our friends individually to faithfulness in occupying the talent received, "as they that must give account;" in dependence upon his grace, and in loving service to Him, who loved them and gave Himself for them; remembering the apostolic injunction, "Ye are not your own, for ye are bought with a price; therefore glorify God in your body and in your spirit, which are God's." We believe that a freer exercise of the various gifts graciously bestowed upon many of our members, might, under, the divine blessing, tend to the instruction, comfort, and edification of the body, and to the spreading of the truth "as it is in Jesus." 1861.

Our attention has been, at various times, seriously turned to the condition of vast numbers of our fellow countrymen in this land, living in ignorance and sin; and we rejoice with thankfulness in contemplating the Christian efforts which have been and continue to be made, for the improvement of their moral and religious condition, by the members of our religious Society. At the same time, believing that much more of devotedness is called for at our hands, and that not a few amongst us are entrusted with gifts and qualifications which ought to be employed in the service of Christ, this meeting feels engaged to encourage Friends to give themselves up in the love of the gospel to the performance of these duties. As in simplicity and in faith, they commit thier efforts to the blessing of the Lord, their labours of love will, we cannot doubt, be graciously accepted of Him. 1861.

SECTION V.—GENERAL CHRISTIAN COUNSEL.

It is much upon us to put Friends in remembrance to keep to the ancient testimony truth begat in our hearts in the beginning, against the spirit of this world; for which many have suffered cruel mockings, beating, stoning, &c., particularly as to the corrupt fashions, dealings, and language of the world, their over-reachings and vain jestings; that the cross of Christ in all things may be kept to, which preserves friends blameless, and honours the Lord's name and truth in the earth. 1675.

Let none strive nor covet to be rich in this world, in these changeable things that will pass away; but let your faith stand in the Lord God who changes not, that created all, and gives the increase of all. 1676.

Friends are advised to be careful of their conduct at all times and on all occasions; that no stumbling-block be laid in the way of honest inquirers, nor offence given to tender young convinced friends. "Let your light so shine before men, that they may see your good works, and glorify your Father which is in heaven." Let us walk wisely towards those that are without, as well as those within; let our moderation and prudence, as well as truth and justice, appear to all men, and in all things; in trading and commerce, in speech and communication, in eating and drinking, in habit and furniture; and, through all, in a meek, lowly, quiet, spirit; that, as we profess to be a spiritually-minded people, we may appear to be such as, being bounded by the cross of Christ, show forth the power of that divine principle we make profession of, by a conversation every way agreeable thereunto. 1731. P. E.

Let none be ashamed of the tendering power of the Lord, but yield to the operation of his Word, which is as a fire to burn up, and as a hammer to break in pieces. It was by this that our ancients became a bright and shining people. The Lord himself hath declared his approbation of an humble and contrite state and condition of soul; so that none need to be ashamed of it. "Thus saith the Lord, the heaven is my throne, and the earth is my footstool: where is the house that ye build unto me? and where is the place of my rest? For all those things hath mine hand made, and all those things have been, saith the Lord: but to this man will I look, even to him that is poor and of a contrite spirit, and trembleth at my word." And the royal prophet says, "The sacrifices of God are a broken spirit: a broken and a contrite heart, O God, thou wilt not despise." 1739. P. E.

We beseech you to stand upon your guard against the allurements and temptations of this evil world: and beware of an ambitious and covetous spirit, by which many are ensnared in an eager pursuit of earthly enjoyments; the danger of which is thus described by the apostle Paul: "They that will be rich fall into temptation and a snare, and into many foolish and hurtful lusts, which drown men in destruction and perdition: for the love of money is the root of all evil; which while some coveted after, they have erred from the faith, and pierced themselves through with many sorrows." Beware, therefore, dearly beloved, lest you also, being led aside by the love of this world, and the deceitfulness of riches, fall from your own steadfastness. 1740. P. E.

And, dear friends, under a consideration of the subtle and continual assaults of the enemy of our souls, we find it necessary to put you in mind, that, whatever your advancement in the work of religion, or your services in the church may have been, you have still as great need as ever to dwell in an humble state of watchfulness. Some, whom the Lord hath favoured with the influences of his love while their hearts remained low and humble in his sight, have, by giving way to the subtle temptations of the enemy, under the specious pretence of enlargement and freedom of spirit, become exalted in their minds, gradually declined from their first love, and from that tender regard and care which once rested upon their minds towards God, and, by an unguarded conduct, have lost their esteem and service in the church, and brought dishonour on the blessed truth which they had long professed. "Wherefore let him that thinketh he standeth take heed lest he fall." 1743. P. E.

We profess to believe in the inward teachings of the Spirit of

Christ Jesus, our Redeemer and Mediator, our Advocate with the Father;—of Him whose precious blood was shed, that He might procure unto us eternal life, and present us holy, and unblamable, and unreprovable unto God. Let us individually inquire, how far we are acting in conformity with the solemn truths of the gospel. Are we seeking, in humble supplication unto the Lord, that our faith may be established therein? Are we, in patient waiting before Him, desiring that we may clearly discover the inshinings of his light upon our understandings, and that, by walking in faith, according to its manifestations, our lives may be spent in the love and fear of our great Creator! 1820. P. E.

If we are really concerned to look into our own hearts, if we do but enough bear in remembrance that our inmost thoughts are beheld by the all-penetrating eye of God, we shall be sensible that there ought to be no relaxation in the great duty of watchfulness unto prayer. The frequent recurrence of this conviction will lead us to look to a higher power than our own faculties, to enable us to work out our salvation, or to aid in promoting the Lord's work on the earth. An increase of gratitude, from a continued sense of the Lord's unmerited goodness, will animate us to serve Him in the performance of our allotted duties; in doing good to our neighbours, or in the concerns of the church. Then will there be a constant reference to Him who has qualified for the work: we shall, in reality, seek no honour one from another; but by our lives as well as by our words, ascribe all to Him to whom it is due. It is equally the duty of all our members, to endeavour, in their daily walk through life, to act consistently with their Christian profession. It is a serious reflection for us to make, that our conduct may, in the eyes of our associates, either adorn or dishonour the principles which we profess. Our views on silent waiting upon God, our belief that pure gospel ministry ought to be exercised from the immediate influence of the Holy Spirit, our testimony to the meek and peaceable nature of the religion of Jesus, and our non-observance of outward ordinances, originate in a conviction that the dispensation of the gospel is a spiritual dispensation. This our religious profession is a loud call upon us for great circumspection of conduct, and deep, inward retirement before the Lord. And, whilst persuaded that these precious testimonies are founded upon the precepts and spirit of the Gospel, we desire especially to press this sentiment upon our friends,—that we are at no time more qualified to bear them, than when we have the ornament of a meek and quiet spirit, and are willing to suffer for the name of Christ. 1821. P. E.

In these days of religious liberty, in which our intercourse with those of other societies is widely different from that which obtained in the times of our pious predecessors, it becomes us to be especially careful that we do not in any way compromise our ancient principles and testimonies. We believe that it is equally incumbent on us, as on those who were made instrumental in the first gathering of our Society, to maintain those views and practices by which they were distinguished. And we feel desirous that, both in the performance of our civil duties and in associating for objects of benevolence, all our dear friends may be concerned not in any way to forfeit the character of consistency, but in all things to adorn the doctrine of God our Saviour. It is, we believe, alike important to our own benefit, and to that of the universal church of Christ, that we do not shrink from filling that station in it which Divine Wisdom has assigned us, but in singleness of heart give ourselves up to what it may be our individual duty to perform. 1828. P. E.

We would remind our friends, that they can never be living members of the church of Christ, without baptism. And what is the baptism which can thus unite them in fellowship with the body? not the performance of any external rite;—but "the washing of regeneration and renewing of the Holy Ghost." Never forget, we beseech you, that vain will be the advantages which you have derived from the teaching of your fellow-men, unless you are truly born of the Spirit, and become new creatures in Christ Jesus. While we confess our continued conviction that all the ceremonies of the Jewish law were fulfilled and finished by the death of Christ, and that no shadows, in the worship of God, were instituted by our Lord, or have any place in the Christian dispensation, we feel an earnest desire that we may all be partakers of the true supper of the Lord. Let us ever hold in solemn and thankful remembrance the one great sacrifice for sin. Let us seek for that living faith, by which we may be enabled to eat the flesh of the Son of man and drink his blood. For, said our blessed Lord, "Except ye eat the flesh of the Son of man and drink his blood, ye have no life in you." Thus will our souls be replenished and satisfied, and our strength be renewed in the Lord. 1835. P. E.

God is faithful, who has called us unto the fellowship of his Son Jesus Christ our Lord. With Him there is bread for the hungry, water for the thirsty, strength for the weak, healing for the sick, and life for the dead. "The grace of God that bringeth salvation hath appeared to all men, teaching us that denying ungodliness and worldly lusts we should live soberly, righteously, and godly, in this present world." Who amongst us, beloved friends, has not been made a partaker of the offers of this grace? To which of us has not been proclaimed, "Behold the Lamb of God, which taketh away the sin of the world?" For which of us hath Christ not died? And who is there amongst us unacquainted with the inward pleadings of the Holy Spirit, softening and contriting the heart, and graciously inviting to the full acceptance and enjoyment, in the obedience of faith, of the plenteous redemption which is in Christ? Seeing then that, in the infinite compassion of our Heavenly Father, his love hath thus abounded towards us in Christ Jesus, fervent are our desires that there may be none in anywise shrinking from the full surrender of the heart unto Him. To be baptized with the Holy Ghost, to experience the circumcision of the heart, is indispensably necessary to a full participation in the privilege of true membership in the church and family of the redeemed. Without this our Christianity is but a name. And if we have a name that we live when we are dead, what will it profit us? How inestimable is the value, how full of woe is the loss, of the immortal soul! May none be loitering as at the threshold of the sanctuary; prepared, it may be, even to rejoice at the entering in of others, without entering in themselves. May none allow the strength and vigour of their days to pass away as though they had no object beyond this transitory life: but may each, in reverence and godly fear, keep continually in remembrance the infinite importance of our present stewardship; and that we are individually called by the most impressive considerations, not to be spectators merely of the Christian race, but to run that race ourselves, if we would, in the end, through unmerited mercy, obtain the incorruptible crown. 1856. P. E.

Beloved friends, have we sufficiently realized the work and power of the Spirit of our Lord, both in its early and in its more abiding manifestations? Have we submitted to its heart-searching, heart-cleansing baptism? Have we, as faithful subjects, been willing-hearted recipients of the grace of our heavenly King? To every member of his church He entrusts a portion of spiritual treasure to be diligently used, not to be buried in the earth or selfishly enjoyed. It is for mutual profit and help that the manifestation of the Spirit is mercifully bestowed. May we, then, be faithful and diligent in our several callings, as good stewards of the manifold grace of God. Whatever be our position in life, may we be concerned to adorn his doctrine in all things, and to commend it to others by an humble and self-denying conversation. So shall the word of Christ dwell in us, not sparingly, but richly; and after our measure of suffering and of service is filled up, it shall be ours, in due season, to reap abundantly, if we faint not. 1858. P. E.

SECTION VI.—EXHORTATIONS TO CHRISTIAN SIMPLICITY, MODERATION AND SELF-DENIAL.

We earnestly desire that Friends everywhere be put in mind to keep under the leadings and guidance of the Spirit of Truth in their outward habits and fashions thereof; not suffering the spirit of the world to get over them, in a lust to be like unto it in things useless and superfluous; lest it prevail upon them, by giving a little way to it, till it leads them from the simplicity and plainness that become the gospel; and so from one vain liberty to another, till they come to lose the blessed liberty that is in Christ, into which they were in measure redeemed, and fall back into the bondage of the world's spirit, and grow up into the liberty of the flesh with the lust and concupiscence thereof; and so lose both their name and place in the truth, as too many have done. 1688. P. E.

It is our tender and Christian advice that Friends take care to keep to truth and plainness, in language, habit, deportment, and behaviour; that the simplicity of truth in these things may not wear out or be lost in our days, nor in those of our posterity; and to avoid pride and immodesty in apparel, and all vain and superfluous fashions of the world. 1691. P. E.

It is the advice of this meeting that all Friends keep to the simplicity of truth, and our ancient testimony, in calling the months and days by scripture names, and not by heathen. 1697. P. E.

This meeting, under a deep sense that pride, and the vain customs and fashions of the world, prevail over some of our profession, particularly in the excess of apparel and furniture, doth earnestly recommend that all who make profession with us take care to be exemplary in what they wear, and what they use, so as to avoid the vain customs of the world, and all extravagancy in colour and fashion; and keep themselves, in respect thereof, spotless and blameless, adorning their profession in all modesty and sobriety; and that all parents be watchful over their children, and careful not to suffer them to get up into pride and excess, but keep them to that decent plainness which becomes the people of God; that their children may not be exposed to ruin by their parents' neglect. 1703. P. E.

Forasmuch as a true Christian practice, and every branch of it, is the fruit and effect of the inward sanctification of the heart, by the Spirit of Christ, for which we are frequently to wait on Him in all humility and lowliness of mind; we tenderly advise, that everything tending to obstruct or divert the minds of children, or those of more advanced years, from this good exercise, may be carefully avoided and taken out of the way. And it being evident, that the glory and vanity of the world, and the pleasures and diversions of it, are of this nature and tendency; we therefore advise that all parents and masters, in the first place, be good examples to their children and families, in a humble and circumspect walking, and with all plainness of habit and speech; and also, that they be very careful not to indulge their children in the use and practice of things contrary thereunto. 1735. P. E.

It is also our concern to exhort all friends, both men and women, to watch against the growing sin of pride, and to beware of adorning themselves in a manner disagreeable to the plainness and simplicity of the truth we make profession of. O that they would duly consider that reproof which the Lord, by the mouth of his prophet, pronounced against the haughty daughters of Zion, where He describes even the particularities of their dressings and ornaments, so displeasing to the Lord, and drawing down his judgments upon them! "I will," saith the apostle Paul, "that women adorn themselves in modest apparel, with shamefacedness and sobriety; not with broidered hair, or gold, or pearls, or costly array; but (which becometh women professing godliness) with good works:" plainly shewing that such adornings are contrary to the profession of godliness. The apostle Peter also is very full in his exhortations on this subject: "Whose adorning," saith he, "let it not be that outward adorning, of plaiting the hair, and of wearing of gold, or of putting on of apparel; but let it be the hidden man of the heart, in that which is not corruptible, even the ornament of a meek and quiet spirit, which is in the sight of God of great price; for after this manner in the old time the holy women also who trusted in God, adorned themselves:" plainly intimating, that those who of old were holy, and did trust in God, placed not their delight in such ornaments. O that ye would weigh and consider these things! "Let your moderation be known unto all men," and, "grieve not the holy Spirit of God;" but, be ye followers of Him, as dear children; walking "circumspectly, not as fools, but as wise, redeeming the time, because the days are evil." 1739. P. E.

As temperance and moderation are virtues proceeding from true religion, and are of great benefit and advantage, we beseech all to be careful of their conduct and behaviour, abstaining from every "appearance of evil;" and as an excess in drinking has been too prevalent among many of the inhabitants of these nations, we recommend to all Friends a watchful care over themselves, attended with a religious and prudent zeal against a practice so dishonourable and pernicious. 1751. P. E.

As to the frequenting of public-houses, we desire that all under our name may be cautious of remaining in them, after the purpose of business or of refreshment is accomplished: but to make them a resort for any other purpose, may it never need to be named among a people who profess the practice of Christian sobriety. 1797. P. E.

It ought to be the frequent concern of every one who professes the name of Christ, by watchfulness unto prayer (a duty often enjoined, but which cannot be too deeply impressed) to follow the example of our blessed Saviour, and to obey his sacred precepts. If thus concerned, he will be anxious by an honest examination to ascertain whether, by a daily course of self-denial, he is evincing his sense of the marvellous love displayed by the coming in the flesh, and as a sacrifice for sin, of the Son of God, who is "the light of the world." We are persuaded, beloved friends, that, if these solemn subjects have their due place in the mind, you will become fearful lest the love of the world should dispossess you of the love of God. In this day of comparative outward ease, and of exemption from great suffering in the support of our views of the pure and spiritual nature of the Gospel, it especially behoves us to be on our guard that we be not gradually drawn aside from the simplicity of the truth as it is in Jesus. 1825. P. E.

This meeting has been brought under renewed concern respecting the dreadful evils which result to the community from intemperance, and especially from the use of ardent spirits: and it recommends to Friends individually, seriously to examine what it is in their power to do towards diminishing this fruitful source of evil. We consider that abstaining from the use of distilled spirits, except for medicinal purposes, would not only preserve many from a snare into which they might otherwise be drawn, but might be highly useful as an example to others more exposed to the temptation: and we believe that those who, from love to God and their neighbour, are willing thus to deny themselves the use of these articles, will find satisfaction therein. 1835.

Our testimony to plainness of speech, behaviour and apparel, rests upon sound, unalterable grounds. It was in the hearty reception of the government of Christ, and in love to Him, and fidelity to his law, that our forefathers, in the light of that truth which the Lord was pleased so largely to shed upon them, were led to the full testimony which they bore against the flattery, pride, and untruth, which had, and still have, so largely insinuated themselves into the established customs and the changing fashions of the world. They were truly an honest, plain, and truth-speaking people; their conduct manifested that they were not of this world; and they believed it right to train up their children in those habits and practices into which the law of Christ had led them. Our present concern is that we may all be brought to follow Christ in the same faithfulness and devotedness of heart. 1842.

"It is required in stewards that a man be found faithful." We had need often to ponder the nature and extent of our stewardship in life, and to call to mind that day of awful reckoning in which every one of us shall give account of himself to God. Happy is that man who, seeking to maintain a good conscience towards God, hath ceased to live unto himself, and is living unto Him who died for us and rose again. Those to whom it is given upon this wise to look upon themselves as bought with a price, and who desire that they may be helped to glorify God in their body, and in their spirit, which are God's, (and is it not to this, dear friends, that we are, every one of us, called?) will be brought to feel that this is not the place of their rest; their hearts being set upon heavenly treasure, that which is earthly and perishable will have less place in their affections; their moderation,—the right and temperate use of the Lord's outward gifts,—will appear unto all men; it will be their concern to be kept from the love of ease, from undue creaturely indulgence, and from the luxuries of life. Regulated by this Christian standard, our personal expenditure, our style of living, the furniture of our houses, the supply of our tables, the plainness and simplicity of our apparel, the right use of our leisure time and of our property, will evince, so far as these things are concerned, that the love of the world is losing its hold upon us, and that the love of Christ is growing stronger and stronger within us. 1844. P. E.

Under the influence of the fear of God, and with a comprehensive view of the requirements of the divine law, we are brought to the Christian standard of truthfulness and simplicity in language, and of plainness and self-denial in clothing, in furniture, and in deportment; and, as becometh men professing godliness, we are led out of a conformity to the varying fashions of the day, and restrained from the pursuits of music and dancing, from theatrical entertainments, and from vain sports and other frivolous and hurtful amusements of the world. Suffer then, we beseech you, the word of exhortation. Be willing to be kept within the bounds of this holy fear. Abide in it all the day long. Allow its restraints to be so laid upon you that, being preserved by it in a quiet and lowly mind, you may, under its influence, and in simple dependence upon Christ, witness for yourselves the evangelical blessing promised by the Lord through his Prophet.—" Unto you that fear my name shall the Sun of righteousness arise with healing in his wings." 1848. P. E.

We have often had to remind our friends of the duties of plainness and moderation in reference to dress. Without any diminution of interest on this point, we feel it right at the present time to advert more particularly to those duties with relation to the furniture of our houses and our general manner of living. We are apprehensive that a degree of display, of luxury and of self-indulgence has crept in amongst us, tending not only to gratify the vain mind, but more or less to benumb the spiritual faculties: and the effect is often not less injurious upon the children of those who, in these particulars, are departing from our testimonies. We fear also that some, who are in moderate, or even in limited, circumstances, being led away by a desire to imitate those whose means are more ample, have been induced to set out in life on a scale of expenditure unsuited to their income, and have thereby been led into a course which has ended in ruin; and where this may not have been the result, their time, their strength and their hearts have, in consequence of the efforts to meet such expenditure, been absorbed by the pursuits of business, to a degree detrimental to their religious growth and to their usefulness in the church. We feel at the same time a concern that, whilst restrained from a vain, a self-indulgent, or an imprudent expenditure on themselves and their families, our dear friends may be preserved from parsimony and the snare of accumulating property, to their own and their children's hurt. Rather let them regard the larger means which the self-restraint we have recommended would leave at their disposal, as adding to their stewardship, for the alleviation of poverty and wretchedness, and for the good of their neighbour. 1849. P. E.

This meeting has been brought under deep concern, in view of the fearful amount of sin and misery existing in our land through the prevailing use of intoxicating liquors. We regard with cordial satisfaction the efforts of many of our members in different parts of the country, to stay the progress of this desolating scourge; and we take comfort in believing that, under the divine blessing, their labour has not been in vain. Whilst we would carefully avoid interfering in any way with the Christian liberty of our dear friends, we would encourage them seriously to consider what may be their individual duty in relation to this important subject. The more we seek to follow the example, and to be imbued with the spirit, of our blessed Redeemer, the less shall we be disposed to shrink from any course of effort or of self-denial, which a compassionate regard for the temporal and eternal well-being of those around us may call for at our hands. 1857. P.E.

Very impressive are the words of our Holy Redeemer, in which He describes his true followers: "They are not of the world, even as I am not of the world." He is the Emmanuel, elect and precious, the image of Him who is invisible; in whom the righteousness and grace of God are revealed to man. And it is the high privilege of his disciples to follow his steps; to be conformed to his holy image; to be, like Him, pure and separated in spirit from the world, meek and lowly in heart, not seeking to gratify self, but in all things given up to spend and be spent for the good of others, to do or to suffer according to the will of God. This is the path which our divine Forerunner hath Himself marked out and consecrated for us; a path of self-denial, humility and holiness. Let none, therefore, deceive themselves by any means. The lust of the flesh, the lust of the eyes, and the pride of life, are not of the Father, but are of the world. And whether it be in our personal habits or attire, in our style of living, in the general tone of our conversation or reading, in the mode of spending our time or our money, in the character of our occupations, or in the manner of conducting our outward affairs; whether it be in that which we do or in that which we leave undone, all that in anywise fosters the desires of the flesh or of the vain and unregenerate mind, impairs the health and vigour of the Christian life. In looking at the holy example of his Lord, the humble believer is made deeply sensible that he has not attained; but as he advances in his course, he will be more and more constrained by the love of Christ, to "follow after" in simplicity and godly sincerity, often faint, yet still pressing forward. May none be satisfied with any lower aim. The standard is a high one, but it is set before us in infinite wisdom and love by Him who is willing graciously to supply all our need. 1857. P. E.

How important, in its connection with the great work of the Holy Spirit, is the duty of cultivating a tender religious susceptibility. Christianity is intended to influence the whole life and conversation. Some of its most precious promises relate to the daily conduct and experience of the believer. "I will dwell in them, and walk in them," saith the Lord. Marvellous condescension! Blessed is he who, in the living sense of it, abides continually in the filial fear of offending God. His tastes and perceptions being renewed from above, he will separate himself from that which the Lord hateth, and which his Spirit reproves. Faithfulness to the divine requirings in the varied details of life leads him into nonconformity with the world; and in this nonconformity he is, of necessity, a marked man amongst the worldly or less restrained. It was a deep consciousness of the essentially practical character of true religion, that led our forefathers to be distinguished from others. Often and feelingly did they declare that they affected no singularity, and imposed no merely human restraints; that they had no pleasure in offending their neighbour, and no stoical indifference to personal suffering; but that it was in the exercise of a good conscience towards God and man, that they were constrained to differ from others in these respects. Like them, we would plead for conformity unto Christ. The testimony which we receive from Him is to simplicity, truth-speaking, and self-denial. These we continue to esteem to be among the distinguishing features of complete, practical Christianity; and by them we trust that our members may ever desire to be known. 1858. P. E.

SECTION VII.—EXHORTATIONS TO LOVE AND UNITY.

DEAR friends, the prosperity of truth, the increase of love, unity and peace amongst all Friends, in their respective meetings and in general, is greatly desired by us; and that every one watch against and shut out all occasions of offences, contentions and divisions, and stop all whisperings, tale-bearing, back-biting and evil-speaking tending thereunto. Be kind and tender-hearted one to another, and earnestly labour for universal love, union and peace, in all the churches of Christ. 1689. P. E.

Where any hath received offence from another, let him first speak privately to the party concerned, and endeavour reconciliation between themselves; and not to whisper, or aggravate matters against them, behind their backs, to the making of parties, and to the widening of the breach. 1692. P. E.

We earnestly recommend an humble and condescending frame of spirit unto all; that with godly fear, wisdom, and meekness, we may be so ordered in all our respective services, that every high and rough thing may be laid low, that all occasions of striving may be prevented, and the peace of the church of Christ preserved and augmented amongst us. 1699. P. E.

Anonymous books, pamphlets and papers, reflecting darkly on Friends, are testified against; and it is desired that no such book, pamphlet, or paper be written, printed, published, or privately handed about, by any under our profession. 1718.

If you hear a report of a friend (to his disadvantage), be careful not to report it again, but go to the person of whom the report is, and inquire if it be true, or not; and if it be true, then deal with such person for it, according to the doctrine of Christ; but if false, then endeavour, as much as in you lies, to stop such report. 1719. P. E.

Among the gospel precepts, we find not any thing more strongly and frequently recommended by our Lord Jesus Christ and his apostles to the primitive believers, than that they should love one another; and as we are sensible that nothing will more contribute to the peace and prosperity of the church than due regard to this advice, so we earnestly desire that it may be the care and concern of all Friends to dwell therein; and, in the unity of the Holy Spirit, to maintain love, concord and peace, in and among all the churches of Christ. 1730. P. E.

It is our earnest desire that a spirit of love and humility may more and more diffuse itself among us, and influence the hearts of all, so that every one may come to seek peace, and pursue it; and that none be apt to take offence, but each, in his own particular, be more careful to rectify his own failings and imperfections, than curious in observing, censuring, and aggravating those of others. This will lead to the exercise of mutual forbearance and forgiveness one of another; by which the occasions of contention will be avoided, and the churches preserved in a state of peace and tranquillity. 1736. P. E.

From love to Christ arises that stream of love to the brotherhood, which, if suffered to flow in our hearts with unobstructed course, would bear away all malice and guile, and cause all complaints of tale-bearing and detraction to cease in our borders. O the precious care that attends the mind in which Christian charity is become habitual! "Charity," saith the apostle, "hopeth all things." It divulges not the faults of others, because, in its unbounded hope, it desires their removal without exposure. For the mind in which it dwells, ascribes its own preservation and the cleansing of its former sins, to the unbounded love of God in Christ Jesus; and it prays that all may partake of the same benefit. How opposite that disposition which delights to report evil, and to accuse! Shun it, dear friends, as the poison of asps. The sacred writings emphatically denominate the grand adversary of mankind by the name of accuser of the brethren. "Follow," therefore, "peace with all men, and holiness, without which no man shall see the Lord: looking diligently, lest any man fail of the grace of God; lest any root of bitterness springing up, trouble you, and thereby many be defiled." 1804. P. E.

Friends, seek peace and pursue it. Ye are called to love. O that the smallest germ of enmity might be eradicated from our inclosure! And verily there is a soil in which it cannot live, but naturally withers and dies. This soil is Christian humility; a state highly becoming and indispensable, for a being who depends continually on the favour of his Lord; a state in which of all others he can most acceptably approach his presence; and which naturally conducts frail man to love and compassion for the companions of his frailty and poverty, yet his fellow-partakers of the offered riches of the gospel. 1805. P. E.

To be "made perfect in love," is a high state of Christian excellence, and not attainable but by the sacrifice of selfish passions. No degree of resentment can consist with this state. Some persons are apt to profess that they can forgive those whom they suppose to have injured them, when such are brought to know and acknowledge their fault. But that is little else than a disguised pride, seeking for superiority. The love which Christ commanded to his church, goes further than that. "This is my commandment, that ye love one another, as I have loved you." And how did the Lord love the world? Let the apostle answer: "God commendeth his love towards us, in that, while we were yet sinners, Christ died for us." And, friends, mark and remember his gracious dying words, when, praying for his very persecutors, He said, "Father, forgive them, for they know not what they do." And shall we expect access for our feeble prayers, at the throne of grace, if we harbour any ill-will to our fellow-travellers towards immortality? Let us hear again the Saviour of men: "And when ye stand praying, forgive, if ye have ought against any." He doth not allow time for seeing the injuring person become submissive; but,—*Standing, forgive:* for, "if ye do not forgive, neither will your Father which is in heaven forgive your trespasses." O, the excellence of Christian love and the temper of forgiveness! 1806. P. E.

Enmity pollutes the mind, and renders it unfit to approach with acceptance that pure and holy Being, of whom the beloved disciple thus emphatically testifies, "God is love." Do we not peculiarly lament the wide-spread distress, which the spirit of contention is, even now, occasioning to suffering humanity? This, though it differs in degree, springs from the same root as private ill-will. Therefore a people abhorrent of war, if they are consistent, will watch against the smallest bud of enmity, as it is conceived, on any occasion, in the heart. And the man who, in the school of Christ, hath learned the useful lesson of self-denial, will often make a sacrifice of his own will and opinion, though he may esteem them to be right, rather than persist in them, at the expense of Christian fellowship. 1808. P. E.

Seeing therefore the infinite value of love, that indispensable qualification of a true disciple, we are desirous of pressing it on every individual to examine impartially, how far he feels it to flourish in his own mind, and to influence all his actions. We believe that nothing will be so favourable to the preservation of this holy disposition as humility of heart; a temper in which we constantly see ourselves unworthy of the least of the Lord's mercies, and dependent only on his compassion for our final acceptance. Seeing also that no awakened mind can be without a view to a better and an enduring state, and that no one knows how soon he may be called to put off mutability, let us bear in perpetual recollection that, in the state to which we aspire, there is nothing but eternal love, joy and adoration, in the presence of Him through whose love we were first awakened.

In contemplating this copious subject, we feel disposed afresh to encourage friends to be prompt in undertaking, and prudent in executing, the blessed office of peace-maker. We believe the patient endeavours of faithful Friends will be generally crowned with success, in proportion as their own minds are seeking to Jesus, for assistance in performing an office on which He has pronounced his blessing; and in endeavouring to lead the minds of contending persons to a sense of the absolute necessity for all true disciples to live in peace one with another, and to forgive one another, even as God for Christ's sake has forgiven them. 1812. P. E.

One of the blessed effects of aspiring after holiness of life, is an increase of true love. This Christian virtue so expands and gladdens the heart, that its possessor having known its value, will be on the watch against any thing that may tend to disturb it: he will strive to yield to heavenly love, when causes of irritation present themselves. Even when he deems himself injured, he will be the more prepared to display the beauty of condescension, and, for the preservation of love and harmony, to relinquish his own right, and to refrain from insisting on his own views. 1821. P. E.

Love and charity towards others are essential features in the religious character. They excite in us a deep interest in the spiritual welfare of our friends; they prompt us to sympathize with them in their troubles, and, in real kindness, to offer a word of encouragement, and to extend a hand of help. When they are the habitual clothing of the mind, they check the first inclination to speak to the disadvantage of another; they enlarge the heart towards the whole human race; they lead us to rejoice in the extension of pure, vital Christianity, whatever may be the denomination amongst men, by which the disciples, engaged in its diffusion, are designated. 1822. P. E.

Dear friends, "be kindly affectioned one to another with brotherly love; in honour preferring one another." May we labour after an increase of that fellowship and sympathy in which we can bear one another's burdens; and in which, if one member of the church suffer, the others can suffer with it, and if one be honoured, the others can rejoice with it. May it be the prayer of us all, that the charity which hopeth, believeth, and endureth all things, may increase and abound amongst us. Bear one with the other in meekness and love, amidst the infirmities of flesh and spirit. "Likewise, ye younger, submit yourselves unto the elder; yea, all of you be subject one to another, and be clothed with humility." And may we every one so hold out to the end, that when the chief Shepherd shall appear, we may each receive a crown of glory that fadeth not away. 1833. P. E.

As the love of God prevails, it leads us to love one another; but how often does the enemy of man's happiness endeavour to scatter and divide! We therefore press it upon every one to examine whether he is distinguished by this badge of discipleship. Maintain that charity which suffereth long, and is kind; put the best construction upon the conduct and opinions one of another which circumstances will warrant. Take heed, with all diligence, dear friends, that the enemy produce no dissensions among you; that nothing like a party spirit be ever suffered to prevail. Let each be tender of the reputation of his brother; let every one be earnest to possess the ornament of a meek and quiet spirit. Watch over one another for good, but not for evil; and whilst not blind to the faults or false views of others, be especially careful not to make them a topic of common conversation. And even in cases in which occasion may require that the failings of others should be disclosed, be well satisfied, before they are made the subject of confidential communication, either verbally or by letter, that your own motives are sufficiently pure.

How beautifully are the origin, the motive, and the effect of love set forth by the apostle John, in the fourth chapter of his first epistle! Meditate again and again upon the comprehensive nature of this heavenly virtue, as there described. 1834. P. E.

Whilst it is at all times the duty of members of the church faithfully to maintain the truth, and whilst some of them may rightly feel themselves called upon openly to oppose error, we believe that there is hardly any thing more inimical to the growth of vital religion than indulgence in the spirit of religious controversy. Satan triumphs when he can make the name of Jesus a word of strife and debate among the professed followers of the Lord. If he, our soul's enemy, can but introduce men into his spirit, he cares little how true may be their words. Let us, therefore, each of us mind our own calling by keeping our eye single to the Lord; and then shall we know that "the fruit of the Spirit" will, in the sight of others, be "in all goodness and righteousness and truth," and to ourselves joy and peace.

It is a precious truth to us in our fallen condition, "that God was in Christ, reconciling the world unto himself, not imputing their trespasses unto them." Christ, who knew no sin, who was a propitiatory offering for our sins and for the sins of all mankind, who enlighteneth every man that cometh into the world, and who is ever present with his people, as "their Teacher to instruct them, their Counsellor to direct them, their Shepherd to feed them, their Bishop to oversee them, and their Prophet to open divine mysteries to them,"* was the foundation of our forefathers; and this foundation is ours. It was to this experimental knowledge of Christ that our early predecessors were engaged to gather all men, that they might really be prepared, sanctified, and made fit temples for Him to dwell in. By one Spirit they were baptized into one body; and, rooted and grounded in love, they were, through the help of their Lord, united one to another in upholding an open and decided testimony to the gospel in its primitive purity. 1846. P. E.

"Let brotherly love continue." It is the token that we are the children of God, who is emphatically love. It is

---

* George Fox's Journal.

the evidence that we belong to Christ. The psalmist compares the unity of the brethren to the anointing oil and the fertilizing dew. Where it is wanting there is no true fragrance or fruitfulness in the church. May the Lord himself cause this fragrance and this fruitfulness to abound yet more and more amongst you to his praise. 1848. P. E.

SECTION VIII.—EXHORTATIONS TO LIBERALITY AND BENEVOLENCE.

Let the Christian duty of visiting the sick be timely remembered and practised; it having often left comfort, ease and sweetness upon the spirits of many, to their very end. 1710. P. E.

We find ourselves at this time engaged to request that Friends, in any part of this kingdom, or other places, where provisions and the necessaries of life are dear and scarce, or sickness doth remarkably afflict, would, in proportion to such scarcity and affliction, exert their charitable assistance to the poor; which is our Christian duty, as stewards of the many mercies wherewith the Lord has intrusted us. 1729. P. E.

Warn those that are rich in this world, that they apply not the blessings of God to the indulging of their appetites in pleasure and vanity; but that they be ready to do good, and to communicate to the relief of those who are in necessity. The principal, if not only, satisfaction a man of a truly Christian disposition can have in affluence and the increase of the things of this world, must arise from the greater opportunities put into his hands of doing good therewith. 1741. P. E.

The great deception of mankind is, that they look for happiness where it is not; are ensnared by the love of the world and the deceitfulness of riches; "which while some coveted after, they have erred from the faith," have abused what they should have made good use of, and hurt themselves with the means given for the help of others; the love of money shutting up their hearts from the exercise of charity, in proportion to the substance bestowed on them. 1746. P. E.

We fear that some of our youth are training in habits of expense in attire, furniture and attendance, which are not only inconsistent with the simplicity of the gospel, but a constant call for much of that property which would be better employed in feeding the hungry, and of that time which might be occupied in visiting and cheering the habitations of human misery. "The trimming of the vain world," said our worthy elder, William Penn, "would clothe the naked one." It is not however with such only that we plead, on behalf of the indigent. We wish those who, in appearance and manners, are generally consistent with our self-denying profession, to be clear that a due proportion of their time and substance is spent in the relief of distress. 1798. P. E.

We warmly desire that the moral and religious improvement of every class of our fellow-men, and the alleviation of their sufferings and distress, may ever obtain that aid and sympathy, which, in the unlimited love of the Gospel of Christ, should be extended towards the whole human race; and that a disposition for active benevolence may be cherished in every heart; each being concerned, to know for himself in what way, consistently with his private and social duties, he may employ his talents for the good of others, and steadily to persevere in what he may have rightly undertaken, with a constant reference to the divine blessing;—not with a view to popularity or ostentation, but simply as acting the part of a wise and faithful servant, who must give an account to his Lord at his coming. 1824—1825. P. E.

The degraded and demoralized state of the poor, in many parts of the United Kingdom, and the great extent of crime, have at this time deeply affected us. We therefore intreat Friends, in their respective situations in town or country, to search out the causes of these evils; and to encourage their neighbours, and unite with them in their endeavours, to apply a remedy to them. And seeing it is sin which separates the soul from God, and that ignorance and intemperance, vice and irreligion, so much prevail among the inhabitants of the British Isles, we are desirous that our members may allow their sympathies to be awakened for these our fellow-subjects. And may their religious concern extend to other parts of Christendom similarly circumstanced, with an earnest desire that, under the blessing of

Providence, they may be made instrumental to effect a real improvement in the domestic, moral, and religious state of our fellow-men. 1833. P. E.

"Blessed is he that considereth the poor." It is our desire that we may all of us be kept in that state of watchfulness from day to day, and in that sense of our responsibility to God, in which we may be enabled to ascertain whether a due portion of our time, our sympathies, and our substance is devoted to the great duty of visiting the poor in our respective neighbourhoods, to the inspection of their condition, and to the relief of their wants; and we wish to put it to our dear young people, to consider whether a larger portion of their time, the means they may have at their disposal, and that which they could spare from the superfluities of life, might not be acceptably devoted to this object. It is important to ourselves, as well as to those who are in need, that the due support of institutions, whose object is the relief of human suffering, should not be substituted for the personal visiting of the poor in their own habitations, and the administering to their wants. 1844. P. E.

SECTION IX.—ADVICE IN RELATION TO THE MINISTRY.

This meeting desires and hopes that you whom the Lord hath gifted with a public testimony for his name and truth will, in this day of liberty, be diligent to visit the heritage of God in their meetings, and more especially those least frequented. 1695. P. E.

Dear brethren and sisters, all of you have a godly care of judging or contradicting one another in public meetings; or showing marks or signs of division therein, amongst ministers or others; it being of a pernicious consequence to bring blame or contempt upon the ministry, and a great hurt to our youth and others. 1716. P. E.

Advised, that ministers, as well as elders and others, in all their preaching, writing, and conversing about the things of God, do keep to the form of sound words, or scripture terms; and that none pretend to be wise above what is there written, and in such pretended wisdom go about to explain the things of God, in the words which man's wisdom teaches. 1728. P.E.

As the Lord in his mercy is breathing afresh on several of our youth, of both sexes, and fitting them for his service, we recommend it to the elders in every meeting, that they tenderly watch over all young ministers, and advise and help them, as they in the wisdom of truth may be opened thereunto: nourishing that which is right, and which comes forth in the savour of life, and discouraging every thing that is unbecoming the ministry. 1736.

We further intreat you, that in all your religious meetings appointed for the worship of Almighty God, you wait in humble reverence for the influence of the Word of life. Be cautious not to move, in acts of devotion, in your own will; set not self to work, but patiently attend and wait for the gift and enlivening power of the Divine Spirit; without which your performances will be unacceptable, and like those of old, of which it was said, "Who hath required this at your hand?" 1742. P. E.

In much love we caution those friends who are rightly concerned in the work of the ministry, to watch over their own spirits, and not to be hasty or censorious in passing judgment respecting the state of those who hear them; but to manifest that, in the exercise of their ministry, they are led by the love of God. 1745.

This meeting recommends to ministers on all occasions, and more especially when about to leave home in the service of the Gospel, to take care that their outward affairs are so conducted and arranged as to prevent any dishonour being brought on our religious profession, through any neglect on the one hand, or, on the other, through their being immersed in the cares of the present life. 1833.

We desire that none may despise the shortness or simplicity of any offerings in the ministry, and that all may be careful not to indulge in a criticising spirit; much less in a disposition to cavil or to judge their brethren, or in controversy. Such things are highly injurious and unbecoming: they lead off from that individual watchfulness and knowledge of ourselves which are essential to a growth in grace, and they are opposed to the meekness and lowliness of a disciple of Christ. Light conversation on the sacred truths of religion is also dangerous. 1835.

A living rightly authorized ministry has ever been a blessing to the church. Our views on the nature and source of gospel ministry have undergone no change. It is the prerogative of Christ Jesus, our Lord, to choose and to put forth his own ministers. A clear apprehension of Scripture doctrine, or a heart enlarged in love to others, are not of themselves sufficient for this work. Whatever may be the talents or scriptural knowledge of any, unless there be a distinct call to the ministry, our society cannot acknowledge it: and except there be a sense of the renewed putting forth and quickening influence of the Holy Spirit, we believe it to be utterly unsafe to move in this office. O! that our dear friends who may be young in the ministry, may take heed to their steps, and keep apart from every thing that would draw them from their own exercises; and that they may be preserved in such a lowly, teachable mind, as to avail themselves of the counsel and encouragement of their more experienced friends. May the diffident and fearful, those who go trembling on their way, be strengthened and encouraged; and may all, both elder and younger, be concerned to minister only in the ability which God giveth. 1835.

At a very early period of the Christian church, a gradual declension crept in, and the truth, as it is in Jesus, was obscured by the corrupt devices of men. Human wisdom and worldly power grievously interfered in spiritual things; a long and dark night of apostacy ensued; but, in the mercy of God, light and truth again broke forth, and we believe that He gave to our predecessors a further insight into the corruptions that had so long reigned among the professors of the Christian name, than had been given to any who had gone before them in the great work of reformation. By the inshining of this light, they saw that the ministry of the gospel of peace and salvation through our Lord and Saviour Jesus Christ is a gift from God himself; that the putting forth of the good Shepherd is to be waited for, from one time to another, in the exercise of this sacred office, and that it ought only to take place under the renewing of the Holy Ghost, and in the ability which God giveth. We thankfully believe that from the early rise of our society, the Lord has been pleased to bestow this gift upon servants and upon handmaidens without respect of persons, and that it has been exercised in his fear, and to the honour of his name; and we would humbly acknowledge that He does not at this day withhold from us this living ministry. We pray that He may be pleased to grant us its continuance and increase, and to keep us from ever desiring any other. That which is uttered under the qualification already set forth, will be delivered in the humiliation of the creature; it may sometimes be only in a few sentences; but as a holy care prevails to move only under the leadings of the Spirit of Truth, unexcited by the activity and affection of the natural man, it will contribute to the edification of the body in love. 1842. P.E.

And you who may believe yourselves called to bear a public testimony to your Lord, let such a call be accepted as a motive to increased watchfulness and humility. Yield up yourselves wholly to the operations of His Spirit, who sitteth "as a refiner and purifier of silver," to "purify the sons of Levi, and purge them as gold and silver, that they may offer unto the Lord an offering in righteousness." Let self be laid low, and your will be given up to the Lord. Move only as He calls you, and be very watchful to know both the outflowing and the staying of the anointing oil. 1861. P. E.

SECTION X.—COUNSEL TO PARENTS AND HEADS OF FAMILIES.

We do intreat and desire all you dear friends that are parents and governors of families, that ye diligently lay to heart your work and calling in your generation for the Lord, and the charge committed to you; not only in being good examples to the younger sort, but also to use your power in your own families in educating your children and servants in modesty, sobriety, and in the fear of God. 1688. P. E.

As touching the education of Friends' children, for which this meeting hath often found a concern, we think it our duty to recommend unto you, that no opportunity be omitted, nor any endeavours wanting, to instruct them concerning the principles of truth which we profess: and there being times and seasons, wherein their spirits are, more than at others, disposed to have such things impressed upon them, so we desire that all parents, and others concerned in the oversight of youth, may wait in the fear of God to know themselves qualified for that service; that in his wisdom they may make use of every such opportunity which the Lord shall put into their hands. 1717. P. E.—1861.

You who are parents of children, labour fervently in the spirit, with supplication unto the Lord, that He may give them an inheritance in the truth, wherein they may be enabled to stand up in their generation after you, to his praise and glory, rather than labour to get great inheritances for them in this world; which have proved a snare and temptation to some to shun the cross, and embrace the glory of this present world. But let those to whom God hath given riches, take the apostle's advice, that they "be not highminded, but fear," and trust not in uncertain riches; but "be rich in good works, ready to distribute, willing to communicate," and therein be good examples to their children. 1725. P. E.

And, dear friends, our advice and exhortation is, that all masters of families, parents, guardians, and tutors of children, would frequently put in practice the calling together of their children and households, to wait upon the Lord in their families; that, receiving wisdom and counsel from Him, they may be enabled seasonably to exhort and encourage them to walk in the way of the Lord, to exercise themselves in reading the Holy Scriptures, and in observing the duties and precepts of holy living therein recommended. 1748. P. E.

To all masters and tutors of children, we affectionately address ourselves; that in a particular manner it may be your care to caution, and, as much as in you lies, to guard the youth committed to your charge, against the dangers and allurements of evil communications, and the reading of profane and immoral writings, those powerful engines of Satan, whether they be such as directly tend to defile the affections, or, with a more specious appearance, to subvert the doctrines of Christianity by a presumptuous abuse of human reason, and by vain and subtle disputations, "after the rudiments of the world, and not after Christ." 1766. P. E.

As, next to our own souls, our offspring are the most immediate objects of our care and concern, it is earnestly recommended to all parents and guardians of children, that the most early opportunities be taken, in their tender years, to impress upon them a sense of the Divine Being, his wisdom, power, and omnipresence, so as to beget a reverent fear of Him in their hearts; and, as their capacities enlarge, to acquaint them with the Holy Scriptures, by frequent and diligent reading therein; instructing them in the great love of God to mankind through Jesus Christ, the work of salvation by Him, and sanctification through his blessed Spirit. For though virtue descendeth not by lineal succession, nor piety by inheritance, yet the Almighty doth graciously regard the sincere endeavours of those parents whose early and constant care is over their offspring for good; who labour to instruct them in the fear of the Lord, and in a humble waiting for, and feeling after, those secret and tender visitations of divine love, which are afforded for the help and direction of all. 1767. P. E.

Among some of the most irksome restraints to the lively dispositions of youth, are often those which relate to speech and dress. But as we know that the ground of our dissent from the world in these things, is Christian simplicity; so we know by experience, that they are often the means of defence against temptation to mingle in the company of such as are unsuitable examples for our youth to observe and to follow. And when, by the gentle intimations of the Spirit of Truth in their ripening understandings, they are entered on a course of self-denial, they will feel you doubly dear to them, for having led them on in the way they should go, and will bless the Lord on your behalf. 1808. P. E.

The habit of a constant attendance of meetings for divine worship forms an important branch of the religious education of our youth; we are therefore desirous of impressing on the minds of those to whom they are intrusted, and who themselves may be diligent, to beware how they deprive their children of such opportunities on the week-day. 1815. P. E.

Our solicitude has at this time been awakened for our young men employed as travellers in business. The exposure of these to the temptations to which they are often unavoidably subjected, has tended to draw aside some from that simplicity, that purity of heart and thought, that strict morality, which our Christian principles require. We would submit to the serious consideration of their parents and employers, the extreme danger of sending forth into such service any young persons whose religious principles are not fixed, nor their habits formed; and we would encourage Friends in different places, where those in this line of employment may travel, to continue and to extend that kind and hospitable notice which has been already manifested. 1816. P. E.

Parents, as they watch the opening capacities of their beloved offspring, may instil into them, during their very early years, (a period when prejudice and worldly temptations present but little obstruction to the work,) the first principles of religion. It is their indispensable duty to seek opportunities for this purpose; that they may impress upon their children the fear and the love of God, and point their early affections to the blessed Jesus, who laid down his life for them, and who has, in a peculiar manner, called them unto Himself.—" Suffer little children to come unto me, and forbid them not."

A highly important means for promoting these objects is instruction in the Holy Scriptures. No study is more interesting to children, when it is judiciously presented to their attention. It is a pleasant and most useful employment to store their tender minds with a knowledge of those sacred histories which so beautifully display the wisdom and love of God; to make them acquainted with the types and prophecies which represented beforehand the coming and character of Christ; and to point out to them those essential truths which were fully brought to light by the gospel. In the course of such instruction, their minds ought to be directed to those parts of Scripture which elucidate our peculiar religious testimonies. Thus, as they advance in life, they will know on what grounds their profession rests. An increasing attachment to that profession will also be promoted in them, by their being led to peruse the history of our Society, and especially the interesting lives of our early predecessors.

As friends are thus concerned to communicate to their tender charge a knowledge of Christian truth, we believe that they will themselves often derive instruction as well as comfort from the work. In prosecuting this work, let us always remember that we cannot, of ourselves, produce religion in the mind. On this principle, we must make it our chief object to direct the early and constant attention of our offspring to the Spirit of Christ within them, from which alone can spring the fruits of righteousness: we must wait upon that Spirit ourselves, for ability to perform our parental duties; and we must seek the Lord, in prayer, for his blessing upon all our efforts. Teach them, dear friends, that of themselves they can do nothing; let them be accustomed, in early life, to religious retirement; and tenderly advise them to lift up their hearts, morning by morning, and evening by evening, to the Author of all their mercies. Thus they will experience preservation, and, as they increase in stature, will increase also in favour with God and man.

But never forget, that it should be your care to set that example of a humble Christian, which so beautifully enforces the pure precepts of the gospel; your own minds must be seasoned with grace; and your labours will only be effectual, as they are carried on and blessed by the power of the Spirit of Christ. If, in the discharge of this duty, discouragements should arise, let not these become a cause of dismay. Even these may teach the important lesson, highly necessary to be learned, that it is only as fresh supplies of holy aid are granted, that we can safely labour in this work. 1818.

In the earliest periods of life, much of the care of children rests with mothers, and we desire that in all cases their pious endeavours may be strengthened by the co-operation of the fathers. The youthful mind is very soon susceptible of serious impressions; and we believe that if parents are careful to watch the most favourable opportunities, they may instil religious truths, lay a foundation for correct principles, and give a right bias to the affections, which may be greatly blessed at a future day. The safe ground on which parents can proceed is, so to live and so to wait before the throne of grace, as to be enabled to pour forth their secret prayers for the blessing of the Most High. Then, instead of looking back with bitter regret, if their beloved offspring should deviate from the path of Christian virtue, they may commit their cause with conscious integrity to Him whom they have desired to serve. 1821. P. E.

Much of the undue liberty indulged in by the youth is often occasioned by the early indulgence granted to them by the parent: wherefore this meeting tenderly, affectionately, yet earnestly, intreats such as are parents, or have the care of children, that they be very early and firm in endeavouring to habituate them to a due subjection of their will; that, having maturely weighed the injunctions which they find necessary to impose, they suffer them not to be disregarded and disobeyed. The habit of obedience, which may thus be induced, will render the relation of parent and child additionally endearing; and as it will prepare the infant mind for a more ready reception of the necessary restraints of the cross, it may be considered, in part, as preparing the way of the Lord: whilst those who neglect to bend the tender minds of their children to parental authority, and connive at their early tendencies to hurtful gratifications, are, more or less, making way for the enemy and destroyer. 1822.

We affectionately exhort parents, and all who have the care of children and young persons, constantly to bear in remembrance the great value of a tender conscience; and to turn their attention to the secret instructions of Divine Grace, reproving for evil, and bringing peace for doing well. Be concerned, dear friends of this class, early to subject the wills of those entrusted to your charge; encourage them to fix their affections on things which are eternal; set before them the necessity of being converted from the evil of their own hearts, and kept clean from the sin which abounds in the world; impress them with a sense of the holiness and purity of God, and of his righteous law; instruct them in the invaluable truths of the Bible, and lead them to seek after the practical application of these precepts and doctrines under the influence of the Holy Spirit. By such a course of religious care and Christian instruction, carried on in simple, humble dependence upon God, you will perform the great duty of bringing them up in the nurture and admonition of the Lord. 1830. P. E.

Our sympathy and esteem are peculiarly due to those who are conscientiously occupied in discharging the responsible duties attached to the care of youth. With the right fulfilment of your trust, dear friends, our hopes of a succeeding generation are intimately connected. Your calling is arduous, but of eminent utility; and one in which you have abundant opportunity to serve the Lord. You have especial need to seek for the wisdom which is from above; but if, through heavenly help, you have been made instrumental in establishing correct moral habits and sound religious principles, however limited your sphere, you may hope to partake of the blessing of those who turn many to righteousness. We are religiously concerned that our young people of every class, whilst they are receiving that education which will fit them for usefulness in after life, may continue to be trained up in the knowledge and love of the Holy Scriptures; and that they may, in humility and the fear of the Lord, examine for themselves the external evidences of the Christian religion. May they ever be preserved in that teachable, watchful, and tender state of mind, in which they will be alive to the perceptible influence of the Holy Spirit, and in which the Lord will be pleased to grant them a right understanding of the way of life and salvation. 1833. P. E.

We have been led at this time deeply to feel how important is the effect of example in the great work of religious training; and we would affectionately intreat those to whom the care of families is entrusted, to ask themselves in the fear of the Lord, how far their conduct and conversation, their self-denial, and godly simplicity, are calculated to attract to, and to lead forward in, the Christian course, the minds of their beloved offspring. Powerful indeed upon others, and especially upon the young, is the influence of a truly religious life. It answers to the witness of God in their hearts and consciences; and by this witness they quickly perceive the inconsistencies with the divine law, which may be exhibited in the practice of those who are around them.

The end of all religious training is to bring the mind under subjection to the will of God, to lead our children unto Jesus, that through Him they may obtain the forgiveness of sins, and be taught in his school who was meek and lowly of heart. How, dear friends, shall we prosecute this work, if we have not ourselves submitted to the yoke of Christ, and been taught of Him? We believe that not a few, who have been measurably thus instructed, and who are religiously concerned for the welfare of their families, will do well to look around them and consider whether anything in their habits of life, the indulgences which they allow themselves, the character of their conversation, the persons with whom their children have intercourse, and the books and other publications which are permitted to enter their houses, are not opposed to the training of their families in a religious life and conversation. Let us not esteem any of these things as insignificant.

Parents should beware that they do not cherish the seeds of vanity in their offspring, by providing them with ornamental attire, or gratify similar dispositions in themselves by thus decorating even their children of the tenderest age. The will should be early subjected in the authority of Christian love; and children accustomed, from their very infancy, to a strict adherence to truth-speaking.

Above all things, dear friends, let us seek to impress upon the susceptible minds of our youth, the fear and love of their Creator and Redeemer, and the minding of those gentle intimations of his will, which are frequently made by the Spirit of Truth, upon the very youthful heart.

Blessed indeed is the child who is thus betimes taught of the Lord, and led onwards, amidst the snares of youth, in his holy way. Well is known to many children that struggle described by the apostle, " the flesh lusteth against the spirit, and the spirit against the flesh; and these are contrary the one to the other." And it may be the privilege of those who have the charge of youth, by example.and by word, to help them in these conflicts, and strengthen them to cleave to the Lord. And O! may it not be, that any of these little ones are offended and stumbled by the conduct of those to whom they look up as their instructors and examples. 1842.

Education, in the largest and most comprehensive sense of the word, constitutes an important branch of Christian discipline: it was strongly enjoined in the precepts of the Old Testament; it held a conspicuous place in the church of Christ in its earliest days; and, in our own Society, it has ever been an object of concern and solicitude. Our forefathers were men fearing God: in this fear it was their honest concern to keep themselves from the corruptions of the world: they had deep experience in that warfare in which " the flesh lusteth against the Spirit, and the Spirit against the flesh;" and through the mercy of God in

Christ Jesus, and by the working of his power, they were brought into that liberty and peace, and that hope for the life to come, which are set before us in the gospel. They had a strong sense of the inherent tendency of the heart of man to pride and vanity, and that these corrupt propensities could not be overcome but by the power of the Spirit of God; hence their great aim in the religious education of their children was to turn their minds to those secret convictions, by which the Lord is pleased, even in very childhood, to visit the soul of man: they sought to bring their little ones to Jesus; and many were those in whom this godly care was eminently prospered. The earlier and later periods of our history furnish us with instances of young people trained up in the nurture and admonition of the Lord, who, having borne the yoke in meek submission to the restraints of that wisdom which is from above, approved themselves in after life good soldiers of Jesus Christ, enduring hardness for his sake. And many have been the instances of children, who, gathered to the bosom of their Saviour in their very tender years, have given testimony, upon the bed of sickness and at the approach of death, to the efficacy of that living faith in Christ, which had been nurtured within them by the watchful and Christian care of their parents. Out of the mouth of babes and sucklings the Lord has perfected praise. 1844. P. E.

To you, dear friends, who are in the position of parents, the condition in the sight of the Lord of your beloved offspring is unspeakably important. Shrink not, we intreat you, from your solemn responsibilities. Remember that your children are born for eternity; and let it be your great concern to lead them to the Saviour, that they may be early trained to bear his yoke, and be prepared for an inheritance in his kingdom. Be tenderly watchful that his holy name may be sanctified among them, through your conversation and example. Seek for opportunities to instruct them in the truth, as it is in Jesus, and be especially concerned that the disciplining of their hearts in righteousness may be steadily going forward. And, under a deep sense of the importance of these duties, may your prayers unto God be fervent for that wisdom and help which will not fail to be found sufficient for all the needs of those who honestly trust in Him. 1852. P. E.

To the Christian mother the precious infant is committed, with the implied charge on behalf of its heavenly Parent,—Take this child and nurse it for Me.

How solemn are the responsibilities thus involved, and how needful that the parental obligations should not be put aside or turned away from, under any feeling of discouragement or want of qualification! It is not on the highly gifted parent alone that the duty is imposed of training up his children in the fear of God, and in the knowledge of the Holy Scriptures; it is a charge laid upon *every* parent; and the sense of our own insufficiency, however deeply felt, will prove no valid plea for neglect, when we are called to account for the trust committed to our keeping. Let none, whilst endeavouring, with single-minded earnestness and in reliance upon higher aid, to discharge this duty, doubt that ability will be granted to them; let them rather believe that they will reap the reward of their efforts in a blessing upon their children and upon themselves. The endearing relation which subsists between parents and their tender offspring ought surely to awaken in the hearts of the former earnest breathings of spirit, that they may be helped to train their children, even from very early years, in tenderness of conscience, in obedience to the restraints and guidance of the Holy Spirit, and in the love of Christ our Saviour.

How appropriate and how interesting would be the occupation of a few minutes each evening before retiring to rest, and of larger portions of time on First-days, in hearing each child of a family repeat to his parent a scripture text learned during the day, or passages from the Psalms and the prophecies, or from the parables and precepts of our Lord. Whilst such exercises would richly store the memory and strengthen the intellect, how many opportunities would they afford to the watchful parent, to impart some lesson of Christian practice, or to present some simple view of divine truth. How might the child's feelings be interested, his sympathies awakened, and his affections warmed and cherished, as he listened to the beautiful narratives of Abraham's faith, of Joseph's filial obedience and purity, of Samuel's early piety, of Jonathan's and David's friendship, of the undaunted faithfulness of Daniel and his three companions to their God; and, above all, of the meek and patient suffering of the Holy Redeemer, his tender love for children, and his wonderful works of beneficence and power. Nor are the warnings conveyed in the narratives of the Flood, of the destruction of Sodom and Gomorrah, of the forty years' wanderings of the Israelites, of Gehazi, of Ananias and Sapphira, and of many others, to be unheeded or unimproved. How often have the lessons of childhood thus given been remembered through life; and how often has the tone of religious feeling, thus early implanted, been the instrument of preservation through youth, and the blessing of manhood and old age! 1857.

SECTION XI.—COUNSEL TO EMPLOYERS.

A RELIGIOUS care is recommended toward our servants, that all appearance of pride, idleness, and vain conversation in them may be discouraged; and that they may be exhorted to attend public worship, and have a sense of God's love upon their spirits, and therein partake of the sweetness of truth; and, in the discharge of their duty to God, and to their masters and mistresses, know peace in themselves. 1718.—1861.

We earnestly intreat that it may be the constant care of all masters and mistresses properly to teach, restrain, and example those whom Providence hath placed under them, for their help, direction and preservation, and for whom an account must be rendered; bringing them up in the fear of the Lord. 1760. P. E.

May those who have the ability to employ servants, whether professing with us or not, sympathize with them in their labours, delight to render them happy, and seek for that disposition that can lead them along as fellow-travellers in the road to the city of God. Various are the means by which this may be attempted. The principal one certainly is, the keeping of the mind attentive to the discoveries of truth; and, as a perusal of the Scriptures is the frequent employ of many families, we desire that the servants may be made partakers of the benefits resulting from the practice, and from occasional opportunities of retirement in spirit. 1805. P. E.

This meeting has been impressed with the importance of the exercise of a due care towards young persons who are taken as apprentices by Friends. It may be thought that an additional responsibility attaches to the taking of members of our Society in that station, or as shopmen or servants; but this meeting trusts that if, from a sincere desire to protect such individuals, Friends were willing to give a preference to our own members, a real satisfaction would arise from it; and we further desire that those who fill the station of master, may endeavour to discharge the important duties which devolve upon them, in a moral and religious care of those who are employed in their service.

We are comforted in the persuasion that the care and instruction which many in early life have received in our public schools have been a blessing to them, and we are anxious that both their employers and other friends in the meetings in which these and other young persons reside, may watch over them for good, and be willing in various ways to show an affectionate interest in their comfort and welfare. A few kind expressions arising from a solicitude for their moral and spiritual good, offered in love as opportunities occur, may have more effect than is at the time apprehended. 1828.

This meeting recommends Friends who have the charge of servants and apprentices, to extend kind attention and care towards them, and to make such domestic arrangements as may enable them to attend public worship duly and punctually, and to promote their employing the portions of the First-day of the week not so occupied, in a manner becoming the professors of the Christian name. 1833.

SECTION XII.—COUNSEL TO THE YOUNG.

BELOVED youth, in an especial manner guard against the first sacrifices of duty to inclination. If ye curb inordinate desires in their infancy, your victory over future temptations will be the more easy; and, through faith in Him that hath loved us, and hath overcome, ye will in time be more than conquerors; but if ye shrink from the conflict, or resign the victory to the tempter, ye will be despoiled of the armour designed to preserve you in future assaults ; and, it may be, unable to resist in your further progress through life, temptations which, in the fresh morning of your day, ye would have held in abhorrence. 1795. P. E.

In considering this subject [the reading of the Scriptures] our younger friends have been brought to our remembrance with warm and tender solicitude. We hope that many of you, dear youth, are no strangers to this practice, and to some we trust it has already been blessed. Hesitate not to allot a portion of each day to read and meditate upon the sacred volume in private: steadily direct your minds to Him who alone can open and apply the Scriptures to our spiritual benefit. In these seasons of retirement, enter into a close examination of the state of your own hearts ; and, as you may be enabled, pray to the Almighty for preservation from the temptations with which you are encompassed. 1815. P. E.

Be very careful, we beseech you, not to read publications which openly, or indirectly, inculcate a disbelief in the benefits procured to us by the sufferings and death of Christ, in the divinity of Him our Lord and Saviour, or in the perceptible guidance of his Spirit. 1820. P. E.

Dear young friends, earnest have been our desires that you may all, not only be professors with us but, by obedience to the Spirit of Christ, become real possessors of the truth as it is in Jesus. We are persuaded that, in the eyes of many amongst you, the truth has indeed appeared lovely : why then is there not a full surrender to its power and to its convictions ? The Lord loveth an early sacrifice. His numberless blessings call for your gratitude, and your allegiance. And mournful indeed will be the reflection, should your days be lengthened to advanced age, that you have slighted the mercies of a gracious Creator, that you have preferred the love of the world and its fading pleasures, and that there can be no peaceful retrospect on devotedness to his cause.

To our young friends who have taken some steps in the right way, we would tenderly offer a few remarks. The youthful mind, in its love for the cause of religion, is readily led into action. Here is a fresh call for watchfulness. A benevolent desire to promote the Lord's work in the earth, and to serve their fellow-men, may have imperceptibly led some from a close and frequent examination of the state of their own hearts. In mixing in public companies, and in witnessing the success of the efforts that are used to promote the common good, our own minds may be gratified, but our quick perception of spiritual instruction may be weakened. Far be it from this meeting to discourage its members from sharing in those excellent labours, in which we can, consistently with our religious principles, unite. In the universal dispersion of the sacred volume, and in the moral and religious instruction of the poor of this and of other countries, we feel a very lively interest. We rejoice in the progress of these good works; but our earnest concern for all is, that each may seek to know and to abide in his proper station; that they whose field of usefulness is principally within the limits of our own Society, may be faithful to their call, and diligent in their Master's service. And may you, whose labours are more extended, be especially careful, that your exertions for the good of others are adorned and enforced by humility, and by that consistency with our principles, which can only be maintained by watchfulness and prayer; that it may be manifest to all, that the love of Christ operating in the heart leads you to seek, not the praise of men, but the glory of God. 1818. P. E.

We recommend to such of our young friends as know and approve what is excellent, and may have been strengthened in some small degree to practise it, not to shrink from modestly, yet faithfully, counselling their associates in early life, when they may be deviating from the path of duty. A tender caution may be received with peculiar advantage, when those to whom it is given know that their counsellors are still alike subject to the same temptations to which they are exposed. 1827. P. E.

The more our young friends are engaged to dwell in true humility, that respect for age and experience which has ever characterised every well-regulated community, both civil and religious, will evince itself. It was an injunction to Israel of old, and we regard it as a standing precept, "Thou shalt rise up before the hoary head, and honour the face of the old man, and fear thy God." 1835.

Our sympathy is awakened for our young men who are sent out as commercial travellers. This occupation renders it highly important to maintain, through holy aid, a firm and Christian course of conduct. The employment leads to the frequenting of inns. The company there met with is often inimical to a growth in grace, and exposes to intemperance and other vices. When young men are thus from home, we affectionately exhort them to seek the company of Friends, and gratefully to avail themselves of those kind and hospitable attentions which are offered to them. It is very important that their arrangements be such as that they can spend the First-day of the week where our meetings for worship are held; and that, as far as practicable, they attend also a week-day meeting. 1834. P. E.

The circumstances of our beloved young friends, whether under the shelter of watchful parental care, or exposed to the temptations of the metropolis and other large towns, have at this time had our very serious consideration. We do not forget the temptations of our early life, and especially those incident to our entrance upon general intercourse with the world; they were slippery paths to us, and with humble thanksgivings to God we call to mind the tender care of his fatherly providence, the pleadings of his warning voice, how He strove with us and his forbearance towards us. We know that, up to this hour, we have nothing to depend upon but the free mercy of God in Jesus Christ our Lord; but, through the aboundings of his grace renewed unto us, we cannot but express our strong solicitude—our prayer, that it may please the Lord to deal graciously with you, dear young friends; that He may never take his Holy Spirit from you, but deepen and strengthen your convictions of the guilt of sin, its hatefulness in his holy sight, and its certain and awful consequences to the impenitent and unconverted. O! that we could induce you duly to appreciate these tokens of our Heavenly Father's love, and that nothing might ever tempt you to call in question the divine origin of those secret checks in the conscience, those monitions and faithful warnings, those pleadings of the Holy Spirit with the mind of man, by which our Heavenly Father would draw us to Himself, and make us rich partakers of that pardon and reconciliation which He grants to his believing and contrite children, through the blessed intercession of our Saviour. Open your hearts to Him that standeth at the door and knocks, suffer his love to prevail, strive to enter in at the strait gate:

we press it upon you with the most earnest and tender intreaty, because we are aware that there is much by which many of our young people are surrounded at the present day, which would draw them away from the humbling discipline of the cross, and induce them to seek an easier path to the kingdom. The words of our Lord are simple, plain, and full; and they commend themselves to the enlightened conscience—" Strait is the gate, and narrow is the way, which leadeth unto life." 1837. P. E.

For you, dear young friends, the objects of our sympathy and love, we would express our strong desire, we believe we may say our fervent prayer, that the ever-watchful care of the heavenly Shepherd may be over you for good: yours is a period of life beset with many and strong temptations; even in the most favoured allotment there are snares both secretly and more openly laid for your feet. O that we could prevail with you all to come unto Christ, to confide in Him as your Saviour, and to enter upon the warfare against the lusts of the flesh and the pride of life! If happily your hearts have been made tender before the Lord, and you know what it is for the hand of God to be upon you, beware that you never resist the working of his power; be frequent in presenting yourselves before the Lord; commune with your own hearts; watch for the gentlest intimations of his Holy Spirit, and in whatever little acts of dedication He may call for the acknowledgment of your love and allegiance, give yourselves up to his service with a willing and a ready mind: think on the blessing pronounced upon the pure in heart; ask of God that He will keep you from evil thoughts and corrupt imaginations; that, in your intercourse with the world and one with another, in your words and all your conversation, you may be blameless and harmless. 1844. P. E.

Strong are our desires for you, our beloved young friends, that you may know the work of the Lord not only to be begun, but to be carried forward in your hearts. Dwell under the power and discipline of the Spirit of the Lord. Give place to no views which would in the least degree weaken your faith in the mysterious, but sacred and all-important, doctrines of that salvation which is in Christ: feeling your own weakness and the limited powers of the human intellect, may you accept these doctrines in reverence of soul, in simplicity, and in godly sincerity. Pray that you may be kept in that humble, dependent state of mind, in which the Lord, by his Spirit, often gradually unfolds the deep things of his kingdom, and grants a holy settlement in the experience of their reality. Love not the world, nor the things of the world. Under a sense of the many temptations which beset your path, earnest is our concern that you may now, in early life, choose the Lord for your portion. Set apart at least a short time daily for private retirement. Seek for the guidance of the Holy Spirit. Thus will you be favoured to escape many trials, and practically to realize the truth, that "Godliness is profitable unto all things, having promise of the life that now is, and of that which is to come." Let not pleasure, profit, or advancement in life, be your first desire, but be concerned above all things to know your calling and election in Christ to be made sure. 1851. P. E.

Tenderly do we sympathize with those beloved younger Friends, who feel that they are, as it were, passing through the wilderness, and whose souls are often discouraged because of the way. To the young disciple the conflict is at times severe. Temptation is strong, whilst the heart is weak; tremblingly halting between Christ and the world. In straits such as these, may you never yield to the suggestions of the carnal mind. Consult not how far you may safely indulge yourselves, or how nearly you may approximate to the ways and habits of the world. Be in earnest to realize a yet closer and more dependent walk with God. The faith that leads you unto Christ will, as it is exercised, give you the victory, through Him. To our fallen nature the path of the cross has ever been a strait and narrow path; but He who hath appointed it will make it easy, and even full of joy, to them that are led by Him; not by widening it, or changing its course, but by bringing their wills into harmony with it. Gently, and at times very gradually, yet surely, does He accustom them to his yoke, and prepare and strengthen them for the difficulties of the way. In submitting to his training, beloved younger friends, is true liberty to be found. In the service of Christ you will find abundant scope for the right employment of every talent, and in the enjoyment of his love your cup will overflow with blessing and praise. 1858. P. E.

Beloved younger brethren and sisters! may you more and

more feel that you are not your own; that you are bought with a price. Where much is given, there, in the great day of final account, will much be required. May all your talents be freely offered unto the Lord, and consecrated to his blessed service. May every crown be cast at the feet of Jesus. Bear in mind that the unfaithfulness or infirmities of others, whatever be their age or station, will furnish no excuse for you; and that with the gospel liberty, which it is your privilege so peculiarly to enjoy in this religious Society, the inconsistency of others, real or apprehended, will not excuse you, as you grow in Christian experience and attainment, from the faithful exercise of all those gifts which it may please the Lord in his mercy to bestow upon you, to your own comfort, to the help of the church, and to the praise of his great and worthy name. The prize is before you: it is a prize not of earth but of heaven; not a corruptible crown, but an incorruptible; to be obtained, not without conflict, through deep repentance, through the forsaking of sin, through the way of the cross, through the life of faith, looking unto Jesus. Press on towards this prize, we entreat you. Shrink not from the warfare: yield up your hearts unreservedly unto Him who will fight for you, the Captain of your salvation. So shall the crown immortal be yours: so shall you for ever rejoice in God your Saviour, and adore his abundant mercy who hath prepared for those that love Him " an inheritance incorruptible, and undefiled, and that fadeth not away." 1851.

SECTION XIII.—ADVICE IN RELATION TO MARRIAGE.

It is our judgment that not only those marriages of near kindred expressly forbidden under the law, ought not to be practised under the gospel; but that we in our day ought not to take first cousins in marriage. And though some have been drawn into such marriages, let not their practice be a precedent or example to any others amongst us for the time to come. 1675.

We earnestly advise and exhort all young and unmarried friends, that they do not make any procedure one with another upon the account of marriage, without first applying to their parents or guardians for their consent and agreement therein. And we also advise, that, in the first place, all young persons concerned seriously wait upon the Lord for counsel and clearness in this weighty concern, before they make any procedure with any, in order to marriage; that they may not be led by any forward or uncertain affections in this great concern, to their own hurt, the grief of their friends, and the dishonour of truth. 1690. P. E.—1801.—1833.

This meeting strongly recommends Friends to avoid and discountenance very early proceedings in regard to marriage after the death of husband or wife; esteeming such conduct as tending to the dishonour and reproach of our Christian profession. 1691. —1833.

Friends are advised against running into excessive, sumptuous, and costly entertainments at marriages; a great part of the cost of which would be better employed in relieving the necessities of the poor. 1718.

Parents are tenderly advised not to make it their first or chief care to obtain for their children large portions or settlements of marriage; but rather to be careful that their children be joined in marriage with persons of religious inclinations, suitable dispositions and temper, sobriety in manners, and diligence in business; and carefully to guard against all mixed marriages, and unequal yoking of their children. 1722. P. E.

Marriage, being a divine ordinance, and a solemn engagement for term of life, is of great importance to our peace and well-being in this world, and may prove of no small consequence respecting our state in that which is to come; yet it is often too inconsiderately entered into, upon motives inconsistent with the evident intention of that unerring Wisdom by which it was primarily ordained; which was for the mutual assistance and comfort of both sexes, that they might be helps to each other, both in spirituals and temporals, and that their endeavours might be united for the pious and proper education of their children, in the nurture and admonition of the Lord, and for suitably qualifying them to discharge their duty in the various allotments in the world. Marriage implies union and concurrence, as well in spiritual as temporal concerns. Whilst the parties differ in religious views, they stand disunited in the main point; even that which should increase and confirm their mutual happiness, and render them helps and blessings to each other.

To prevent falling into such engagements, it is requisite to beware of the paths that lead to them—the sordid interests, and the ensnaring friendships of the world, the contaminating pleasures and idle pastimes of earthly minds; also the various solicitations and incentives to festivity and dissipation; likewise especially too frequent and too familiar converse with those from whom may arise a danger of entanglement, by their alluring the passions, and drawing the affections after them.

For want of due watchfulness, and obedience to the convictions of Divine grace in their consciences, many have wounded their own souls, distressed their friends, injured their families, and done great disservice to the church, by these unequal connexions; which have proved an inlet to much degeneracy, and mournfully affected the minds of those who labour under a living concern for the good of all, and the prosperity of Truth upon earth. 1777. P. E.

We think it right at this time to remind our members of the ancient testimony of our Society, that marriage is not a mere civil contract, but a religious act; that it is God's ordinance and not man's; and therefore seeing that the legislature has fully confirmed us in our privilege of solemnizing marriage according to our own long-established religious usages, we desire that none of our members may be found departing therefrom. And we further think it right explicitly to state our judgment, that marriages of our members before the Superintendent Registrar, though not open to the special religious objections connected with marriages by a priest, are, nevertheless, inconsistent with the good order of our discipline, and with our aforesaid testimony to the true nature and character of the marriage ordinance. 1848.

This meeting is impressed with a sense of the vast influence, either for good or for evil, which marriage exercises on both the temporal and the spiritual condition of man, and earnestly desires that, in the choice of a companion for life, all may seek unto the Lord for his guidance; not allowing any merely exterior advantages to be the primary motive, and bearing in mind that an accordance in religious principles and practice is essential to the perfectness of such a union.

And seeing that the real enjoyment of life is far more effectually secured by contentment, with simple habits, than by any appearance or mode of living which entails anxiety or risk, we would strongly advise parents, whilst they exercise a prudent care over the interests of their children, not to be unduly anxious to secure worldly advantages for them on entering the marriage state. And we would affectionately encourage our younger members, when looking towards this most important step, to be satisfied to set out in life in a manner befitting their circumstances, instead of seeking to imitate, in their style of living, the example of those who possess larger resources: they would thus, on the one hand, avoid the necessity of unduly deferring their union; and, on the other, be less exposed to the temptation of launching into business beyond their means.

Many, we fear, have, under these circumstances, been induced to enter into trade on their own account with borrowed capital, who, had their views been more moderate, might, with greater safety and more real comfort to themselves, have continued, at least for a time, in the employ of others.

And may it ever be borne in mind that, marriage being a Divine ordinance, its solemnization should in all cases be conducted in the fear of the Lord, and in humble dependence on his blessing. On these deeply interesting occasions, let there not be in the attire of the parties themselves, or in that of their relatives and friends attending, any display unbecoming an assembly of Christian worshippers; and may the subsequent proceedings of the marriage day, whilst characterized by cheerful enjoyment, never pass the boundary line of Christian simplicity, moderation, and self-restraint. 1857.

SECTION XIV.—ADVICE IN RELATION TO THE AFFAIRS OF THIS LIFE.

LET friends and brethren in their respective meetings watch over one another in the love of God and care of the Gospel; particularly admonishing that none trade beyond their ability, nor stretch beyond their compass; and that they use few words in their dealings, and keep their word in all things, lest they bring, through their forwardness, dishonour to the precious truth of God. 1675.

As it hath pleased God to bring forth a day of liberty and freedom to serve Him, let every one have a care so to use this liberty, as that the name of God may be honoured by it; and not an occasion taken by any, because of the present freedom, to launch forth into trading and worldly business beyond what they can manage honourably and with reputation; and so that they may keep their words with all men, and that their yea may prove yea indeed, and their nay may be nay indeed. 1688. P. E.

It is advised, and earnestly desired, that the payment of just debts be not delayed by any professing truth beyond the time promised and agreed upon; nor occasion given of complaint to those they deal with, by their backwardness of payment where no time is limited; nor any to overcharge themselves with too much trading and commerce, beyond their capacities to discharge with a good conscience towards all men; and that all Friends concerned therein be very careful not to contract extravagant debts, endangering the wronging of others and their families; which some have done, to the grieving the hearts of the upright; nor to break their promises, contracts or agreements, in their buying or selling, or in any other lawful affairs, to the injuring themselves and others, occasioning strife and contention, and reproach to truth and Friends. And it is advised, that all friends that are entering into trade, or that are in trade, and have not stock sufficient of their own to answer the trade they aim at, be very cautious of running themselves into debt, without advising with some of their ancient and experienced friends. 1692. P. E.

Knowing how quickly many are removed by death, it is weightily recommended that care be taken in each Monthly Meeting, that friends who have estates to dispose of, by will or otherwise, be advised to make their wills in time of health, and strength of judgment; to prevent the inconveniences, loss, and trouble that may fall upon their relations and friends, through their dying intestate. Making such wills in due time can shorten no man's days, but the omission or delay thereof has proved very injurious to many. 1691.—1695. P. E.—1703. P. E.

Recommended, that Friends who have young children do in

their wills appoint faithful friends to be guardians to them, till they come to the age of twenty-one years. 1706.

Executors and trustees, concerned in wills and settlements, are advised to take especial care that they faithfully discharge their respective trusts, according to the intent of the donors and testators; and that all charitable gifts, legacies, bequests, and settlements of estates, by will or deed, intended and given for the use of the poor, the aged, the impotent, or putting poor Friends' children to education or apprenticeships, may not be appropriated or converted to other uses than such as the donors and testators have directed and enjoined by legal settlement, will or testament. 1715.

Advised, that Friends in making their wills have a strict regard to justice and equity, and be not actuated by caprice and prejudice, to the injury of those who may have a reasonable expectation from their kindred and near connexion; nor (although occasion may have been given or taken) carry any resentment to the grave, remembering that we all stand in need of mercy and forgiveness: also that none postpone making their wills to a sick-bed, an improper season to settle our outward affairs, in the painful struggles of nature, even if we should be favoured with a clear understanding; which ought not to be diverted from a solemn consideration of the approaching awful period of life.

Friends are earnestly recommended to employ persons skilful in law, and of good repute, to make their wills; as great inconvenience and loss, and sometimes the ruin of families, have happened through the unskilfulness of some who have taken upon them to make wills. And all Friends who may become executors or administrators, are advised to make a full, clear and proper inventory of the estate and effects of the deceased as soon as possible after the interment, as many difficulties and disputes have arisen for want of it, where it has been deferred; and seeing also that in the affirmation made at proving a will, there is a promise to make such inventory. 1782.—1801.

It is our earnest desire that Friends be very careful to avoid all pursuit after the things of this world, by such ways and means as depend too much on hazardous enterprises; but rather labour to content themselves with such a plain way and manner of living, as is most agreeable to the self-denying principles of truth which we profess, and most conducive to that tranquillity of mind that is requisite to a religious conduct. 1724. P. E.

It is the sense and judgment of this meeting, if any fall short of paying their just debts, and a composition be made with their creditors to accept a part instead of the whole, that, notwithstanding the parties may look upon themselves legally discharged of any obligation to pay the remainder, yet the principle of universal righteousness enjoins full satisfaction to be made, if ever the debtors are of ability. And in order that such may the better retrieve their circumstances, we exhort them to submit to a manner of living in every respect the most conducive to this purpose. 1759. P. E.

We warn all against a most pernicious practice, too much prevailing, which hath often issued in the utter ruin of those concerned therein, viz., that of raising and circulating a fictitious kind of paper-credit (by what are called accommodation bills) with indorsements and acceptances, to give an appearance of value without an intrinsic reality; a practice highly unbecoming that uprightness which ought to appear in every member of our religious Society; and of which practice we think it our incumbent duty to declare our disapprobation, and disunity therewith, as absolutely inconsistent with the truth we make profession of. 1771. P. E.

We are engaged to caution every individual against imprudently entering into joint securities with others; for by these practices many innocent wives and children have been inevitably and unexpectedly involved in ruinous and deplorable circumstances. We therefore earnestly desire Friends to keep strictly on their guard, that none, through any specious pretences of rendering acts of friendship to others with safety to themselves, may risk their own peace and reputation, and the security of their families. In order hereunto, we recommend this salutary advice of the wise man to their especial notice and regard: "Be not thou one of them that strike hands, or of them that are sureties for debts. If thou hast nothing to pay, why should he take away thy bed from under thee?" 1771. P. E.

In times of outward prosperity there are snares to be avoided, as well as duties to be fulfilled. One of these snares seems to us to be a too eager, and therefore unlawful, pursuit of lawful things.

Such a pursuit prevents the mind from rising in living aspirations to God, the giver of every good and perfect gift; indisposes for duly assembling to wait upon and worship Him, as well as for the perusal of the sacred Scriptures, that record of truth, which was written aforetime for our instruction; and tends to spread devastation over religious society. But, friends, we intreat you, "Seek ye first the kingdom of God and his righteousness; and all these things," said our blessed Redeemer, speaking of necessary things, "shall be added unto you." 1802. P. E.—1861.

We do not tax all who embark in large concerns in trade with an undue desire after riches; but we much fear that the effect which their schemes are likely to have upon themselves and their connexions, as affecting their condition, both religious and civil, is not duly regarded. The love of money is said in Scripture to be "the root of all evil;" and we believe it may be shown that honest industry and moderation of desire are roots of incalculable benefit to the humble Christian. We feel for many of our friends in limited circumstances, in this day of increased, and possibly increasing, expense; but we would caution such, and particularly those who are setting out in life, against imitating the manner of living of those whose means are more abundant. We wish, friends, to call you, not to penuriousness, but to economy; and we particularly desire that all such as have families of children, even if in more affluent circumstances, would inure them to early industry, and not to habits of depending too much on the services of domestics. 1805. P. E.

It is earnestly recommended, that Friends frequently inspect the state of their affairs, and, when any find themselves unable, or have not more than sufficient, to pay their just debts, that they immediately disclose their circumstances to some judicious friends, or principal creditors, and take their advice how to act, and be particularly careful not to pay one creditor in preference to another. 1782.

It is the duty of all frequently to inspect the state of their affairs; and, if reverses should occur, to ascertain and know for themselves, that they are fully justified, as honest, upright men, in going on with their business. Such an examination would be greatly facilitated by all being very careful to keep clear accounts; that, whether they be taken off by death, or it may be needful to exhibit those accounts to others, the same may appear perspicuous and intelligible.

And we would affectionately encourage friends, who find themselves in embarrassed, or even in doubtful circumstances, not to hesitate, not to be ashamed, to disclose their affairs to men of upright character, in whom they can confide. Such a timely procedure would, we believe, often save the reputation of individuals, call forth the respect and compassion of their creditors, and prevent the keen sufferings of tender wives and innocent children, and such reproach as, in some instances, has been brought upon our high profession. 1819.

Those who, whilst honestly and diligently endeavouring to provide for their families, have to encounter many difficulties, have a strong claim on the sympathy of their friends: yet they need not fear, as they continue to place their whole trust in our Heavenly Father, but that He will care for them in such a way as He sees meet. But if any, whether of the more affluent, or of those who cannot be ranked in this class, are deviating from safe and regular methods of business, if they are carried away by uncertain and hazardous, though plausible, schemes for getting rich, if they yield to a desire rapidly to enlarge their possessions —such are in imminent danger. They cannot justly expect the blessing of the Most High on such pursuits; their spiritual eye becomes dim; and they do not perceive with clearness that light which would enable them to perfect holiness in the fear of God. 1825. P. E.

And may you, dear friends, who are favoured with' outward prosperity, so live that, when riches increase, you set not your hearts upon them. Be very careful how you venture to increase your ways of accumulating wealth; but walk as ensamples to those around you, evincing that you are redeemed from the inordinate pursuit of lawful things. You will then be more prepared to enter with kindness into the situation of others, when they may consult you; you will be more qualified, in a brotherly way, to advise your brethren to take such measures as may prevent those sufferings to which we have alluded. He that is concerned to support the character of a follower of Christ, —and who amongst us would disclaim this character?—ought to be earnest in his endeavour that accessions of wealth do not disqualify him for the discharge of any duty. 1819—1825. P. E.

We would tenderly invite those who may have acquired a competency of outward substance, to watch the proper period at which they may withdraw from the cares of business, and, when disengaged from the regular concerns of trade, to beware how they employ their property in investments which may involve them anew in care and anxiety. We affectionately desire that neither these nor other cares may disqualify them from acting the part of faithful stewards in the employment of their time, their talents, and their substance, or from being concerned above all things, through watchfulness unto prayer, to have their lamps trimmed, and oil in their vessels; that when the solemn close of life shall come, they may, through redeeming love and mercy, be prepared to enter into the joy of their Lord. 1826.

Those who hold the property of others—and this may be said to be the case more or less with most who are engaged in trade —are not warranted, on the principles of justice, in neglecting to inform themselves from time to time of the real situation of their affairs. If men conceal from their nearest connexions in life a knowledge of the actual state of their property, they may deprive themselves of salutary counsel and of a kind participation in trouble; family expenses may be incurred, and subsequent distress may ensue, which might have been avoided. And we particularly advise young persons to be cautious not to enter too hastily into business, and from the time of their being thus engaged, to be very careful to make themselves well acquainted with their annual income and expenditure. This would be greatly facilitated by their early adopting, and regularly pursuing, a clear and methodical system of keeping their accounts, in regard both to trade and domestic expenses. 1826.

We would advise all our members, especially those about to establish themselves in business, seriously to weigh the numerous evils obviously connected with trading in spirituous liquors. And, believing that the prevalence of what are usually termed dram-shops in this country is amongst the most fruitful causes of crime and misery, this meeting is of the judgment that it is inconsistent for any member of our Society to be engaged in such shops. 1835.

Every period of life, every variety of circumstances in the condition of man, has its peculiar temptations. The schemes now afloat for the employment of capital, some of them holding out the promise of large and rapid accumulation of wealth, render the present to many a day of great danger. Our desires are strong that those engaged in trade and commerce, and such as already possess a competency in life, may be duly aware of the snares which surround them, and that we, all of us, may stand open to the secret checks of the Spirit of the Lord which are at times sensibly felt, even whilst we are actively engaged in our daily avocations, and which would often hold us back from prosecuting our own purposes. And may those of our dear friends, whether in earlier or more advanced life, who may be endued with talents peculiarly adapted to the affairs of this life, and whose temptation it may be to enter very largely into its concerns, duly appreciate this inward restraint thus graciously vouchsafed. This would set limits to their pursuit of the things that perish, and bring them to that quiet and contented mind, in which, taught of the Lord, they would see the paramount value of heavenly over earthly things, and seek to devote the whole man to Him. Some of the speculations by which individuals have been betrayed into haste to become rich, may appear for a time to have been prospered; yet if by these undertakings they have been leavened into a worldly mind, and the ease of affluence has deadened their sense of the transcendent excellence of heavenly things, instead of their having been fruitful to God,—we speak it with sorrow, —leanness has entered into their souls. We are therefore engaged to offer the word of pressing exhortation to Friends, and particularly to our younger brethren in their outset in life, that they endeavour to be satisfied with the moderate gains and profits of the ordinary course of trade, that they be not ashamed of those lawful callings in which Divine Providence may have placed them, and that, as honest Christian tradesmen, their uprightness and circumspection in all things may adorn the high profession we make of our obligation to serve the Lord in our outward concerns. 1845. P. E.

We feel a concern that none of our dear friends may be tempted, by the prospect of high rates of interest, to risk their property in hazardous engagements; and that they may be very careful, before making any investment, to ascertain the extent of the responsibility involved, that their peace of mind may not be endangered, or the cause of truth be evil spoken of. 1849.

An earthly mind shows itself in various forms. It is obvious in many of the lawful pursuits of trade and commerce, and it is by no means excluded from those of agriculture. The enemy of man's peace knows how to suit his baits to the various circumstances of life. Markets and fairs may be lawfully frequented for the purchase and sale of produce, but they have their peculiar snares; and he who is seeking to live as a consistent Christian, will, in attending them, endeavour, as far as practicable, to avoid all those places of resort and that association which endanger the maintenance of either pureness, temperance, or integrity.

Amid the multiplied variety of pursuits in the present day, we would caution our dear friends, how they enter into engagements which may subject them, by close and frequent intercourse, to the influence and example of individuals or bodies of men whose minds are not under the regulating power of the truth; lest thereby a worldly standard should be substituted for that true tenderness of conscience, which would not only preserve from injustice in dealing, but would lead us, in all things, to do unto others as we would that they should do unto us. 1846. P.E.

For you, dear friends who, from whatever cause, are brought into pecuniary difficulties, and for your families, we feel an earnest desire that you may be preserved from yielding to the peculiar temptations incident to your situation; that you may be enabled to make a right use of your trials, and that, through the help of the Lord, these trials may work together for your good. We believe that your comfort and peace of mind, and your future success in life, will be materially promoted by a willingness to come down at once to the true level which your altered circumstances require. 1848. P.E.

Our brethren who are employed in agriculture, and those who are engaged in the various branches of trade, claim our sympathy. The latter especially are at times exposed to close competition and to the temptation to pursue their own interest in a way inconsistent with true justice in dealing; they may be much tried by the small profits often resulting from a course of honest industry and diligent attention to business; but it should never be forgotten that there is a sterling integrity which the Christian trader should always maintain; that there is a standard set before him in the New Testament which he should always keep in view. As this is the case, he will be honourable and just in his transactions, he will have a true support under all his difficulties, and he may ask the blessing of the Lord on his efforts to provide things honest in the sight of all men: and as he is concerned that his wants may be few, that his affections may in the first place be set on things above, and that he may not be ensnared by the love of money, he will escape many a bitter pang and many an anxious toil. Bright have been the examples in our Society of men who have been enabled to maintain this Christian character amongst their neighbours. May all our members, renouncing the spirit of the world, and living under the government of Christ, have their possessions in "bags which wax not old, a treasure in the heavens, that faileth not." 1851. P. E.

The love of money is apt to increase almost imperceptibly. That which was at first laboured after under the pressure of necessary duty may, without great watchfulness, steal upon the affections, and gradually withdraw the heart from God. The danger depends not upon how much a man has, but upon how much his heart is set upon what he has, and upon accumulating more. The trafficker in hundreds may be no less involved in the spirit of the world, than the trafficker in thousands. Therefore watch, dear friends, we intreat you, not only in the beginning, but in the midst of your active career, yea, even to the very end of life, lest you reap from earthly care nought but vanity and vexation of spirit, or sink at last into the grave weary and oppressed, laden as with thick clay. In all your business engagements, whether in smaller or larger concerns, as individuals or as partners with others, keep within the restraints of a tender and enlightened conscience, quick to discern where the desire to serve the Lord in all things ceases, and the service of self begins. Seek to have your hearts raised above the world, that you may live as strangers and pilgrims upon earth. Encourage a spirit of Christian bountifulness. Let them that have but little to give, give that little cheerfully, according to their ability; and let those to whom a larger stewardship has been committed, be largely liberal in proportion to their means. 1858. P. E.

SECTION XV.—ADVICE TO EMIGRANTS.

This meeting has been introduced into feelings of sympathy in behalf of our members who may contemplate emigration, either singly or in families, to distant countries. We strongly recommend our friends, on all such occasions, to take counsel of their brethren before entering on an undertaking of such importance. We also desire, in much affection, to offer a word of caution to such, that they be not hastily induced by the prospect of outward advantage to engage in a movement so fraught with important consequences, but that in singleness of heart they seek for divine direction, whereby they may be favoured to know the place of their right allotment, whether at home or abroad. We would especially intreat them to guard against the influence of an impatient or restless spirit, which would lead them, under the pressure of present difficulties or discouragement, to seek in foreign lands those supposed temporal advantages which may not seem to be easily attainable at home, and whereby they may expose themselves and their families to much disadvantage in reference to their religious interests. Many are the dangers attending a hasty and unadvised movement of this kind : our safety consists in being willing to commit all our ways to the Most High. In reference to this subject, as well as other important undertakings connected with the affairs of this life, we desire to remind our dear friends of the gracious promise to those who seek first the kingdom of God and his righteousness, even that all things necessary shall be added. 1839.

We would intreat those who may establish themselves in newly-settled countries to reflect upon the responsibility which attaches to them when they are the neighbours of uncivilized and heathen tribes. It is an awful but indisputable fact, that most settlements of this description, besides dispossessing the natives of their land without equivalent, have hitherto been productive of incalculable injury to the moral and physical condition of the native races; which have been thereby more or less reduced in numbers, and in some instances completely exterminated. Earnestly, therefore, do we desire that all those under our name who may emigrate to such settlements, may be careful neither directly nor indirectly to inflict injury upon the natives, but that they may, on the contrary, in their whole conduct, exhibit the practical character of that religion, which breathes "Glory to God in the highest, and on earth peace, good will toward men." As this is their aim, they will not only exert themselves to check the evils which are but too generally inflicted by the whites upon their feebler neighbours, but will be solicitous to do their part in endeavouring to diffuse amongst them the blessings of civilization and Christianity; which will prove the best means of preventing their extermination, and of raising them to the full enjoyment of their rights. 1840.

SECTION XVI.—AMUSEMENTS AND RECREATIONS.

We earnestly beseech our friends, and especially the youth, to avoid all such conversation as may tend to draw out their minds into the foolish and wicked pastimes with which this age aboundeth, particularly balls, gaming-places, horse-races and play-houses, those nurseries of debauchery and wickedness, the burden and grief of the sober part of other societies, as well as of our own; things wholly unbecoming a people under the Christian profession, contrary to the tenor of the doctrine of the gospel, and the examples of the best men in the earliest ages of the church. 1739. P. E.

This meeting strongly advises against the practices of hunting and of shooting for diversion. The awakened mind may see that the leisure of those whom Providence hath permitted to have a competence of worldly goods, is but ill filled up with these amusements: therefore, being not only accountable for our substance, but also for our time, let our leisure be employed in serving our neighbour, and not in distressing, for our amusement, the creatures of God. 1795.—1861.

This meeting has repeatedly testified against vain sports, and places of diversion, as so many allurements tending to draw the mind from its watch, and to lay it open to further temptation. The best recreation of a Christian is the relief of distress; and his chief delight to promote the knowledge, and to exalt the glory, of his heavenly Master: and this is most effectually done, under his holy influence, by a life of faith, purity, and general benevolence. 1799. P. E.

We have been at this time introduced into much concern with reference to the well-known testimony of our religious Society against the attendance of places of diversion. Earnest have been our desires, that Friends everywhere, and particularly those in younger life, may seriously reflect on the injury and, in many instances, the moral ruin, which pursuits of this description bring with them. It is our conviction that, in proportion as the mind is renewed by Divine grace, all those vain amusements will be felt to be inconsistent with the restraints of the Gospel, and incompatible with that quietness and peace of mind which are the portion of the watchful Christian. Our attention has also been turned to the increased exposure of our young Friends to the temptations of music, both in its acquisition and in its practice. Serious is the waste of time to those who give themselves up to it; and what account can they render of those precious hours which might otherwise have been devoted to the glory of God and to the good of their neighbour? It does not, however, merely involve the absorption of time; it not unfrequently leads into unprofitable and even pernicious association, and, in some instances, to a general indulgence in the vain amusements of the world. 1846. P. E.

It was the prayer of one of old,—may it be the prayer of every one of us, "Lord, make me to know mine end, and the measure of my days, what it is; that I may know how frail I am." Our time, our day upon earth, is fast passing away; its duration is altogether uncertain; and few, very few, are the working hours of even the longest day. Shall any, then, allow the precious moments that can never be recalled to pass unimproved, or spend them upon occupations or amusements inconsistent with the great object of their being? The life of the Christian is not a dull and cheerless existence. There are no joys here below to be compared with those of which the renewed soul is permitted to partake, even upon earth, in the faithful service of the Lord. It is not then for the diminution, but for the increase, of their happiness, that we would affectionately invite our dear friends everywhere unreservedly to submit all their pursuits, even those which may be intended as recreations, to the restraints and holy government of the Lord's Spirit. As this is the case, the various duties and enjoyments of the present life will be placed in their true relation to the life to come. And not only will the engagements of business be brought within their just limits, and the mind be thereby enabled to perform the duties and to bear the anxieties connected with them with greater alacrity and firmness, in simple confidence in the Lord, but the desires, the affections, the very tastes will be "renewed." The occupations of our leisure hours,—and with many of our dear friends they make up a large amount in the sum of their responsibilities,—our associations, our reading, our varied engagements of a social or more public nature, will be baptized into the Christian spirit.

Of the various means of allowable recreation and mental improvement placed within our reach, few call for the exercise of greater circumspection than travelling, especially in foreign countries. In excursions or in tarrying at watering places, whether at home or abroad, the time may be wasted, and the mind insensibly drawn into habits and associations more or less undesirable or pernicious. It especially behoves the true disciple of Christ,—and who among us would not wish to bear that blessed name?—to be careful, when thus separated from his home associations, to maintain a course of conduct in all things consistent with his high profession. He is not warranted in lowering the Christian standard, by doing, amongst strangers, that which he would hesitate to do amongst his friends. Nor can he consistently countenance, by his presence or his conformity, either the superstitions or the follies which may prevail around him. And we would encourage our dear friends, whilst thus absent from home, and deprived of opportunities of meeting with their brethren on the First-day of the week for the purpose of waiting upon the Lord, not to shrink from acting upon their own religious principles; but, at stated times, whether alone or with their companions, to present themselves in reverence of soul before Him. Let them never forget that his all-seeing eye is upon them, and that, in whatever circumstances they may be, the worship that is in spirit and in truth is his due. 1853. P. E.

Amongst those gratifications of sense from which the members of our religious Society, by common consent growing out of what we believe to be a root of Christian principle, have, with much unanimity, felt themselves restrained, are the study and practice of music. That which is of the character ordinarily designated as sacred music not unfrequently stimulates expressions and feelings which are far from being the genuine breathings of a renewed heart, and tends to produce an excitement often unhappily mistaken for devotion, and to withdraw the soul from that quiet, humble and retired frame, in which prayer and praise may be truly offered with the spirit and with the understanding also. And as to those musical exhibitions in which an attempt is made to combine religion with a certain amount of amusement, it is hard to understand how a truly Christian mind can allow itself to sanction the profanation of the sacred name by the attendance of such performances; where the most awful events recorded in Holy Scripture are made the subject of professed entertainment to an indiscriminate assembly, many of whom make no pretensions to religion. That music, on the other hand, which does not in any degree partake of the character usually designated as sacred, has, we fear, in innumerable instances, allured the feet of the young to the lightness, the gaiety and even the dissipation of the world, and thus proved among the many snares against which we are enjoined fervently to pray, "Lead us not into temptation." 1854. P. E.

To look upon this life as the training-school for Heaven, is at once the Christian's duty and consolation. The sense of his responsibilities and of his dangers is too strong to allow him to court temptation. He has no time to squander upon trifles. His renewed tastes have no relish for vain or frivolous pursuits. He asks not how near he can approach without danger to the gaieties or amusements of the world. Rather does he seek to know how closely he can follow that Saviour by whom the world is crucified unto him and he unto the world. With these views of the practical effect of the religion of Jesus, we cannot learn without sorrow the increased interest taken by several of our members in musical entertainments. There are amusements, and we consider these performances to be among them, the object of which is principally, if not entirely, the gratification of sense, which possess a fascination sufficient more or less to withdraw the mind from worthier objects, and the pursuit of which almost necessarily distracts the attention from the sober realities of life and the duties of religion. As the heart becomes truly given up to the love of Christ, the services of pure and undefiled religion, the improvement of the mind, and the varied duties which we owe to our fellow-men, will be found abundantly sufficient to employ the energies of the renewed soul; whilst the sweet consolations of the Lord's Spirit will give far truer and more abiding refreshment than can be met with in any mere gratification of taste or sense. 1860. P. E.

SECTION XVII.—ON BOOKS AND READING.

This meeting, considering that some in the present age do endeavour, as well by certain books, as by a licentious conversation, to lessen and decry the true faith in our Lord and Saviour Jesus Christ — even that precious faith once delivered to his saints, which by the mercy of God is also bestowed upon us — doth therefore earnestly advise and exhort all parents, masters and mistresses of families, and guardians of minors, that they prevent, as much as in them lies, their children, servants, and youth, under their respective care and tuition, from having or reading books or papers that have any tendency to prejudice the profession of the Christian religion, to create in them the least doubt or question concerning the truth of the Holy Scriptures, or those necessary and saving truths declared in them; lest their minds should be poisoned thereby, and a foundation laid for the greatest evils. 1723. P. E.

This meeting, being sorrowfully affected under a consideration of the hurtful tendency of reading plays, romances, novels and other pernicious books, earnestly recommends to every member of our Society to discourage and suppress the same; and particularly to acquaint all booksellers, under our name, with the painful anxiety occasioned to this meeting by a report of some instances of selling or lending such books, entreating them to avoid a practice so inconsistent with the purity of the Christian religion. And Friends are desired to be careful in the choice of all books which their children read, seeing there are many, under the specious titles of the promotion of religion and morality, containing sentiments repugnant to the truth as it is in Christ Jesus. 1764.

We earnestly recommend to all the frequent perusal of the

Holy Scriptures, according to repeated exhortations; and we at this time also recommend the writings of our faithful predecessors, and the accounts that are published of their experiences, labours, travels and sufferings in the cause of Christ. 1789. P. E.

We desire to offer a word of caution to our dear friends on the subject of reading. Books may be regarded as companions, which insensibly infuse somewhat of their spirit and character into those who converse with them. It behoves us to exercise a sound discretion as to what publications we admit into our houses; that neither we nor our children may be hurt by that reading which would have a direct, or even a remote, tendency to leaven our minds into the spirit of the world, and to unfit us for the sober duties of life. The books which we introduce to the young require particular care: they may give a bias to the mind, and materially influence the future character. Some of those which, we fear, find access to our families, are calculated to give false views of real life, and to lower that standard of morals which Christianity upholds; and others, though they may not stimulate evil passions, are adapted to lessen the attachment of our youth to the principles of their education, or even to rob them of the tenderness of their consciences, and alienate them, it may be by slow gradations, from the fear of God. 1839. P. E.

Dear younger Friends, we feel a lively concern that none of you may be in anywise beguiled from the simplicity which is in Christ. And we would affectionately desire that, in your intellectual pursuits, you may be guarded against publications, or any other vehicles of opinion, of which there are so many in the present day, in which the deep questions of moral truth are so treated, that the natural depravity of man and the absolute need of redemption, as set forth in the Gospel, are almost, if not altogether, set aside or overlooked. In however captivating a form the opinions thus set forth may appear, and however nearly in some instances they may seem to approach to those glorious views of Gospel freedom which, as a Christian Church, we have ever maintained, we are persuaded that no sound or permanent reformation, either in ourselves or in others, can be expected from them. Depraved and corrupted in the fall, the human heart cannot cleanse itself; and they that would thus work upon it in its unregenerate state, without regard to the great truths of Christian Redemption, however plausible may be their professions, can do no more than propose the substitution of one mode of selfishness for another. The evil may change its form, but it is not eradicated. The soul, still weary and restless, is drawn no nearer to its God. 1851.

SECTION XVIII.—ON THE RIGHT OCCUPATION OF THE FIRST-DAY OF THE WEEK.

Whilst the remembrance of our Creator ought at all times to be present with us, it is our concern that the day more particularly set apart for public worship may be rightly observed. It is no small privilege to be living in a country where much more regard is paid to this duty than in many others; and it highly becomes us to be careful that our example in this respect be consistent with the profession we make to the world.

May all our friends seriously examine whether the mode of spending that portion of the day not occupied with the attendance of our meetings for worship is that which is likely to contribute to the eternal interests of the soul, and whether the character of their pursuits, and even of their conversation, be such as may not tend to dissipate any religious impression that may have been received.

Many have derived great increase of spiritual strength, both on this and on other days, from private retirement, from reading the Holy Scriptures with minds turned to their Divine Author, in desire that He would bless them to their comfort and edification; and from reading the lives and experience of the Lord's faithful servants.

On this day of the week especially ought the households of Friends to be assembled for the reading of the Scriptures, and for waiting upon the Lord—a practice to which we wish particularly to call the attention of those who live in remote and secluded situations. 1817. P. E.—1828. P. E.

SECTION XIX.—ECCLESIASTICAL DEMANDS.

Our testimony against tithes and forced maintenance in this Gospel day, being received from Christ our head and high priest, is not of our own making or imposing, nor from the tradition of men; but what we have from Him, by whose divine power we were raised up to be a people, and by which we have been preserved to this day; knowing that his ministry and Gospel are free, according to his own express command, "Freely ye have received, freely give." 1701. P. E.

It seems incumbent upon us to repeat our exhortation to faithfulness, in supporting our testimony against the antichristian yoke of tithes; and we entreat that all, who suffer either upon that account or for any other demands inconsistent with the principles of truth, may demonstrate, by their whole conduct and conversation, that they really suffer for conscience sake, and may keep close to the guidance of that good Spirit, which will preserve in meekness and quiet resignation, under every trial. For if resentment should arise against those whom you may look upon as the instruments of your sufferings, it will deprive you of the reward of faithfulness, give just occasion of offence, and bring dishonour to the cause of truth. Cavilling, or casting reflections upon any, because of our sufferings, doth not become the servants of Christ, whose holy example and footsteps we ought in all things faithfully to follow. 1759. P. E.

We have uniformly entertained the belief, on the authority of Holy Scripture, that when in the fulness of time, according to the all-wise purposes of God, our blessed Lord and Saviour appeared personally upon earth, He introduced a dispensation pure and spiritual in its character. He taught, by his own holy example and divine precepts, that the ministry of the Gospel is to be without pecuniary remuneration. As the gift is free, the exercise of it is to be free also: the office is to be filled by those only who are called of God by the power of the Holy Spirit; who, in their preaching, as well as in their circumspect lives and conversation, are giving proof of this call. The forced maintenance of the ministers of religion is, in our view, a violation of those great privileges, which God, in his wisdom and goodness, bestowed upon the human race, when He sent his Son to redeem the world, and, by the power of the Holy Spirit, to lead and guide mankind into all truth.

Our blessed Lord put an end to that priesthood, and to all those ceremonial usages connected therewith, which were before divinely ordained under the law of Moses. The present system of tithes was not in any way instituted by Him, our Holy Head and High Priest, the great Christian Lawgiver. It had no existence in the purest and earliest ages of his church, but was gradually introduced, as superstition and apostacy spread over professing Christendom, and was subsequently enforced by legal authority. And it appears to us that, in thus enforcing, as due "to God and Holy Church,"* a tithe upon the produce of the earth, and upon the increase of the herds of the field, an attempt was made to uphold and perpetuate a divine institution, appointed only for a time, but which was abrogated by the coming in the flesh of the Lord Jesus Christ. The vesting of power by the laws of the land in the king, assisted by his council, whereby articles of belief have been framed for the adoption of his subjects, and under which the support of the teachers of these articles is enforced, is, in our judgment, a procedure at variance with the whole scope and design of the Gospel; and, as it violates the rights of private judgment, so it interferes with that responsibility by which man is bound to his Creator.

In accordance with what has been already stated, we of course conscientiously object also to all demands made upon us in lieu of tithes. We likewise object to what are termed Easter-dues, demands originally made by the priests of the church of Rome, but continued in the Protestant church of England, for services which we cannot accept. We also object to mortuaries, sums applied for and still enforced in some places, as due to the incumbent of a parish on the death of the head of a family. In the example or precepts of our blessed Lord and his apostles, no authority can be found for these claims, or others of a kindred nature, which all had their origin in times of the darkness and corruption of the Christian church. And we consider, that to be compelled to unite in the support of buildings where a mode of religious worship is observed in which we cannot conscien-

* 27 Henry VIII. c. 20.

tiously unite, and in paying for appurtenances attached to that mode of worship from which we alike dissent, is subversive of that freedom which the Gospel of Christ has conferred upon all. 1832.

We continue to desire that our testimony against ecclesiastical demands may be maintained in the spirit of meekness, and in consistency with our profession. We intreat Friends to be careful that no political considerations disqualify them from rightly supporting this testimony, and to bear in mind that it is not upheld, and that it never was upheld, by us on any other than Christian grounds. Our religious Society has always maintained a stedfast attachment to the government of our country, and has enjoined and practised a cheerful submission to its laws when conscience was not violated. We caution Friends everywhere to cherish a peaceable and quiet spirit, and on all occasions of popular excitement to act as becometh meek, humble, self-denying Christians. 1834. P. E.

We believe that the refusal of all ecclesiastical demands was laid upon our forefathers, as a testimony against the corruptions of the church and to the spiritual reign and government of Christ, and that, in the patient endurance of persecution in consequence of this part of their Christian profession, they were evidently owned of their Lord. We desire that all Friends may continue firmly, yet meekly, to bear an open testimony against those ecclesiastical encroachments and that interference with the rights of conscience which still prevail. It is at the same time our desire, in relation to this duty, that all our conduct may prove that it results from the exercise of a tender and enlightened conscience. 1841. P. E.—1861.

This meeting thinks it right to encourage Friends generally to take all suitable opportunities of making known, in a right spirit, the principles of our religious Society on the subject of demands in connexion with ecclesiastical establishments. 1841.

The blessings and privileges of the Christian dispensation are, in our apprehension, greatly interfered with by the systems of human invention introduced into the worship of God, under which a certain order of men assume a power in the church, inconsistent with the free exercise of those gifts which it may please the Lord to confer. This assumption was one of the earliest, and it continues to be the source of some of the most grievous, corruptions of the professing church.

We feel truly grateful to Almighty God for that large measure of religious liberty which, after a protracted period of cruel sufferings, has long been afforded to our Society. We love our country, and we are, in the largest sense of the term, a Protestant church. But we believe that, in continuing to usurp authority over conscience in the exercise of the civil power, by maintaining established forms of worship, and by obliging men to contribute to those which they conscientiously disapprove, one of the worst features of the apostacy is retained. We think that, with a right sense of the inestimable value of religious truth, no truly conscientious man could join in supporting rites and practices which he believes to be contrary to the law of Christ and to the spirit of his religion; and still less could he impose the maintenance of his own religious opinions and practices upon those who differ from him. True religion undoubtedly leads us to do to others as we would that they should do to us. The establishment by law of one system of faith and observance as the recognized religion of the state, and a legal provision for the use of all the sects into which a nation may be divided, appear to us to be both unwarranted; the former as being an assumption of exclusive rule, the latter as treating the great questions of religion as matters of indifference. 1845. P. E.—1861.

This meeting advises Friends against repurchasing goods distrained to satisfy ecclesiastical or military demands. 1848.—1861.

In arrangements for the letting or hiring of land, it is desirable that Friends avoid making stipulations or covenants in relation to the payment of the tithe rent-charge which they cannot conscientiously fulfil, and which may afterwards hamper them in the faithful maintenance of their testimony. A like care should also be exercised not to be active in inducing the other party in the transaction to covenant to do that which the Friend himself is uneasy to do in his own person. 1851.

In the year 1836, the legislature passed an Act for effecting the commutation of all tithes in England and Wales into a tithe rent-charge, issuing out of the lands previously subject to them.

This Act, by taking away the jurisdiction of the Ecclesiastical Courts, and most of the other costly processes for the enforcing of the demand, and creating a direct and inexpensive mode of recovering it, lessened the amount of pecuniary suffering inflicted by this oppressive system. But although it has thus removed some of the branches, it has left the root untouched. The title, by which the tithe was claimed, was, in every particular, impressed upon the substituted rent-charge; and the demand for the support of a priesthood is still a compulsory demand, and in payment of services which we believe to be inconsistent with the freedom and spirituality of the New Covenant. We believe it to be our duty, as the result of repeated deliberations on the subject on various occasions, to express our solid judgment that the Christian testimony which our forefathers had to bear against tithes, we, their successors in religious profession, are called upon, in meekness, consistency and firmness, to support, against the payment of the impost secured to the priesthood, under the altered name, and with the somewhat modified incidents, of tithe rent-charge. 1851.

SECTION XX.—ON WAR.

As it hath pleased the Lord, by the breaking forth of the glorious light of his Gospel, and the shedding abroad of his Holy Spirit, to gather us to be a people to his praise, and to unite us in love, not only one unto another, but to the whole creation of God, by subjecting us to the government of his Son, our Lord and Saviour Jesus Christ, the Prince of Peace, it behoveth us to hold forth the ensign of the Lamb of God, and, by our patience and peaceable behaviour, to show that we walk in obedience to the example and precepts of our Lord and Master, who hath commanded us to love our enemies, and to do good even to them that hate us. Wherefore we intreat all who profess themselves members of our Society to be faithful to that ancient testimony, borne by us ever since we were a people, against bearing arms and fighting; that, by a conduct agreeable to our profession, we may demonstrate ourselves to be real followers of the Messiah, the peaceable Saviour, of the increase of whose government and peace there shall be no end. 1744. P.E.

And, dear friends, as it hath pleased the Almighty to reveal unto mankind his Son Jesus Christ, the peaceable Saviour, let it be our steady concern to demonstrate to the world that we are his followers, by bringing forth the fruits of the Spirit, "love, joy, peace, long-suffering, gentleness, goodness, faith, meekness, temperance." And, as we are called out of wars and fightings, so let them be as seldom as possible the subjects of our conversation; but let a holy care rest upon us, to abide in that power which gives dominion over the hopes and fears that arise from the concerns of an unstable world, and tend, as they are admitted into the mind, to lessen its trust on that rock which is immovable. Thus, like faithful Abraham, may we hope for preservation, and be qualified to approach the throne of mercy in intercession for others, at a time when the tokens of divine displeasure are manifest. Let us keep in mind that declaration of our Lord, "My kingdom is not of this world;" for they whose kingdom is of this world, will only strive for the thin s thereof. Therefore, we beseech you, mind your calling; that it may be evident you are not seeking a city here, but one to come which hath everlasting "foundations, whose builder and maker is God." 1757. P. E.

We are sorrowfully affected to find that some Friends have failed in the maintenance of our Christian testimony against wars and fighting, by joining with others to hire substitutes, and by the payment of money to exempt themselves from personal service in the militia: a practice inconsistent with our testimony to the reign of the Prince of Peace. 1760.

It is recommended to Friends everywhere, to take into their serious consideration the inconsistency of any under our profession suffering their temporal interest to induce them in any manner to contribute to the purposes of war. 1781.

We intreat that, when warlike preparations are making, Friends be watchful lest any be drawn into loans, arming or letting out their ships or vessels, or otherwise promoting the destruction of the human species. And let all be careful not to seek or accept profit by any concern in the preparations so extensively making for war; for how reproachfully inconsistent would it be, to refuse an active compliance with warlike measures, and, at the same time, not to hesitate to enrich ourselves by the commerce and other circumstances dependent on war! 1790.—1798. P. E.

Our testimony against bearing arms is a testimony for the Messiah, of whose reign it is predicted that "the wolf and the lamb shall feed together." Most, if not all people admit the transcendent excellency of peace. All who adopt the petition, "Thy kingdom come," pray for its universal establishment. Some people then must begin to fulfil the evangelical promise, and cease to learn war any more. Now, friends, seeing these things cannot be controverted, how do we long that your whole conversation be as becometh the Gospel; and that, while any of us are professing to scruple war, they may not in some parts of their conduct be inconsistent with that profession! It is an awful thing to stand forth to the nation as the advocates of inviolable peace; and our testimony loses its efficacy in proportion to the want of consistency in any. And we think we are at this time peculiarly called to let our light shine with clearness, on account of the lenity shewn us by government, and the readiness of magistrates to afford us all legal relief under suffering. We can serve our country in no way more availingly, or more acceptably to Him who holds its prosperity at his disposal, than by contributing, all that in us lies, to increase the number of meek, humble, self-denying Christians.

Guard against placing your dependence on fleets and armies; be peaceable yourselves, in words and actions; and pray to the Father of the universe, that He would breathe the spirit of reconciliation into the hearts of his erring and contending creatures. 1804. P. E.—1805. P. E.

Friends are advised against aiding and assisting in the conveyance of soldiers, their baggage, arms, ammunition, or military stores. 1810.—1861.

The continuance of the blessing of peace to this nation has warmed our hearts with gratitude. Our refusal to bear arms is a testimony, not only against the violence and cruelty of war, but against a confidence in what is emphatically termed in Scripture, the "arm of flesh;" it is a testimony to the meekness and gentleness of Christ, and a resignation to suffer, in reliance on the power, the goodness, the protection and the providence of the Almighty. Let us, even now, seek to have our trust so firmly fixed on this unfailing source of help, that, if our faith should be again put to the test, we may have ground to look with humble confidence to Him in whom we have believed. 1819. P. E.

We rejoice in the belief, that a correct appreciation of the peaceable principles of the Gospel of Christ is spreading in our own and in other lands. We hail, as a symptom of this enlightened view, many instances of later years, in which disputes between nations have been settled by arbitration, and not by a recourse to the anti-christian practice of war. May a sense of the wisdom and true policy of arbitration increase, until it shall become the ultimate rule for the determination of such differences. And O! that all nations that take upon them the name of Christ may be brought, by the light of his Spirit, to see that, in having recourse to arms to settle disputes, and in gratifying the love of conquest and power, they give occasion for his holy name to be blasphemed by Mahomedans and Pagans. 1846. P. E.

Our minds have been deeply affected by the awful consideration that, after the lapse of so many years of comparative tranquillity, the nations of Europe are again plunging into the horrors of war. Whilst not insensible of the solemn responsibility of the profession which we are making before men, we feel bound explicitly to avow our continued unshaken persuasion that all war is utterly incompatible with the plain precepts of our Divine Lord and Lawgiver, and with the whole spirit and tenor of his Gospel; and that no plea of necessity or of policy, however urgent or peculiar, can avail to release either individuals or nations from the paramount allegiance which they owe unto Him who hath said, "Love your enemies." To carry out such a profession consistently is indeed a high attainment, but it should be the aim of every Christian. May this testimony never be advocated by us in the spirit of political zeal, or of mere worldly expediency. Let us honestly examine our own hearts, whether we are ourselves so brought under the holy government of the Prince of Peace, as to be willing to suffer wrong and take it patiently, and even, if required, to sacrifice our all for the sake of Him and of his precious cause. In this frame of mind, we shall be kept in watchfulness and humility, and be best preserved from any participation in that excitement, and that tendency to exasperation against those who may be called our enemies, which are among the many fruits of bitterness fostered by war.

Under existing circumstances, we would intreat our friends everywhere to be on their guard against entering into any engagements in business which would be likely to involve them in transactions connected, more or less directly, with the maintenance of war or of a military establishment. We would also offer a word of caution (though we trust there are but few for whom it is needful) that none of you, whilst professing the principles of peace, allow yourselves to be present on any of those occasions of military or naval display which are calculated to kindle a martial spirit amongst the inhabitants of this favoured land. And greatly do we desire that, through the help of the Lord, our Society may be enabled steadily and faithfully to maintain this precious testimony with clean hands, and with a conscience void of offence toward God and toward men. 1854. P. E.

If war is to be prevented, the spirit from which war proceeds must be excluded. As with individuals, so with nations, the beginnings of strife must be watchfully guarded against. To give occasion of offence or jealousy to the governments or to the inhabitants of other countries, whether by imputing evil motives, by needless alarms of invasion, or by anything approaching to a hostile attitude, is inconsistent alike with Christian duty, and with true patriotism. May the members of our religious Society be so watchful over their thoughts, their words, and their actions, as not only to be themselves preserved from the contagion of a martial spirit, but to be enabled, by example and by precept, to do their full part towards counteracting it.

We observe with pain the arrangements extensively made in various localities to organize Rifle Clubs and Volunteer Corps. Great is the force of example and the seductive influence of companionship; and some who, in their moments of serious reflection, would refuse to take the life of a single fellow-creature even to save their own, may, either through the excitement of emulation, or the want of moral courage to withstand a sneer, be tempted to enter into pursuits, the object of which is to acquire, for the professed purpose of national defence, dexterity and certainty in the destruction of human life. May our dear young friends have the courage to resist the temptation; and may they remember that, if herein they faithfully confess their Lord and Master before men, He will sustain them in the hour of trial.

The Christian and truly scriptural testimony of our Society against all war is as precious to us as ever it was. We dare not believe that our Lord and Saviour, in enjoining the love of enemies and the forgiveness of injuries, has prescribed for man a series of precepts which are incapable of being carried into practice; or of which the practice is to be postponed till all shall be persuaded to act upon them. We cannot doubt that they are incumbent upon the Christian now; and that we have in the prophetic Scriptures the distinct intimation of their direct application, not only to individuals, but to nations also.

Great indeed must be the change before our fellow-countrymen generally, and the subjects and citizens of other professedly Christian States, are brought to admit that all war, defensive as well as offensive, is unlawful for the followers of the Lamb: but how is this change to be brought about unless by faithfulness in word and deed on the part of those who are already convinced in their consciences, that both the precepts and the example of our Lord enjoin an adherence on the part of his disciples to the principles and the practice of inviolable peace? 1859. P. E.— 1861.

SECTION XXI.—SLAVERY AND THE SLAVE-TRADE.

It is the sense of this meeting, that the importing of negroes from their native country and relations by Friends, is not a commendable nor allowed practice, and is therefore censured by this meeting. 1727.

We fervently warn all in profession with us, that they be careful to avoid being any way concerned in reaping the unrighteous profits arising from the iniquitous practice of dealing in negroes and other slaves; whereby, in the original purchase one man selleth another, as he doth the beast that perisheth, without any better pretension to a property in him than that of superior force; in direct violation of the Gospel rule, which teacheth all to do as they would be done by and to do good to all; being the reverse of that covetous disposition, which furnisheth encouragement to those poor ignorant people to perpetuate their savage wars, in order to supply the demands of this most unnatural traffic, whereby great numbers of mankind, free by nature, are subjected to inextricable bondage; and which hath often been observed to fill their possessors with haughtiness, tyranny, luxury and barbarity, corrupting the minds and debasing the morals of their children, to the unspeakable prejudice of religion and virtue, and the exclusion of that holy spirit of universal love, meekness and charity, which is the unchangeable nature, and the glory, of true Christianity.   1758.   P. E.

This meeting, having reason to apprehend that divers under our name are concerned in the unchristian traffic in negroes, doth recommend it earnestly to the care of Friends every where to discourage, as much as in them lies, a practice so repugnant to our Christian profession; and to deal with all such as shall persevere in a conduct so reproachful to Christianity, and to disown them, if they desist not therefrom.   1761.

It appears that the practice of holding negroes in oppressive and unnatural bondage hath been so successfully discouraged by Friends in some of the colonies, as to be considerably lessened. We cannot but approve of these salutary endeavours, and earnestly entreat they may be continued, that, through the favour of Divine Providence, a traffic so unmerciful and unjust in its nature to a part of our own species made equally with ourselves for immortality, may come to be considered by all in its proper light, and be utterly abolished, as a reproach to the Christian profession.   1772.   P. E.

Our testimony against the inhuman practice of slave-keeping gains ground amongst our brethren in the American colonies, and hath had some happy influence on the minds of considerate people of other denominations, in opposition to that flagrant injustice to our fellow-creatures; for whom, as well as for others, our Saviour shed his precious blood, and to whom He dispenseth a measure of his grace in common with the rest of mankind. 1774.   P. E.

We lament the slow progress in this country of the cause of our fellow-men, the oppressed black people, but we do not despair of its success: and we desire Friends may never suffer the cause to cool on their minds, through the delay which the opposition of interested men hath occasioned, in this work of justice and mercy; but rather be animated to consider that, the longer the opposition remains, the more necessity there is, on the side of righteousness and benevolence, for steadiness, perseverance, and continued breathing of spirit to the God and Father of all, who formed of one blood all the families of the earth. 1793. P. E.

A feeling hath been witnessed amongst us at this time, which directs the mind in pity towards the deplorable state of those men who promote, procure and execute the tearing away of the Africans from their parent soil: and, seeing we believe that a just and dreadful retribution awaits the unrepenting and obdurate oppressor at that awful tribunal where sophistry will not prevail to exculpate, let us, amidst our sympathy for the sufferers, give place in our minds to a true concern for the traders in negroes; and let us seek for and cherish that disposition of mind, which can pray for these enemies of humanity. 1795. P. E.

We are inclined to express our thankfulness for an event which concerns not us only, but incalculable multitudes of our fellow-creatures, our fellow-possessors of the faculty of reason, our fellow-objects of the redemption which comes by Christ. We scarcely need name the abolition of the slave-trade. We view it as one of the most important acts of public, national righteousness, which ever dignified the councils of any government; and our minds have been directed in secret prayer to the Almighty Parent of the universe, that He may be pleased to regard this kingdom for good, and direct its future councils to such further acts of justice and mercy as may promote his glory, in the harmony of his rational creation. 1807. P. E.

Although the infamous traffic with Africa in slaves has been abolished by law, we desire Friends not to forget that slavery still exists within the British empire, and to suffer their sympathy still to flow towards its oppressed victims. 1812. P. E.

The cruelties and horrors of the slave-trade have at this time deeply interested our feelings. We have heard with sorrow that this trade, with all its attendant evils and miseries, is still pursued by the subjects of several foreign powers, to a very great extent. As a testimony of our belief that it is a disgrace to any people professing the Christian name, we have been engaged to issue an address to the inhabitants of Europe on the iniquity of the traffic. 1822. P. E.

It has been very acceptable to find that our brethren on the other side of the Atlantic are in various places alive to the enormities of slavery, and diligent in their endeavours to expose the iniquity of the internal slave-trade, carried on in the southern and south-western states of the Union. The desolating and widely extended effects of this dreadful traffic, whether we turn our attention to Africa, to America, to the West India Islands, or to other parts of the globe, are indeed enormous and mournfully distressing. 1827. P. E.

This meeting has felt deep regret and sorrow in reflecting upon the continuance of slavery and all the evils connected with it. And under a full conviction of the iniquity of such a system, it desires the Meeting for Sufferings to embrace the earliest opportunity, which it may judge suitable, to petition the legislature for the immediate and total abolition of slavery within the British dominions. 1830.

The bill for the abolition of slavery in the British colonies, which was before parliament when we last met, has passed into a law; and on the first of the Eighth Month next slavery is to cease in the colonies of Great Britain. Some provisions are attached to this Act, the insertion of which we regret. We, at the same time, think it right to express our gratitude to God, in that He has been pleased to incline the hearts of our rulers to this act of national justice and mercy. Look back to the faithful, persevering labours of our dear friends of former days, when, simply following those principles of justice and equity which the Gospel enjoins, they bore their testimony to the unrighteousness of man holding his fellow man in bondage. To the spread of this view of the subject we attribute, under Divine Providence, the removal of this system of iniquity. It may truly be said to have been hastened in the Lord's time; such were the singular providences brought to bear upon the public feeling and upon the Legislature, that none could point to the result as arising from their individual efforts; and the lesson was renewedly sealed on the Christian mind, that the Lord ruleth amongst the children of men. We commend the moral and religious condition of these our long-injured fellow-subjects to the continued interest of our members. 1834. P. E.

This meeting thinks it right to record its thankfulness to

Almighty God, in that it has pleased Him to crown with success the efforts made for the extinction of the last remnant of slavery, by the termination of the system of negro apprenticeship in the British colonies, with the exception of the island of Mauritius, from whence no information of the event has yet reached us. May this happy consummation be followed by multiplied blessings to the long oppressed negro race, not only temporally, but in their being made, more generally than has yet been the case, rich partakers of that knowledge which is life eternal.

It is our desire that we may not dismiss from our sympathy those who, in such large numbers, still remain subject to all the hardship and cruelty inseparable from a state of slavery, both in the nations of the American continent, and in other parts of the world. 1839.

Our sympathy has been awakened for our brethren in the United States in their peculiarly trying position, with warm desires that they may be strengthened, in meekness and boldness, to uphold our well-known testimony on this subject. To live under a government and amongst a people who profess the religion of our blessed Saviour, and at the same time uphold and strengthen by law the system of negro slavery, must necessarily bring the Christian mind into deep sorrow. We commiserate the degraded and suffering condition of the enslaved; we feel much for our dear friends who are brought into immediate contact with this state of society, and we feel, in brotherly love, for the inhabitants of that widely-extended and rapidly-rising country, who are more or less implicated in the sin of slavery. We should rejoice to hear of the immediate and peaceable termination of this iniquitous system: earnest are our desires that it may please Him, who in his love has created all men, and who, as the almighty and all-wise Parent of the universe, has bestowed upon the slave natural and inalienable rights of which he is unjustly deprived, rapidly to advance the coming of the day when justice and mercy shall so prevail in the councils of all governments, that slavery shall utterly cease, not only in the United States of America, but throughout the nations of the earth. 1851. P. E.

SECTION XXII.—OATHS.

ADVISED, that our Christian testimony be faithfully maintained against the burthen and imposition of oaths, according to the express prohibition of Christ, and also of the apostle James: "Ye have heard that it hath been said by them of old time, thou shalt not forswear thyself, but shalt perform unto the Lord thine oaths; but I say unto you, Swear not at all; neither by heaven, for it is God's throne; nor by the earth, for it is his footstool; neither by Jerusalem, for it is the city of the great King; neither shalt thou swear by thy head, because thou canst not make one hair white or black: but let your communication be, Yea, yea; Nay, nay; for whatsoever is more than these cometh of evil." "But above all things, my brethren, swear not; neither by heaven, neither by the earth, neither by any other oath; but let your yea, be yea; and your nay, nay; lest ye fall into condemnation." 1693. P. E.

In the year 1833 an Act was passed (3 and 4 William IV., c. 49) giving, in all cases, to the affirmation of Friends, the legal force and effect of an oath.* Thus has this testimony of our religious Society against all swearing been, through progressive steps, recognised by the legislature, until at length, in this respect, every obstacle is removed to a full participation with our fellow-countrymen in all civil duties and privileges. We cannot but regard this important result, although not solicited by us, as happily indicating more enlarged and enlightened views than have heretofore prevailed, in regard to Christian liberty and the rights of conscience. It is probable, however, that some of our dear friends may, in consequence of the enactment in question, be subjected to trying and even to painful circumstances; yet we trust, that, as they are engaged to watch unto prayer for the

---

* By the Act 1 and 2 Victoria, c. 77, the same privilege is extended to persons who have been Friends or of the persuasion of Friends, and who entertain conscientious objections to the taking of an oath. And, under the Common Law Procedure Act, 1854, section 20, judges and other persons qualified to take affirmations or depositions may, in all civil cases, permit witnesses and others having conscientious objections to the taking of an oath, to make a solemn affirmation instead thereof. And by an Act passed in the session of 1861 (24 and 25 Vict. c. 66) the same power has been extended to criminal cases.

guidance and help of the Holy Spirit in all their conduct, they will be preserved from evil; and, by faithfulness in the support of our various religious testimonies, be made instrumental in advancing still further those views of Christian truth which our religious Society has, in accordance with Holy Scripture, maintained from the beginning. 1834.—1861.

The following is an extract from the Act referred to :—

"Whereas it is expedient and reasonable that the solemn affirmation of persons of the persuasion of the people called Quakers, and of Moravians, should be allowed in all cases where an oath is or shall be required; be it therefore enacted by the King's most excellent majesty, by and with the advice and consent of the lords spiritual and temporal, and commons, in this present parliament assembled, and by the authority of the same, That every person of the persuasion of the people called Quakers, and every Moravian, be permitted to make his or her solemn affirmation or declaration, instead of taking an oath, in all places and for all purposes whatsoever where an oath is or shall be required either by the common law or by any Act of Parliament already made or hereafter to be made, which said affirmation or declaration shall be of the same force and effect as if he or she had taken an oath in the usual form; and if any such person making such solemn affirmation or declaration shall be lawfully convicted, wilfully, falsely and corruptly to have affirmed or declared any matter or thing, which, if the same had been in the usual form, would have amounted to wilful and corrupt perjury, he or she shall incur the same penalties and forfeitures as by the laws and statutes of this realm are enacted against persons convicted of wilful and corrupt perjury, any law, statute, or custom to the contrary notwithstanding: Provided always, that every such affirmation or declaration shall be in the words following: (that is to say)

'*I* A. B. *being one of the people called Quakers* [*or one of the persuasion of the people called Quakers, or of the United Brethren called Moravians,* as the case may be,] *do solemnly, sincerely, and truly declare and affirm.*'"

By the Act 22 Vict. c. 10 the following is settled as the form of affirmation, to be made by Friends and other persons permitted by law to affirm, instead of the oath required to be taken in certain cases by way of substitution for the oaths of allegiance, supremacy and abjuration formerly in force.

" I, A. B. do solemnly, sincerely, and truly declare and affirm, that I will be faithful, and bear true allegiance to Queen Victoria, and to her will be faithful against all conspiracies and attempts whatever, which shall be made against her person, crown, or dignity; and I will do my utmost endeavour to disclose and make known to Queen Victoria, her heirs and successors, all treasons and traitorous conspiracies which I shall know to be formed against her or them; and I will be true and faithful to the succession of the crown, which succession, by an Act intituled 'An Act for the limitation of the Crown and better securing the rights and liberties of the subject,' is, and stands limited to the Princess Sophia, Electress of Hanover, and the heirs of her body, being Protestants, hereby utterly renouncing and refusing any obedience or allegiance unto any other person claiming or pretending a right to the Crown of this Realm; and I do declare that no foreign prince, person, prelate, state, or potentate hath, or ought to have, any jurisdiction, power, superiority, pre-eminence, or authority, ecclesiastical or spiritual, within this realm." 1861.

We entreat that, when any Friend has occasion to make an affirmation, he be very considerate and sure of the truth of what he is about to affirm, remembering that "a false witness shall not be unpunished, and he that speaketh lies shall not escape," and that the command, "thou shalt not bear false witness," is as well in the Gospel as in the law. If a due sense of the obligation to truth-speaking adequately rest upon the mind, its effect will be manifest, even in the deportment of those who are giving evidence. 1833.

SECTION XXIII.—ADVICE IN RELATION TO CIVIL GOVERNMENT.

ADVISED to walk wisely and circumspectly towards all men, in the peaceable spirit of Christ Jesus, giving no offence or occasions to those in outward government, nor way to any controversies, heats, and distractions of this world, about the kingdoms of it; but to pray for the good of all, and submit all to that divine power and wisdom, which rules over the kingdoms of men. 1689.

The corrupt and immoral practices which have frequently attended public elections, are a scandal to the Christian name, and would be very reproachful to any of our profession. We know that drunkenness, riot and confusion, are frequently attendant on these contests; and how can any in profession with us expose their minds, which it is their duty to keep unspotted from the world, to such contamination? 1774.—1790.

We have ever maintained that it is our duty to obey all the enactments of civil government, except those by which our allegiance to God is interfered with. We owe much to its blessings; through it we enjoy liberty and protection in connexion with law and order; and whilst bound by our sense of religious conviction not to comply with those requisitions which violate our Christian principles, we desire ever to be found of those who are quiet in the land; a condition favourable to true Christian patriotism, and in which services highly valuable and useful may be rendered to the community. 1834. P. E.

The position of our members in connexion with the laws which have rendered them eligible for civil offices, from which they have long been excluded, has excited our concern. We are not about to discourage any one from taking his proper share in those services, which, as a member of the community, he may be rightly called to perform, and which do not require or involve a compromise of our Christian principles. But we desire that, when the opportunity of choice is afforded, our dear friends may seriously consider the responsibilities which they are required to take upon themselves, and the temptations to which they may be exposed. Do not satisfy yourselves, dear friends, that it is merely lawful; but also ascertain whether it is for you expedient. Beware lest you be influenced by any other motives than those which will bear the test of Christian principle acting on an enlightened conscience. Be especially careful not to yield to the temptation of indulging the love of distinction, or of seeking to promote a party.

And let those who enter on any public office be concerned, in the first place, to fulfil its duties in the fear of the Lord, seeking for his help, and diligently and faithfully performing the trust reposed in them, as those who have to render an account, not to man only, but to God. We desire that our dear friends may, on these occasions, support in simplicity and fidelity all those testimonies which distinguish us from others. We are anxious, however, that it should ever be borne in mind, that these testimonies rest on no other foundation than the great principles of Christianity. Fulfil the law of immutable righteousness; uphold the standard of truth-speaking and inflexible integrity in all things; watch over your spirits, that you be not leavened into the spirit of the world, if so be you have known what it is to be raised above it; shun all party combinations, and pursue in humility the course of Christian independence. In thus discharging your duties among men, you would be made rich in the inestimable treasure of a good conscience, be enabled to grow in Christian vigour and experience, and be of those preachers of righteousness who, bringing forth the fruits of the Spirit, do, by their good works, glorify our Father who is in heaven. 1836.

The difficulties to which Friends are liable in taking office in Municipal Corporations, and also in accepting magisterial and other offices under the Crown, more especially with reference to one of the declarations which the law prescribes in such cases, have been closely under the consideration of this meeting. The declaration alluded to is that of the 9 Geo. IV. c. 17, modified by two Acts passed during the present session of Parliament, (1 & 2 Vict. c. 5, and 1 & 2 Vict. c. 15,) and which declaration now stands as below :*—This declaration contains an engagement so binding in its character, as respects the conduct of our members with reference to the Christian testimony of our religious Society in regard to ecclesiastical establishments, that we feel engaged to press upon Friends, individually, to weigh well the full import of such an engagement before they consent to make it, and to caution them to be very careful, whilst commendably desirous to fulfil their duties in civil society, that they have an especial reference to the admonitory language of the apostle :—" Happy is he that condemneth not himself in that thing which he alloweth."

By a clause introduced into an Act, passed in 1836, (6 and 7

---

* "I, A. B., being one of the people called Quakers, [or one of the persuasion of the people called Quakers, or of the United Brethren called Moravians, or of the denomination called Separatists, as the case may be], having conscientious scruples against subscribing the Declaration contained in an Act passed in the Ninth Year of the Reign of King George the Fourth, intituled *An Act for repealing so much of several Acts as imposes the necessity of receiving the Sacrament of the Lord's Supper as a qualification for certain Offices and Employments,* do solemnly, sincerely, and truly declare and affirm, That I will not exercise any power or authority or influence which I may possess by virtue of the office of   to injure or weaken the Protestant Church as it is by Law established in England, nor to disturb the said Church, or the Bishops and Clergy of the said Church, in the possession of any right or privileges to which such Church or the said Bishops and Clergy may be by Law entitled."

Wm. IV. c. 104) it is provided, that no person, enabled by law to make an affirmation instead of taking an oath, (in which description Friends are included,) shall be liable to any fine for non-acceptance of office in any borough, by reason of his refusal, on conscientious grounds, to take any oath, or make any declaration required by the Municipal Corporation Act, or to take upon himself the duties of such office. 1838.

The liability of Friends, in the present state of the law, to be called upon to fill magisterial offices, has led us to take a serious review of the character of such offices, and of the nature of the duties connected with them. We continue, as our Society has always done, to entertain a very high sense of the just authority of civil magistracy. The nature, however, of some of the duties which, in the present state of the civil and political institutions of our country, are attached to the magisterial office, is such, that if performed by a Friend, they would decidedly infringe upon several of our Christian testimonies: in particular,—the administration of oaths, the issuing of orders and warrants in reference to ecclesiastical demands, the calling out of an armed force in cases of civil commotion, the discharge of functions relative to the army and the militia, and some other matters of a similar nature, would, in the view of this meeting, render it impracticable for a member of our religious Society, executing the office, to maintain our testimonies consistently, without subjecting himself to the risk of liabilities from the breach of his duties as a magistrate. Under all the circumstances of the case, this meeting thinks it right to recommend Friends seriously to consider whether it is right for them to accept an office which involves such alternatives. 1838.—1847.—1861.

The awful subject of the punishment of death has at this time deeply impressed our minds. We believe that, where the precepts and spirit of our great Lord and Lawgiver have a complete ascendancy, they will lead to the abolition of this practice. The situation of those who have forfeited their liberty by the commission of crime, has also claimed our consideration. We regard such as objects of great compassion, and desire that they may receive the kind assistance of Friends who may have it in their power to help them; but this should be coupled with due prudence and discretion, and with that respect to the laws of our country, and to those who administer them, which we have ever believed it our duty to enjoin. 1818. P. E.

The punishment of death, to a very great extent, fails to produce the effect of deterring others from the commission of crime; and we believe that it is even the means of hardening in sin many who witness public executions. But a far more serious objection to it is, that man thus undertakes to determine the period at which his fellow man shall cease to exist in this world; when all opportunity for repentance terminates, and when, in consequence of the laws and decisions of fallible men, the criminal, however unprepared he may be, is hurried into the presence of the Judge of the whole earth. We recommend this solemn subject to the very serious attention of our members, and would encourage them to seek, under the influence of the wisdom which is from above, to promote that close examination of the matter by our countrymen and our rulers, which may so enlighten their understandings, as to hasten the day when the punishment of death shall be wholly abolished. 1847. P. E.

In fulfilling the duties of life, when occasions occur in which you may consistently serve the community in a civil capacity, be concerned to know whether it is right for you to be thus engaged; and be watchful that such undertakings do not mar the work of the Lord in your hearts, or interfere with your line of service in his church. The like watchfulness should be maintained, when taking a public part with others in associations for the purpose of lessening the mass of vice and misery which may prevail around you, or in works of more extended philanthropy. When we consider the seductive influence of popularity, and the self-satisfaction consequent upon the successful efforts of the intellectual powers, even in a good cause, we feel bound, with affectionate earnestness, to caution our friends against being led to take an undue part in the many exciting objects of the day. 1841. P. E.

SECTION XXIV.—NATIONAL FASTS AND REJOICINGS.

Advised, that Friends keep to their wonted example and testimony against the superstitious observance of days. 1691. P. E.

It is well known that we regard it as a Christian testimony, to refrain from uniting in many of those demonstrations of joy, which prevail on occasions of public rejoicing. They not unfrequently lead to practices inconsistent with that meek and quiet spirit which should clothe the disciple of Jesus, and they are often an inlet to excesses which estrange the mind from God. It is not in this way that we should manifest our gratitude for national blessings; but by endeavouring, through redeeming love and power, to live more and more in the spirit of the Gospel, and thus to hold out an example of genuine Christian conduct. 1814. P. E.—1861.

We believe that at times the Lord is pleased, in an especial manner, to visit nations by his judgments, and that they call for deep humiliation before Him, and for that repentance which includes a real turning away from all our evil works. This was the great feature of that memorable fast which obtained the divine favour for Nineveh, after the prophet had been sent to pronounce its destruction. The true and acceptable fast to the Lord was declared by the prophet Isaiah to be, not the bowing of the head for a day, but the right performance of acts of justice and mercy. How loudly then are we, as Christians, called upon to beware of depending upon any temporary or external performances, and to observe that daily and continual fast, which consists in the obedient homage of the soul to its Almighty Creator and Redeemer.

The imposition of religious exercises by the civil government, we conceive to be an infringement of the rights of conscience, and an intrusion on his prerogative, whose right it is to rule there. We have thought it right, as a Society, to abstain from the observance of days set apart, without a divine direction, for the religious commemoration of particular events, or for national humiliation under peculiar trials; and when we consider that the orders for such observances in this country are issued under the authority of the Sovereign, as head of the church of England, we feel additionally bound, with meekness, to refuse compliance with such orders, and thereby to testify against that usurpation which we believe to be anti-christian.

Whilst supporting these our views of the liberty of the Gospel, let us be careful to prove, by our conduct and conversation, that we walk in the fear of God, and do indeed believe that He rules in the kingdoms of men. May we increasingly cherish that true love of our country, which would lead us frequently to the throne of grace on its behalf; that so, whilst we cannot lift up the sword in its defence, our prayers and intercessions may ascend availingly to Him in whose hand are the prosperity of nations, and the issues of life and death. 1833.—1861.

The believers in Christ are spoken of as a royal priesthood. To the great privilege of offering "spiritual sacrifices acceptable to God by Jesus Christ," we are all invited under the new covenant. As we come to enjoy this privilege, we are brought not to depend one upon another, or upon stated performances in the public worship of God, and are confirmed in the truth, that typical rites and ceremonies are no part of the spiritual dispensation under which we live.

The spirituality and freedom of the Gospel lead also to the non-observance of days enjoined by the civil or ecclesiastical authority, as those of humiliation or thanksgiving. Whilst endeavouring faithfully to obey all laws which do not infringe upon the divine law, we continue to believe that to impose such observance, in the name of any ecclesiastical rulers whatever, is an interference with the prerogative of Christ, who alone is the head over his own Church. It is the great duty of Christians so to live, that when public calamities visit a nation, their sense of the chastening which is laid upon them may be manifested by humiliation of soul, under a feeling of that constant dependence upon God in which our spiritual strength so greatly consists. 1851. P. E.

SECTION XXV.—BURIALS AND MOURNING HABITS.

Advised against imitating the vain custom of wearing or giving mourning, and all extravagant expenses about the interment of the dead. 1724. P. E.

It is advised that women Friends should not be induced by the desire to imitate prevailing customs or otherwise, to refrain from attending the burial of their relations, agreeably to the practice of our worthy predecessors, and as a becoming token of respect to the deceased. 1782.—1861.

Our attention has been turned to the practice of wearing mourning garments on the occasion of the decease of relatives and friends; and we feel concerned to offer an affectionate caution to our members against this obvious conformity to the vain and oppressive customs of the world. It tends to occupy the thoughts with useless and frivolous subjects, at a time when it is peculiarly important that nothing should interfere with those precious visitations of the love of God to the soul, which often, in an especial manner, accompany the afflictive dispensations of the Most High in the death of our near connexions, contriting the hard heart and comforting the true mourner. It is, moreover, in many instances a token of a sorrow not really felt; and thus includes a departure from that strict truthfulness which, in deed as well as in word, ought ever to mark the Christian character. We are also desirous of cautioning our friends against those progressive deviations from simplicity of dress in other respects, and that gradual assimilation with the world, which we believe often render it additionally difficult for them to resist its customs in this particular. 1845. P. E.

Burials of persons not members of our religious Society may take place in our burial grounds, provided they be in all respects conducted as the burials of Friends are conducted. Friends are to exercise discretion as to complying with any application that may be made in such cases; and as to appointing a meeting for worship on the occasion. 1832.—1861.

This meeting, after serious and deliberate consideration of the subject, is renewedly of the judgment, that our religious Society has a sound Christian testimony to bear against the erection of monuments, as well as against all inscriptions of a eulogistic character over the graves of their deceased friends. Nevertheless, it is of the opinion, that it is no violation of such testimony to place over or beside a grave a plain stone, the inscription on which is confined to a simple record of the name, age and date of the decease of the individual interred. The object in this instance is simply to define the position of the grave, with a view to the satisfaction of surviving relatives, and the preventing of its premature re-opening.

Friends are therefore left at liberty to adopt the use of such stones in any of our burial grounds; it being distinctly understood that, in all cases, they are to be provided and put down under the direction of the Monthly Meeting; so that, in each particular burial ground, such an entire uniformity may be preserved, in respect to the materials, size and form of the stones, as well as in the mode of placing them, as may effectually guard against any distinction being made in that place between the rich and the poor. 1850.—1861.

CHAPTER III.

CHRISTIAN DISCIPLINE.

INTRODUCTION. — ON THE ORIGIN OF THE CHRISTIAN DISCIPLINE ESTABLISHED AMONG FRIENDS.

By the term discipline, is to be understood all those arrangements and regulations which are instituted for the civil and religious benefit of a Christian church. The meetings for discipline are, of course, for the purpose of carrying those objects into effect: their design was said by George Fox to be—the promotion of charity and piety.

It cannot be said that any *system* of discipline formed a part of the original compact of the Society. There was not indeed, to human appearance, any thing systematic in its formation. It was an association of persons who were earnestly seeking after the saving knowledge of Divine Truth. They were men of prayer, and diligent searchers of the Holy Scriptures. Unable to find true rest in the various opinions and systems which in that day divided the Christian world, they believed that they found the Truth in a more full reception of Christ, not only as the living and ever-present Head of the Church in its aggregate capacity, but also as the light and life, the spiritual ruler, teacher, and friend, of every individual member.

These views did not lead them to the abandonment of those doctrines which they had heretofore held, in regard to the manhood of Christ, his propitiatory sacrifice, mediation, and intercession. They did lead them, however, to much inward retirement and waiting upon God, that they might know his will, and become quick of understanding in the fear of the Lord; and they were very frequent in their meetings together for mutual edification and instruction, for the purpose of united worship in spirit and in truth, and for the exercise of their several gifts, as ability might be afforded by Him who has promised to be with the two or three disciples who are gathered together in his name.

From these meetings, in which the love of God was often largely shed abroad in the hearts of those who attended them, even when held in silence, most of those ministers went forth, who, in the earliest periods of the Society, proclaimed to others the truth as they had found it, and called them from dependence on man to that individual knowledge of Christ and of his teachings, which the Holy Scriptures so clearly and abundantly declare to be the privilege of the Gospel times. As these views struck at the very root of that great corruption in the Christian Church, by which one man's performances on behalf of others had been made essential to public worship, and on which hung all the load of ecclesiastical domination and the trade in holy things; so it necessarily separated those who had, as they believed, found the liberty of the Gospel, from those who still adhered to that system which was upheld by the existing churches of the land.

Being thus separated from others, and many being every day added to the church, there arose of course peculiar duties of the associated persons towards each other. Christianity has ever been a powerful, active, and beneficent principle. Those who truly receive it no more "live unto themselves;" and this feature and fruit of genuine Christianity was strikingly exhibited in the conduct of the early Friends. No sooner were a few persons connected together in the new bond of religious fellowship, than they were engaged to admonish, encourage, and, in spiritual as well as temporal matters, to watch over and help one another in love.

The members who lived near to each other, and who met together for religious worship, immediately formed, from the very law of their union, a Christian family or little church. Each member was at liberty to exercise the gift bestowed upon him, in that beautiful harmony and subjection which belong to the several parts of a living body, from the analogy to which the apostle Paul draws so striking a description of the true church; "Ye are the body of Christ and members in particular."

Of this right exercise of spiritual gifts, and thereby of an efficient discipline, many examples are afforded in the history of the earliest period of the Society: we shall select one which we believe may be considered as fairly illustrating the practice of early times. Stephen Crisp, in his Memoirs, speaking of his

own state soon after his convincement, which was in 1665, and within a few years of the establishment of a meeting at Colchester, the place of his residence, thus expresses himself:—
"The more I came to feel and perceive the love of God and his goodness to me, the more was I humbled and bowed in my mind to serve Him, and to serve the least of his people among whom I walked; and as the word of wisdom began to spring in me, and the knowledge of God grew, so I became a counsellor of those that were tempted in like manner as I had been; yet was kept so low, that I waited to receive counsel daily from God, and from those that were over me in the Lord, and were in Christ before me, against whom I never rebelled nor was stubborn; but the more I was kept in subjection myself, the more I was enabled to help the weak and feeble ones. And, as the church of God in those days increased, and my care daily increased, and the weight of things relating both to the outward and inward condition of poor Friends came upon me; and being called of God and his people to take the care of the poor, and to relieve their necessities as I did see occasion, I did it faithfully for divers years, with diligence and much tenderness, exhorting and reproving any that were slothful, and encouraging them that were diligent, putting a difference according to the wisdom given me of God, and still minding my own state and condition, and seeking the honour that cometh from God only."

Thus, then, we believe it may be safely asserted, there never was a period in the Society, when those who agreed in religious principles were wholly independent of each other, or in which that order and subjection which may be said to constitute *discipline* did not exist. But, as the number of members increased, those mutual helps and guards which had been, in great measure, spontaneously afforded, were found to require some regular arrangements for the preservation of order in the church.

The history of these proceedings affords no small evidence that the spirit of a sound mind influenced the body in its earliest periods. Contending, as they did, for so large a measure of individual spiritual liberty, and placing the authority of man, in religious matters, in a position so subordinate to that of the one Great Head of the Church, they nevertheless recognized the importance and necessity of arrangements and of human instrumentality, under the direction of the Spirit of Christ; and they were led to establish a system of order at once so simple and efficient, that, notwithstanding the varying circumstances of the Society, and the power of every annual meeting to alter it, it has been found, in its main particulars, adapted to those changes, and it remains to this day essentially the same as it was within forty years of the rise of the Society. Previously, however, to the establishment of that regular system of discipline, and of that mode of representation in the meetings for conducting it, which now exist, there had been many General Meetings held in different parts of the nation, for the purpose of providing for the various exigencies of the Society. George Fox mentions, in his journal, that some meetings for discipline were settled in the north of England so early as 1653. The first General Meeting, of which we are aware that any records are extant, was held at Balby, near Doncaster, in Yorkshire, in the year 1656; and from this meeting a number of directions and advices were issued, addressed "To the Brethren in the North." This document refers to most of the points which now form the chief subjects of our discipline. It contains instructions as to the Gospel order of proceeding with delinquents, and advices to husbands and wives, parents and children, masters and servants, as to the discharge of their relative duties, and also in regard to strict justice in trade, and a cheerful and faithful performance of civil offices in the commonwealth. George Fox mentions attending a General Meeting in Bedfordshire, in 1658, which lasted three days; at which, he says, "there were Friends present from most parts of the nation, and many thousands of persons were at it." He also mentions attending a meeting at Skipton in 1660, "for the affairs of the church, both in this nation and beyond the seas;" and he says that he had recommended the establishment of this meeting several years before, when he was in the north; "for many Friends suffered in divers parts of the nation; their goods were taken from them contrary to law, and they understood not how to help themselves, or where to seek redress." "This meeting," he adds, "had stood several years, and divers justices and captains had come to break it up; but when they understood the business Friends met about, and saw Friends' books, and accounts of collections for the use of the poor; how we took care one county to help another, and to help our friends beyond sea, and to provide for our poor, so that none should be chargeable to their parishes, the justices and officers confessed we did their work, and would pass away peaceably and lovingly."

Next to General Meetings we must notice the establishment of Quarterly Meetings, which were constituted of friends deputed by the several meetings within a county. These meetings, in several of the counties at least, had existed prior to the establishment of Monthly Meetings, and they appear to have had much the same office in the body, as the Monthly Meetings now have amongst us. George Fox, in an epistle of an early date, writes thus respecting them: "In all the meetings of the county two or three may be appointed from them to go to the Quarterly Meetings, to give notice if there be any that walk not in the truth, or have been convinced and gone from the truth, and so have dishonoured God; and likewise to see if any that profess the truth follow pleasures, drunkenness, gaming, or are not faithful in their callings and dealings, nor honest, but run into debt, and so bring a scandal upon the truth. Friends may give notice to the Quarterly Meetings (if there be any such), and some may be ordered to go and exhort them, and bring in their answers to the next Quarterly Meeting. And to admonish all them that be careless and slothful to diligence in the truth and service for God, and to bring forth heavenly fruits to God, and that they may mind the good works of God, and do them in believing on his Son, and showing it forth in their conversation, and to deny the devil and his bad works, and not to do them; and to seek them that be driven away from the truth into the devil's wilderness by his dark power; seek them again by the truth, and by the truth and power of God bring them to God again."

It appears to have been with our Society as it had been with the primitive church, that the care and provision for its poor members was amongst the earliest occasions of disciplinary arrangements. The occasion for this provision was much increased by the cruel persecutions and robberies to which, on their first rise, the Friends were almost everywhere exposed. It was no rare occurrence, at that period, for the father of a family to be thrown into a dungeon, and for the house to be spoiled of the very children's beds and all their provisions. Nor was it uncommon to seek their entire proscription and ruin, by refusing to deal with them. Well may we say, with reverent thankfulness, in reference to those times, "If it had not been the Lord who was on our side, when men rose up against us, then they had swallowed us up quick, when their wrath was kindled against us."

The members of the persecuted society were far from opulent; but they proved themselves rich in charity, as well as in faith and hope: and the illustration of these virtues, by the sacrifices which they made for the relief of their more afflicted associates, and their unbroken constancy in the sufferings which they endured for the testimony of a good conscience, were doubtless amongst the practical arguments which at length extorted the commendation even of their enemies.

A second, and perhaps contemporaneous, object of the meetings for the discipline of the society, was the obtaining of redress for those illegally prosecuted or imprisoned. Though so patient in suffering, they deemed it their duty to apprise magistrates, judges and the government, of illegal proceedings, and to use every legal and Christian effort to obtain redress. Several friends in London devoted a large portion of time to this object, and regular statements of the most flagrant cases were sent to them, and were frequently laid by them before the king and government. Their constancy in suffering was hardly exceeded by their unwearied efforts to obtain relief for their suffering brethren, and for the alteration of the persecuting laws; and through these means the cause of religious liberty was essentially promoted.

A third object, which at a very early period of the society pressed upon its attention, was the proper registration of births and deaths, and the provision for due proceedings relative to marriage. Their principles led them at once to reject all priestly intervention on these occasions, and hence the necessity for their having distinct arrangements in regard to them. In some of the meetings of earliest establishment regular registers are preserved from the year 1650 to the present time. Great care was taken in regard to proceedings in marriage; investigation as to the clearness of the parties from other marriage engagements, full publicity of their intentions, and the consent of parents, appear to have been recommended in early times as preliminaries to the ratification of the agreement between the parties; and this act took place publicly in the religious meetings of the society. Marriage has always been regarded by Friends as a religious, not a mere civil compact.

The right education of youth, the provision of suitable situations for them as apprentices or otherwise, and the settlement of differences without going to law one with another, were also among the early objects of the society's care.

The last object of the discipline, in early times, which we shall enumerate, was the exercise of spiritual care over the members. As the society advanced it was soon reminded of our Lord's declaration: "It must needs be that offences come." Evidencing, as the society did to a large extent, the fruits of the Spirit, there were those who fell away from their Christian profession, and walked disorderly; and sound as was the body of Friends in Christian doctrine, there were members who were betrayed into false doctrines and vain imaginations; and pure, and spiritual, and consistent with true order and Christian subjection as were the principles of religious liberty advocated by the society, there were those who appear to have assumed them under the false expectation of an entire independence.

To all these cases the discipline was applied in very early times; yet the spirit of tenderness, which breathes through the writings of George Fox in regard to the treatment of delinquents, and which there is good reason to believe was practically illustrated, to a large extent, in the conduct of the Friends of those days, is worthy of especial notice. From one of his epistles we make the following extracts: "Now concerning Gospel order, though the doctrine of Jesus Christ requireth his people to admonish a brother or sister twice, before they tell the church, yet that limiteth none, so as that they shall use no longer forbearance. And it is desired of all, before they publicly complain, that they wait to feel if there is no more required of them to their brother or sister, before they expose him or her to the church. Let this be weightily considered, and all such as behold their brother or sister in a transgression, go not in a rough, light, or upbraiding spirit, to reprove or admonish him or her; but in the power of the Lord and spirit of the Lamb, and in the wisdom and love of the truth, which suffers thereby, to admonish such an offender. So may the soul of such a brother or sister be seasonably and effectually reached unto and overcome, and they may have cause to bless the name of the Lord on their behalf, and so a blessing may be rewarded into the bosom of that faithful and tender brother or sister who so admonished them. And so keep the church order of the Gospel, according as the Lord Jesus Christ hath commanded; that is, 'If thy brother shall trespass against thee, go and tell him his fault between thee and him alone: if he shall hear thee, thou hast gained thy brother: but if he will not hear thee, then take with thee one or two more, that in the mouth of two or three witnesses every word may be established: and if he shall neglect to hear them, tell it unto the Church.'"

We now proceed to notice the more regular and systematic establishment of Monthly and Quarterly Meetings, and of the Yearly Meeting. Though the history of those times bears ample testimony to the useful part which was taken in this important work by many faithful friends, yet it is clear that George Fox was the chief instrument in the arrangement and establishment of these meetings. There was doubtless much reference to his individual judgment, but it is worthy of notice how carefully he sought to keep the body from an improper dependence upon him. As in his preaching he directed his hearers to Christ for themselves, as alike *their* and *his* teacher, so in the discipline of the society he laboured diligently that the body might be strengthened to help itself.

Under the date of 1666, George Fox says in his journal: "Whereas Friends had had only Quarterly Meetings, now truth was spread and Friends were grown more numerous, I was moved to recommend the setting up of Monthly Meetings throughout the nation." In 1667 he laboured most diligently in this service, under much bodily weakness from his long confinements in cold and damp prisons. In 1668 he thus writes: "The men's Monthly Meetings were settled through the nation. The Quarterly Meetings were generally settled before. I wrote also into Ireland, Scotland, Holland, Barbadoes, and several parts of America, advising Friends to settle their men's Monthly Meetings in those countries, for they had their Quarterly

Meetings before." These Monthly Meetings, so instituted, took a large share of that care which had heretofore devolved on the Quarterly Meetings, and were no doubt the means of bringing many more of the members into a larger sphere of usefulness and the exercise of their respective gifts in the church, the free course for which he was so anxious to promote. With reference to this subject, he observes, in one of his epistles: "The least member in the church is serviceable, and all the members have need one of another."

The Quarterly Meetings from this time received reports of the state of the society from the Monthly Meetings, and gave such advice and decisions as they thought right, but there was not, until some years after this period, a general Yearly Meeting, at which all the Quarterly Meetings were represented. Of the establishment of that meeting we come now to speak.

In the year 1672 a General Meeting of ministers was held at Devonshire House, London: amongst its proceedings we find the following minute, in which we trace the origin of the Yearly Meeting, constituted as it now is of representatives from various parts of the kingdom. "It is concluded, agreed, and assented unto, by friends then present, that, for the better ordering, managing, and regulating of the public affairs of Friends relating to the truth and service thereof, there be a General Meeting of Friends held at London once a year, in the week called Whitsunweek, to consist of six friends for the city of London, three for the city of Bristol, two for the town of Colchester, and one or two from each of the counties of England and Wales respectively."

This representative Yearly Meeting met at the time proposed in 1673, and came to the conclusion, that the General Meeting, constituted as it then was, "be discontinued till Friends, in God's wisdom, shall see a further occasion; and it was further agreed, that the General Meeting of friends who labour in the work of the ministry, do continue as formerly appointed. This meeting of friends in the ministry appears to have been regularly held annually from this time to the year 1677 inclusive.

In 1675 a series of important advices and instructions were agreed upon, and sent forth to the several meetings: they are contained in an epistle, and are thus introduced: "At a solemn General Meeting of many faithful friends and brethren concerned in the public labour of the Gospel and service of the church of Christ, from the most parts of the nation." This document is signed by eighty-one friends, most of whom are well known as conspicuous in the early history of the Society; and the spirit of fervent piety and charity which it breathes is well worthy of their character. In 1677, it was agreed again to convene the meeting of representatives in the ensuing year, and then to advise respecting its continuance. Accordingly in 1678 the representative Yearly Meeting assembled in London, and, after agreeing upon several matters, the substance of which was conveyed to the various meetings of Friends in the form of an epistle with much Christian counsel, concluded to meet again the next year after the same manner; and these meetings have continued to assemble once a year in London, with unbroken regularity, to the present time.

When the General Meeting of ministers transferred much of its duties to the representative Yearly Meeting, of which they formed a part, there were some portions of the service of these meetings which more particularly belonged to the ministers. Although the power to approve and disapprove of ministers rested with the members of the church to which they respectively belonged, in the capacity of a Monthly Meeting, yet it was deemed fitting that the ministers should have an especial oversight of each other, and that they should meet together for mutual consultation and advice in regard to those of their own station.

George Fox, in 1674, writes thus: "Let your general assemblies of the ministers [in London, or elsewhere] examine, as it was at the first, whether all the ministers that go forth into the counties do walk as becomes the Gospel; for that you know was one end of that meeting, to prevent and take away scandal, and to examine whether all who preach Christ Jesus, do keep in his government and in the order of the Gospel, and to exhort them that do not." Meetings for these purposes, in which friends in the station of elder are now united, continue to be regularly held.

All the meetings which have been hitherto described were conducted by men; but it was one of the earliest features of our religious economy to elevate the character of the female sex, by recognizing them as helpers in spiritual, as well as in temporal things; holding, in the former as well as in the latter, a distinct place, and having duties which more peculiarly devolved on them. For this purpose meetings were established among them, with a special regard to the care and edification of their own sex. The views of George Fox in regard to the establishment of these meetings are conveyed in the following passages: "Faithful women, called to a belief of the truth, and made partakers of the same precious faith and heirs of the same everlasting Gospel of life and salvation, as the men are, might in like manner come into the profession and practice of the Gospel order, and therein be meet-helps to the men in the service of truth, and the affairs in the church, as they are outwardly in civil and temporal things; that so all the family of God, women as well as men, might know, possess and perform their offices and services in the house of God: whereby the poor might be better taken care of; the younger sort instructed, informed, and taught in the way of God; the disorderly reproved and admonished in the fear of the Lord; the clearness of persons proposing marriage more closely and strictly inquired into in the wisdom of God; and all the members of the spiritual body, the church, might watch over and be helpful to each other in love."

Thus was a system of order and government, in conformity with the spirit of Christianity, established amongst us in early times; and thus a field was opened for the exercise of the various gifts, by which the church, the body of Christ, is edified.

SECTION I.—YEARLY MEETING.

For better managing, ordering, and regulating the public affairs of Friends relating to truth and the service thereof, it is agreed that a General Meeting be held in London annually. 1672. *Object and Character.*

The good and blessed intent and end of this and all our assemblies, is, with the Lord's assistance, for his honour; in the promoting and maintaining of our Christian society and religion, in life and practice, in all the parts and branches thereof. 1695. P. E.

The intent and design of our annual assemblies, in their first constitution, was for a great and weighty oversight and Christian care of the affairs of the churches pertaining to our holy profession and Christian communion; that good order, true love, unity and concord may be faithfully followed and maintained among us. 1718. P. E.

It is the fervent desire of this meeting, that the business and concerns thereof be solidly, in the fear of God, managed and carried on, without contention or striving, and with as few words, and in as pertinent expressions to the matter in hand, as may be, for expediting the affairs thereof without loss of time, or any ways disordering the meeting; but one at a time speaking, and standing up, that all things may be done decently, and in order. 1710.

Constitution.
It is concluded that this meeting consist of all the members of the Quarterly and General Meetings in Great Britain, and of representatives from the Yearly Meeting in Ireland. In order to provide for the due attendance of this meeting, each Quarterly and General Meeting is to appoint not more than eight nor less than four representatives, where they can conveniently be found; but the Quarterly Meetings of Lancashire and Cheshire, London and Middlesex, and Yorkshire, in consideration of their numbers, are each allowed to send twelve. 1728.—1782.—1833.—1861.

Regulations.
The Yearly Meeting is to begin at ten o'clock on the Fourth-day after the third First-day in the Fifth month. Meetings for worship are to be held at ten o'clock on Sixth-day Morning in the same week, and, at the same hour, on Fourth-day morning in the week following.* 1798.—1861.

Advised, that no representatives withdraw, or go out of town, before the meeting end, without leave first requested and granted; that the service of the meeting may not be neglected. 1709.

This meeting desires that all propositions from any Quarterly or General Meeting to this meeting be delivered in writing, and signed by order of such meeting. 1735.

* For the time of holding the meeting of ministers and elders, see Section XI.

All letters directed to this meeting, except from such meetings as regularly correspond therewith, are to be first perused by two or three friends to be appointed, who are to consider and report whether the same be proper to be read in this meeting or not. 1736.

Agreed that two or three friends be appointed to revise the minutes of each day's transactions, and to correct any slight inaccuracies that may be observed; and, if any alterations or corrections in things of moment appear necessary, to propose the same to the meeting at its next sitting, previously to any other business; in order that the minutes may be entered with due accuracy, and in a manner clearly to be comprehended. 1762.

This meeting having been informed that some friends have been engaged, in this and the previous sittings, in taking notes of its proceedings, thinks it right to express its judgment that such practice is a violation of good order; as being inconsistent with the state of mind becoming the occasion, and with the object and character of our meetings for discipline. 1837.

It is agreed that the representatives shall meet at the close of the first sitting of this meeting in each year, and shall, when so met, nominate a clerk and two assistants for the current year, from amongst the members of this meeting. The said nomination is to be reported to the next sitting of this meeting previously to any other business: and the former clerk is not to consider himself discharged until another be chosen. The representatives are also to consider of suitable friends to act as clerk and assistants of the large Committee (if such should be appointed), and to submit such nomination to the large Committee, at its first sitting, for its approval. 1807.—1833.—1861.

A committee is to be annually appointed to audit the accounts of the national stock, and is to consist of one friend from each Quarterly Meeting, such friend being a representative to the Yearly Meeting, and nominated by his Quarterly Meeting for that special service. By this means all the Quarterly Meetings may have an opportunity of being informed how the money collected for the general service of the Society is expended. 1752.—1861.

SECTION II.—QUARTERLY MEETINGS.

Care of Subordinate Meetings. This meeting recommends to the attention of our Quarterly Meetings the circumstances of the very small Meetings for Worship and the small Monthly Meetings within their limits. We desire that the condition of these meetings may obtain the care of well concerned friends, and that a brotherly and christian intercourse, so far as practicable, may be kept up between all the members of a Quarterly Meeting. 1842.

This meeting has had under its consideration the important place which Quarterly Meetings hold in the arrangement of our meetings for discipline. It has often been found to be of great advantage for those meetings to appoint committees who should, in Christian love, attend the Monthly Meetings as well as the particular meetings within their limits, extending this service sometimes to the families of Friends, under a concern for the growth of their members in the truth, and for the faithful maintenance of our religious testimonies. These visits are found to be a means of strengthening the bond of Christian fellowship, and especially so if occasionally repeated; they bring the visitors to a more thorough knowledge of the trials and cares of their fellow members, and afford an opportunity to enter into sympathy with them, and to administer counsel, encouragement, or help. Such a service may sometimes be acceptably rendered by Monthly Meetings when they include several Preparative Meetings and spread over an extensive district. Well concerned friends are encouraged to manifest their love for their brethren by accepting of the appointment, and we believe that, as it is done in the fear of the Lord and in the simplicity of faith, it will contribute to their own religious benefit. 1852.

It is the judgment of this meeting, when any Monthly Meeting thinks it right to establish any new Meeting for Worship, or any Preparative Meeting, or to discontinue, either wholly or in part, any such meeting already settled, that the same be reported to the Quarterly Meeting for its approbation, before it be carried into effect. 1822.

The several Quarterly Meetings are to transmit annually in the Spring to the Meeting for Sufferings, information of any meetings which have been settled, discontinued, or united in the course of the year; in order that such information may be duly communicated to this meeting. And when any Quarterly Meeting thinks it right, under special circumstances, to give permission to a Monthly Meeting to be held less frequently than once in the month, the same is to be reported to the Yearly Meeting. 1833.—1861.

This meeting is of the judgment, that ministering friends who have a concern to travel in Ireland or Scotland, or on the islands adjacent, with a view of holding meetings among those of other religious Societies, should have the concurrence and unity of their Quarterly Meetings, in addition to that of their Monthly Meetings, when the same can be had with convenience; apprehending that such procedure will be of considerable advantage to friends under an exercise of so important a nature. Nevertheless, it is not meant that this rule shall apply to friends travelling in the work of the ministry, whose concern is chiefly to the members of our own Society. 1812.—1861. *Concerns of Ministers to travel.*

This meeting, having considered the case of ministers who have to apply to their Quarterly Meetings for concurrence in their concerns to travel in religious service, concludes that the said meetings are at liberty to enter upon the consideration of such concerns in a joint Quarterly Meeting of men and women friends, if they should think it desirable to pursue such a course. 1830.

SECTION III.—MONTHLY MEETINGS.

AGREED, that no Monthly Meeting shall be allowed to divide itself into two separate Monthly Meetings, without the consent or concurrence of the Quarterly Meeting. 1715. *Their division and junction.*

Wheresoever it appears that any Monthly Meetings, through the smallness of the number of friends attending them, are not sufficiently qualified for carrying on the discipline of the church, we wish that such small meetings might join some other neighbouring Monthly Meetings; that by such union they might be assisted and strengthened. 1752.

Care of small meetings.

This meeting, being of the judgment that it would be an acceptable and useful service, if friends were occasionally to attend the smaller meetings for worship, held on First-days, and on other days of the week, in the districts in which they reside, recommends the subject to the attention of Monthly Meetings. Such an intercourse would enable friends to enter more closely into the peculiar circumstances of their brethren; and would, we believe, tend to strengthen the precious bond of Christian fellowship. 1826.

Lending meeting-houses.

It is the judgment of this meeting that Monthly Meetings, or committees of their appointment, should exercise a sound discretion in either lending, or refusing to lend, our meeting-houses for the purpose of worship to persons of other religious denominations. 1861.

Membership.

On the subject of the right of children to membership in the Society, this meeting considers it proper to define that such right is to be understood as extending to any child born of parents in membership; also to any child either the father or mother of whom is at the time of its birth a member, provided such father and mother were both of them members at the time of marriage. 1820.—1861.

Although we recognise the children of our members as objects of our care, and partakers of the outward privileges of Christian fellowship, we would earnestly remind all that such recognition cannot constitute them members of the Lord's spiritual Israel. Nothing can effect this but the power of the Holy Spirit working repentance towards God, and faith towards our Lord Jesus Christ; therefore let the words of our Divine Master have their due place with us all—"Ye must be born again." May all our members become such on the ground of true convincement, and be prepared in their several places to bring forth fruit unto God. 1861.

In cases where both the parents or the surviving parent of children in membership may, by resignation or disownment, have ceased to be members or a member of our Society; and where it does not appear probable that such children will be educated in accordance with our religious principles, Monthly Meetings are left at liberty, in their discretion, and after communicating, when practicable, with their parents or guardians, to declare any such children, not being above fourteen years of age, to be no longer members of our Society. In every such case, information of the conclusion of the Monthly Meeting is to be communicated in writing to the parents or guardians of the child or children to whom the same shall relate. 1861.

Monthly Meetings are to keep an alphabetical list of their members, and annually to appoint a committee for the purpose of examining such list by comparing the entries with the Monthly Meeting's minutes.* After being thus examined, it is recommended that the said list be read over once a year, either by a committee of the Monthly Meeting, or by that meeting in its collective capacity. 1812.—1861.

Advised, that Monthly Meetings lay hands on no man suddenly, nor speedily admit into membership any who may come to Friends' meetings as convinced persons, especially such as discover an earnestness for a speedy admission into communion with us, without a seasonable time to consider their conduct. Let the innocency of their lives and conversation first be manifested, and a deputation of judicious friends be made, to inquire into the sincerity of their convincement of the truth of our religious principles; and let this appear to the Monthly Meeting previously to their admission. 1764. *[Non-members.]*

This meeting has derived satisfaction from the attention which has been paid in the respective Quarterly Meetings, to the children of parents not in affluence, not members of our Society, which children are brought up in the attendance of our religious meetings; and wishes to encourage friends of the respective Quarterly and Monthly Meetings to continue to extend a friendly care and interest towards the parents of such children, and towards the children themselves as regards their moral and religious education. 1829.—1833.

This meeting, under a concern for the religious oversight of children and young persons who may be in profession, though

---

* The same committees may also with advantage examine the marriage registers, and compare the birth and burial notes with the check margins.

Non-members. not in membership, with us, and especially of those who have received their education in some of our public schools, recommends to Monthly Meetings that provision be made for bringing such young persons under the notice of Friends. Separate lists of the names of such, as well as of all other attenders of our meetings not in membership, are recommended to be kept and read, for the purpose of maintaining a Christian interest on their behalf. 1851.

Monthly Meetings are left at liberty, in their discretion, to admit into membership, in their infancy, any children whose parents are, or may have been, members, or who may be otherwise connected with our Society, in cases where a reasonable probability appears that such children will be educated in accordance with our religious principles. 1861.

Delinquencies. In the love of Christ, we earnestly exhort you to watch diligently over the flock, and deal in due time, and in a spirit of Christian love and tenderness, with all such as walk disorderly amongst you, in order to reclaim and restore them by brotherly counsel and admonition; and when any one of our members commits an offence, and after due private labour it has been communicated to the Monthly Meeting, that meeting shall appoint some well qualified friends to visit the offending member, and to inquire carefully into the matter, and labour for the restoration of the brother or sister who may have been overtaken in a fault. The friends appointed are to report as early as convenient to the Monthly Meeting.

In the case of delinquency by a Friend who is not a member of the meeting in which he resides, care should be taken, after due inquiry and private labour, that the meeting to which he belongs be informed of the case. The meeting of which he is a member is then to proceed to visit and deal with him, unless by reason of distance it be not convenient; in which case, it is to apply to the Monthly Meeting in which the offender resides, to act for it and visit him, and report its proceedings to the meeting of which he is a member; which meeting is to receive his acknowledgment, or disown him, as in its judgment the case shall require, reporting either conclusion to the other meeting. If a testimony of disownment be issued, a copy thereof is to be sent to the meeting in the compass of which the offender resides, which is to acquaint him therewith, and acknowledge the receipt thereof to the meeting that sent it.

If the offender remove after dealing be commenced, the meeting that had him under its care shall continue the same, if he be equally within its reach, or otherwise is at liberty to write to the meeting into the compass of which he is removed; which meeting is to proceed therein, and report to the meeting of which he is a member, which shall receive his acknowledgment, or proceed to disown him as aforesaid.

In case offenders shall remove to places not within the acknowledged limits of any Monthly Meeting, it is agreed that they may be placed under the care of the meeting to which they are the nearest situated.

If an offender cannot be found, the meeting to which he belongs shall issue a testimony against him, if the nature of the case require it. Information of disownments is to be sent to the women's Monthly Meeting, and also to the Preparative Meeting (if there be one) to which the disowned person belonged: and in all cases a copy is to be delivered to the person disowned, if access can be had to him. When a person, having been disowned, is desirous of re-admission into the Society, and is not resident within the compass of the Monthly Meeting which disowned him, it is advised that any committee appointed in the case do communicate with the meeting which disowned him. 1782.—1801.—1861.

If there be any such gross errors, false doctrines, or mistakes held by any professing truth, as are either against the validity of Christ's sufferings, blood, resurrection, ascension, or glory in the heavens, according as they are set forth in the Scriptures; or any ways tending to the denial of the heavenly man Christ; such persons ought to be diligently instructed and admonished by faithful friends, and not to be exposed by any to public reproach; and where the error proceeds from ignorance and darkness of their understanding, they ought the more meekly and gently to be informed: but if any shall wilfully persist in error in point of faith, after being duly informed, then such to be further dealt

Delinquencies. with according to gospel order; that the truth, church, or body of Christ, may not suffer by any particular pretended member that is so corrupt. 1694.

Persons professing with us, who habitually absent themselves from our religious meetings, and disregard the repeated advice and endeavours of friends to stir them up to this necessary duty, are to be dealt with by the Monthly Meeting to which they belong, even to disowning, if the case require it. 1770.—1861.

A complaint being made about some ship-masters, who profess the truth, and are esteemed Quakers, carrying guns in their ships, supposing thereby to defend and secure themselves and their ships, contrary to our principle and practice, and to the endangering of their own and others' lives thereby; also giving occasion of more severe hardships and sufferings to be inflicted on such Friends as are pressed into ships of war, who, for conscience' sake, cannot fight or destroy men's lives; it is therefore recommended to the Monthly Meetings whereunto such ship-masters belong, to deal with them in God's wisdom, and tender love, to stir them up and awaken their consciences; that they may seriously consider how they injure their own souls in so doing, and what occasion they give to make the Truth and Friends to suffer by their declension, and acting contrary thereunto through disobedience and unbelief, placing their security in that which is altogether insecure and dangerous: which we are really sorry for, and sincerely desire their recovery, and safety from destruction, that their faith and confidence may be in the arm and power of God. And if any be concerned in fabricating or selling instruments of war, let them be treated with in love; and if by this unreclaimed, let them be further dealt with as those whom we cannot own. 1693. P.E.—1790.

We recommend to Friends in their respective Quarterly and Monthly Meetings to have a watchful eye over all their members; and where they observe any deficient in discharging their contracts and just debts in due time, so as to give reasonable suspicion of weakness or negligence, that Friends do earnestly advise them to a suitable care and necessary inspection into their circumstances, in order that they may be helped; and if any proceed contrary to such advice, and by their failure bring open scandal and reproach on the Society, that then Friends justifiably may and ought to testify against such offenders. Nevertheless it is not intended to prevent Monthly Meetings from exercising the discipline in cases in which no advice may have been given prior to insolvency. Those friends who may be appointed by Monthly Meetings to visit those who have failed, should always inquire of their assignees or trustees how they have acted in the above respects,* and report to the meeting. 1732. P. E.—1782.—1816.

It is the judgment of this meeting, that Monthly or other Meetings ought not to receive collections or bequests for the use of the poor, or other services of the Society, from persons who have fallen short in the payment of their just debts, though legally discharged by their creditors; for until such persons have paid the deficiency, what they possess cannot in equity be considered as their own. And Monthly Meetings are desired to exercise due caution against too early admitting such individuals to take an active part in the discipline. 1782.—1833.

We desire, pursuant to former advices, that meetings would appoint suitable friends as overseers of the flock, who are intreated to enter into and discharge this labour with a ready mind. And, dear friends, we earnestly recommend that, in all your meetings, in the choice of elders or overseers of the flock, you be especially careful to choose such as are themselves of upright and unblamable conversation; that the advice which they shall occasionally administer to other friends may be the better received, and carry with it the greater weight and force on the minds of those whom they shall be concerned to admonish. 1752. *Overseers.*

When an appointment of overseers is necessary, the matter is to be referred to a committee of judicious friends who are to report to the Monthly Meeting, for its approbation, the names of such friends as are thought suitable for that service. 1789.—1801.

It is the judgment of this meeting that, as far as circum-

---

* This refers to their having been careful not to pay one creditor in preference to another, and to their having kept clear and accurate accounts.

Overseers. stances will admit, at least two men and two women friends be appointed as overseers in each particular meeting; and Monthly Meetings are recommended to revise the list of friends on this appointment once in three years. 1833.—1861.

Ministers. We earnestly desire the increase of true gospel labourers amongst us, for the edification of our own body, and the spreading of the truth as it is in Jesus. At the same time let us remember the apostolic advice, " Lay hands suddenly on no man ;" for we have cause to believe that injudicious encouragement hath tended to promote an unsound ministry in some places. It is therefore recommended, that the ministers and elders, in the several Monthly Meetings, would tenderly advise those who come forth in public testimony, to wait patiently under a deep consideration of their state of infancy and childhood: and when their fruits afford sufficient evidence of their qualifications for so important a service, that the cases of such ministers be reported to their Monthly Meetings ; which, upon solid and deliberate consideration, may, as in the wisdom of truth shall seem meet, record them as ministers. 1773.—1833.

This meeting recommends, when a proposition for acknowledging a minister is made to a Monthly Meeting, as pointed out by the preceding rule, that the same be brought forward in the men's Monthly Meeting, previously to its entering upon any other business. The men's meeting on receiving it, is either then, or at a suitable time, to proceed, in conjunction with the members of the women's Monthly Meeting, to the consideration and conclusion of the case. If the case originate in the meeting itself, the men's meeting is to determine whether the time be come for it to be laid before a general conference of men and women Friends. 1810.—1822.—1861.

Friends of judgment and experience are advised to watch with fatherly care over such especially as may be young in the ministry; that whilst, on the one hand, nothing tending to the glory of God and the edification of his church and people may be discouraged, so, on the other hand, where counsel may appear to be called for, it may be wisely and faithfully administered. 1720.—1861.

If any person appearing as a minister shall give cause of uneasiness or dissatisfaction to Friends, in doctrine, behaviour, or conversation, the person so offending is to be dealt with privately in a gospel spirit and manner. If this shall not take effect, then let complaint be made of such person to the Monthly Meeting to which he or she may belong; in order that proceeding thereon may be had accordingly, and the affair settled with all possible expedition. 1723.

If any individuals feel disunity with the communications of any minister, let them not make any public demonstrations of their disapprobation, but rather impart their uneasiness privately, either to the party concerned, or to an elder or overseer, according to gospel order; and if private counsel be unavailing, the matter should be made known to the meeting to which the minister belongs. 1699.—1723.—1861.

It is recommended to Monthly Meetings to be careful that all friends. travelling from or among them in the work of the ministry, do go in the unity of the meeting to which they belong; and with written testimonials therefrom. And we advise all Monthly Meetings, to take due care in giving such testimonials; to prevent the uneasiness which sometimes falls on the church, from a weak and unskilful ministry. 1720.—1731.—1861.

It is the judgment of this meeting, when either men or women friends have a concern to travel in the work of the ministry, and have occasion to apply to their Monthly Meeting for a written testimonial of its concurrence, that they communicate their views to men and women friends collectively assembled, on notice being given at the close of the preceding meeting for worship for the women to remain until the men's meeting is regularly constituted; when, on the concern of the individual being communicated, it is to be made the subject of joint deliberation and conclusion; after which, if the concern be united with, a written testimonial of concurrence is to be prepared, and signed by the clerk of the Monthly Meeting. Nevertheless the friends thus collectively assembled are at liberty to postpone the decision, or refer the subject to a committee for consideration, whenever they may apprehend such delay or reference desirable; and any committee so appointed is to make report at another joint conference, previously to the

Ministers. ordering or granting of a certificate. 1811.—1816.—1822.—1861.

This meeting recommends, when Monthly Meetings liberate friends to travel in the work of the ministry, and the places at which their labours are likely to commence are at a considerable distance from their respective residences, as may particularly occur in the case of visits to Ireland and Scotland, that such meetings provide for the discharge of the necessary travelling expenses of such friends, and of a guide where needful, until they enter upon their service, in like manner as if the distance were less; and that similar expenses of any friends so travelling and returning home from a place considerably remote, be defrayed by any Monthly Meeting in Great Britain in the compass of which their service may terminate.

If, in any of the cases which may come within the preceding recommendation, neither the Monthly Meeting, nor the Quarterly Meeting of which it forms a part, should be in a situation suitably to bear the expenses so incurred, it is agreed that the latter shall be at liberty to apply to the Meeting for Sufferings; which meeting may, in its discretion, reimburse the whole or any part thereof out of the national stock. 1827.

Testimonies. Monthly Meetings are advised to exercise due care and deliberation before they conclude on issuing testimonies or minutes concerning deceased friends, whether ministers or others, whose lives have been marked by devotedness to the cause of their Lord, and to the service of the church. In drawing up such documents, when it is judged proper to issue them, Monthly Meetings are desired to pay due regard to conciseness, and especially to bear in mind that the object is not eulogy, but to preserve a record of the power of divine grace in the lives of the Lord's faithful servants. Testimonies, when drawn up, are to be presented by the Monthly Meeting to its Quarterly Meeting, which meeting is recommended, in each case, to revise the testimony so presented (by the appointment of a committee or otherwise); and it is left to the discretion of the Quarterly Meeting either to send forward the same, or a new testimony prepared by itself, to this meeting; or, if thought expedient, to withhold altogether any such testimony.* 1861.

Monthly Meetings are desired to appoint some serious, discreet, and judicious friends, who are not ministers, tenderly to encourage and help young ministers, and advise others, as they, in the wisdom of God, see occasion; and where there are meetings of ministering friends, the friends so appointed are to be admitted as members of such meetings of ministers, and to act therein for the good purposes aforesaid. 1727.   *Elders.*

In the appointment of elders, age or wealth is not to be an inducement in the choice; but let such be appointed as fear God, love his truth in sincerity, are sound in Christian doctrine, and of clean hands. 1761.—1833.

In order to assist in a suitable choice, when an appointment of elders appears to a Monthly Meeting to be desirable, application is to be made to the Quarterly Meeting for the assistance of a few friends; and the Quarterly Meeting of women friends is to have the opportunity of appointing some of its number. The Monthly Meeting is to appoint a few judicious men and women friends previously to this application, who, with those appointed by the Quarterly Meeting, are to form a committee for judging of the gifts and qualifications of such as may be then proposed for this important station. Their report is to be presented to the Monthly Meeting for its consideration; and such friends as may be thus nominated, if approved by the Monthly Meeting, are to be appointed to the station of elder. Information thereof is to be conveyed to the Meeting of Ministers and Elders; as from the period of their appointment they become members of that meeting. 1784.—1796.—1812.—1833.

Monthly Meetings are at liberty, after the exercise of due care and admonition, to displace from the appointment, such elders as appear to be either incompetent to their station or unfaithful in it. 1772.—1776.—1801.

When a friend appointed to the station of elder in any Monthly Meeting removes into another, it is the judgment of

---

* It is advised that all testimonies, intended for the next ensuing Yearly Meeting, be transmitted not later than to the winter Quarterly Meeting.

Elders. this meeting that such station is not lost, provided such removal be within the same Quarterly Meeting; but in case the removal of an elder be out of the limits of the Quarterly Meeting to which he or she belongs, such elder shall not be continued in that station, unless a re-appointment be made, pursuant to the rules for the choice of elders. 1801.

Appointments for various purposes. We are concerned to recommend to Monthly Meetings, the appointment of suitable friends to visit the families of their brethren in Christian love, and therein to inform, admonish, and advise, as occasion may be; and we beseech you, brethren, let the tender advice of such as shall undertake so brotherly an office, meet with a kind and open reception, that, in the mutual giving and receiving of wholesome counsel and advice, you may co-operate to the help and furtherance of each other's faith. 1752. P. E.

This meeting recommends to general practice what hath been found of great use in many places, viz., an annual appointment in each Monthly Meeting of suitable friends, to apply for an account of distraints to each of their members liable to ecclesiastical or military demands, and, where weakness or unfaithfulness appears in any, to administer such advice and admonition as may be necessary for their help. 1780.—1861.

This meeting directs Monthly Meetings annually to make appointments of suitable friends to impart to those of their members to whom it may be applicable advice on the subject of keeping clear and correct accounts, and on that of carefully inspecting the state of their affairs at least once in the year, as well as to recommend them to make their wills and settle their outward concerns in time of health. In the discharge of this service, opportunities are afforded for a kind and brotherly intercourse, which, without intruding into the private affairs of individuals, may be productive of real benefit. 1793.—1833.—1845.—1861.

Libraries. It is desired that Monthly Meetings would request their particular meetings to revise the catalogues of their libraries once in the year, and report their having done so to the Monthly Meeting; and then to consider what additions may be suitably made, as well as the best means of giving publicity to the collection, promoting the circulation of them, and affording ready access to the books to all who may wish to peruse them, whether members of our religious society or not. 1821.—1833.

This meeting desires that Monthly Meetings may maintain a correspondence with such of their members as have removed out of the reach of the oversight of their friends, and beyond the limits of any recognized Meetings for Discipline, so as to bring them under the Christian notice and sympathy of these meetings, and that they have a special regard to them when their lists of members are annually read and revised; also that they may be careful that the names and residences of such persons are furnished to the Meeting for Sufferings. 1844. *Correspondence with Members abroad.*

SECTION IV.—PREPARATIVE MEETINGS.

It is the judgment of this meeting, that the holding of Preparative Meetings, under suitable regulations, may be of real advantage, where Monthly Meetings consist of two or more particular meetings; and that the proper business of such meetings is;—

To inquire after births, burials, and removals, in order to carry accounts thereof to the Monthly Meeting:

To read and consider the queries, as settled by the Yearly Meeting, and conclude on answers in writing to the Monthly Meeting:

To appoint representatives to the Monthly Meeting. 1794.—
—1833.

This meeting is of the judgment, that advantage would accrue to our small Preparative Meetings, by their being encouraged, in the discretion of Monthly Meetings, to act as a united Preparative Meeting of men and women Friends. The answers therefrom to be sent to the men's and, as far as applicable, to the women's Monthly Meeting also; and representatives appointed to each when practicable. 1799.—1833.—1861.

When a Preparative Meeting is omitted to be held, information of the same should be sent from the Monthly to the Quarterly Meeting; but it is not necessary for such information to be transmitted to this meeting. 1828.

It is apprehended that advantage might be derived from occasionally reading in Preparative Meetings portions of the counsel issued by this meeting, contained in the volume "Rules of Discipline and Advices." 1833.

It is suggested that Preparative Meetings may, with advantage, refer business of a financial and secular character to an adjournment of such meetings, or to a committee of men friends appointed for the service. 1861.

SECTION V.—WOMEN'S MEETINGS.

Establishment. It is our Christian advice that you do encourage faithful women's meetings, and the settling of them where they are wanting, and may with convenience be settled; knowing their service, and what need there is also of their godly care in the church of Christ, in divers weighty respects proper to them. 1691. P. E.

The several Quarterly and General Meetings of women friends are at liberty to appoint two or more of their members to meet in London, at the time of holding this meeting; nevertheless so that the number from any women's meeting do not exceed that of the representatives allowed to be appointed by the men's meeting, for the same district. The meeting so appointed shall be denominated the Yearly Meeting of women friends held in London.

This meeting agrees, that the meeting of women friends held annually in this city be at liberty to correspond in writing with the Quarterly Meetings of women friends, to receive accounts from them, and to issue such advice as, in the wisdom of truth, may from time to time appear necessary and conducive to their mutual edification.

And this meeting is further of the judgment, that the several women's Quarterly Meetings should annually send to their Yearly Meeting, answers in writing to the queries proper for the women friends. The said meeting is not at liberty to make or alter any rules of discipline or queries. 1784.—1790.

Duties devolving on them.

On considering the nature and extent of the discipline committed to women friends, it is our judgment, that its nature is, as expressed by the minutes of the Yearly Meeting, to come up to the help of their brethren in the discipline of the church.

As to its extent:

1. They are to inspect and, in their discretion, to relieve the wants of the poor of their own sex; and to apply to the men's meeting for the means, and for its concurrence, as cases shall require.

2. They are to take cognizance of proposals for marriage, conformably to the rules on that subject.

3. They are to join in certificates of removal for women friends, when about to be recommended with their husbands. In such cases the women's Monthly Meeting, on notice from the men's meeting, is to appoint one or two of its members to make the necessary inquiry, and to report the result thereof to the friend or friends appointed to inquire by the men's meeting. But when it may appear proper to issue a certificate of removal on behalf of a woman friend other than as above, the women's meeting is to appoint two of its members to make the needful inquiry. If no obstruction arise, the friends so appointed are to prepare a certificate, agreeably to the rules for removals, which, after being read and approved in the women's meeting, and signed by the clerk, is to be sent to the men's meeting, for its approbation, and to be recorded and signed by the clerk, by whom it is to be forwarded.

4. They are also, on receiving from the men's meeting certificates for women friends removed into the compass of the Monthly Meeting, to make appointments to visit them.*

5. They are to have overseers; in order to which, when it is necessary that women overseers be appointed, the women's

* See 4th Rule under "Removals." Sec. XVII.

Duties devolving on them. Monthly Meeting is to appoint a committee, which is to join a committee to be appointed by the men's Monthly Meeting. The joint committee is to nominate the overseers, and the names of the women then nominated are to be reported to the women's Monthly Meeting, and, if approved by that meeting, sent to the men's meeting for confirmation.

6. The women's Monthly Meeting, at the desire of the men's Monthly Meeting, should make appointments to join the men in visiting such women as apply for admission, or reinstatement, into membership; and the report of the committee is to be made to the men's Monthly Meeting, which is to inform the women's meeting of the conclusion.

7. In cases of delinquency of women friends, when, after due exercise of private labour, the women's Monthly Meeting believes it necessary that any of its members be dealt with as delinquents, it is to inform the men's meeting thereof. That meeting may, if it think fit, request the women's meeting to proceed to deal with the delinquent, and report the result of their labours to the men's meeting; but, if the men's meeting should see it expedient to join them in the dealing, the report of the joint committee is to be made to the men's meeting, which, in either case is to inform the women's meeting of its determination. No proceedings of the women only are to be a sufficient ground for a testimony of disownment; unless, after mature deliberation, and from any peculiar circumstances which may attach to the case, the men's meeting, feeling satisfied that the discipline has been fully exercised by the labour of the women friends, shall be convinced that it is not its place to make any appointment on the case of delinquency. 1792.—1802.—1822.—1861.

N.B.—In reference to the duties of these meetings, see also "Advices," p. 165—and "Women's Queries," p. 170.

SECTION VI.—AUSTRALIAN MEETINGS FOR DISCIPLINE.

The Meetings for Discipline established in Tasmania, Victoria, and South Australia,* are respectively recognised as regularly constituted meetings. They are encouraged to unite in forming

* At Hobart Town, Melbourne, and Adelaide.

one General Meeting, having the same relation to the meetings constituting it, as our Quarterly Meetings in this country have to their Monthly Meetings, and, so far as the greater distance will admit of it, having the same relation to the Yearly Meeting of London as the Quarterly Meetings of which the latter is composed. The three meetings constituting the General Meeting are to be still at liberty to correspond with this meeting or its committee, and one or two friends in each of the said meetings are to be appointed as correspondents.

The following are to be the arrangements in respect to certificates of removal between Monthly Meetings in this country and the aforesaid meetings in Australia.

1. Every friend going from Great Britain, with the intention of residing within either of the three colonies above-mentioned, as well as every friend who has heretofore gone, is to be recommended by certificate to the Meeting for Discipline of such colony. The certificate is in all cases to be forwarded by the regular mail, addressed to one of the correspondents.

2. On the acceptance of such certificate, the individual in question is to cease to be a member of the recommending Monthly Meeting in Great Britain.

3. The Australian Meeting for Discipline, under either of the following circumstances, is to be at liberty to return certificates:—first, the individual failing, within a reasonable time after his arrival, to place himself in communication with the members of the meeting:—secondly, his settlement at such a distance from it as to preclude the possibility of that degree of intercourse, without which Christian care and interest cannot be availingly exercised.

4. In the event of the occurrence of the first-named contingency, the recommending Monthly Meeting is to be at liberty, in the exercise of its discretion, and after giving due notice, when practicable, to the individual, to discontinue him as a member of our religious Society.

5. In the event of the other contingency, that of the certificate being returned, in consequence of the party settling at such a distance from either of the said meetings as to preclude the exercise of Christian care, he is to remain a member of the recommending Monthly Meeting in Great Britain, so long as he maintains a satisfactory correspondence with that meeting. But,

in the event of his ceasing to correspond, or of his communications being of an unsatisfactory character, the Monthly Meeting is to be at liberty, in the exercise of its judgment, and after notice being given, when practicable, to the individual, to discontinue him as a member of our religious Society.

6. In the event of a member of any of the three meetings aforesaid removing to Great Britain, furnished with a properly authenticated certificate addressed to a Monthly Meeting in this country, he is, on the acceptance of his certificate, to become a member of such Monthly Meeting. 1861.

SECTION VII.—GENERAL COUNSEL IN RELATION TO MEETINGS FOR DISCIPLINE.

IT is our judgment and testimony, that the setting up and establishment of men's and women's meetings is according to the mind and counsel of God. 1675.

It is our advice in the love of God, that, after any friend's repentance and restoration, he abiding faithful in the truth that condemns the evil, none among you so remember his transgression, as to cast it at him, or upbraid him with it; for that is not according to the mercies of God. 1675.

Let all your affairs be managed in your meetings in the peaceable wisdom and spirit of our Lord Jesus Christ; not striving, but bearing one with and for another; that the power of Christ may rest upon you, and rule in all your assemblies. 1696. P. E.

Keep all your meetings, as well those for good order, charity, and Christian discipline, as those set apart entirely for the worship of God, in his love, and in the name, power, and peaceable Spirit of his dear Son Jesus Christ, which is the alone true authority of all our meetings; for without Him we can do nothing. And Friends are tenderly desired and advised, carefully to keep to, and in that authority; and therein manage all the business and affairs of the said meetings, in discharge of their duty to God and his church; and not expect or depend upon this meeting for particular direction, from time to time, how they shall proceed in the management of the concerns of those meetings, relating to truth's testimony and service; but wait for, and depend upon, the power and wisdom of God for counsel and direction in such matters and cases as may come before them; which will be to the great ease of this meeting, and despatch of the proper concerns thereof. And let the man's part, and natural wisdom and attainments, be subject to the power and Spirit of God, which will truly edify the body in love, righteousness and peace.

It is recommended unto faithful friends, and elders especially, to watch over the flock of Christ in their respective places; that they faithfully and diligently walk up to the testimony of the blessed truth, to which the Lord hath gathered us in this latter age of the world; that so where any are found short, weak, or faulty, they may be admonished and sought in the spirit of love, which is the spirit of the gospel—that divine charity, wherein mercy is not only mixed with judgment, but may appear over all our works; that it may be seen by all that church-love abounds before church-censure comes, and that a gospel spirit is the spring and motive to all our performances, as well in discipline as worship. 1700. P. E.—1703. P. E.

Recommended, that friends concerned in Meetings for Discipline do labour to know their own spirits subjected by the Spirit of Truth; that, thereby being baptized into one body, they may be truly one, in the foundation of their love and unity; and that therein they may all labour to find a nearness to each other in spirit; this being the true way to a thorough reconciliation, wherever there is, or hath been, any difference of apprehension. Hereby Friends will be preserved in that sweetness of spirit, that is, and will be, the bond of true peace throughout the churches of Christ. 1717. P. E.

Advised, that nothing be done through strife and contention, or vain-glory, murmuring or disputing; but in the spirit of meekness, love and humility, carry yourselves towards one another. And ye younger brethren, endeavour to know your places, as living members of one body, and preserve a due regard to your elders in Christ Jesus. 1718. P. E.

We recommend that such friends as are concerned in the affairs of the church, in Quarterly, Monthly, or Particular Meetings, be careful to act therein in the wisdom of God, whereby they will be exemplary to the young: and, as such young persons are found to be qualified with a real sense of truth upon their spirits and subjection thereunto, and thereby made capable to come up to a service in their respective meetings, friends are desired to encourage and bring them forward therein; whereby they may be helpful to the ancients and brought up in a life of righteousness, to walk and act to the praise of God's holy name; and, standing in their lot, may supply the place of the elders in such meetings, through the same Spirit, when they are gone. 1722. P. E.

Advised, that Friends, in Meetings for Discipline, watch over their own spirits; that no indecent warmth get in, whereby the understanding may be hurried, and hindered from a regular judgment on the affairs before the meeting. 1724. P. E.

As the promotion of piety and charity is the end and intent of our meetings for the discipline of the church, a weighty concern rests upon us, that Friends be careful diligently to attend those meetings; and, when there, to act in the wisdom given them of God, with a real and living sense of truth upon their spirits; that so the affairs of the church may be carried on in brotherly love, and in that sweet, calm and Christian disposition of mind, which tends to the mutual comfort and edification one of another, and of the church in general. 1733. P. E.

In order to unite us the more nearly one to another, as members of the same body, and to strengthen our hands to promote the general cause of truth, it is recommended to friends to stand open to the leadings of the love of God through Jesus Christ our Lord: and when they feel drawings in their minds to sit with any of their neighbouring Monthly or Quarterly Meetings, that they attend thereto; and that such Monthly or Quarterly Meetings as are visited receive such as they know to be well approved at home, in the love of God, and not look upon them as intruders: so shall mutual help be given and received amongst us, and we truly be a people led by one and the same spirit. 1759.

This meeting is impressed with a sense of the important duties which devolve upon Quarterly and Monthly Meetings, and, under this impression, feels that small Meetings for Worship and small Preparative Meetings ought peculiarly to claim their attention. We desire that Quarterly or Monthly Meetings may, from time to time, consider whether these meetings are held in such a manner, under such regulations, and at such times, as are best adapted to answer the end designed; and whether there may not be a propriety in appointing suitable committees occasionally to visit them. 1815.—1821.—1822.

This meeting has been afresh impressed with the benefits resulting from our Christian discipline, that salutary provision for the exercise of gospel love and care, and for the purpose of reclaiming and restoring those who may be overtaken with a fault. We believe that it had its origin in Divine authority; that it was founded on love one towards another; and that it has been a great blessing to our Society. We therefore affectionately recommend that, where any are deficient, they should, in tenderness and love, be invited to assemble with their brethren in meetings held on these occasions. If it be the concern of all, when thus met, to seek to have their minds settled in that state in which they are most fit to perceive the gentle intimations and restraints of the Spirit of Truth, these meetings will often prove times of great instruction, of close self-examination, and of a renewal of strength; they would then tend to unite us still more strongly one unto another in the bond of Christian love; and they would be a means of increasing our esteem for those salutary restraints which our religious testimonies require. Some who may have far to travel to attend such meetings, whilst careful not to neglect their outward affairs, would do well, on the recurrence of these occasions, to consider whether it would not be for their good thus to be separated from the cares of this life, and to breathe, in tender aspirations, for strength to rise above them; and these would, we believe, often be permitted to feel that such acts of dedication are followed by a peaceful reward. 1819.—1820.

We recommend that, in making appointments, care be taken to judge of the respective qualifications of those who are employed in the service of the church, and not to introduce friends to matters which may be beyond their religious strength. 1821.

As one means of preserving a quiet, settled frame of mind, we exhort friends to consider whether it may not be injurious to enter into conversation, when about to attend a meeting for discipline, after having previously been at a meeting for worship;

and we desire that this care may prevail with regard to conversation, both before entering, and on leaving, all our religious meetings. The meeting for divine worship, previous to a meeting for discipline, affords an opportunity for retirement in spirit before the Lord, a state in which we are best qualified to enter upon the concerns of the church: and, if friends endeavour to settle down in this collected state of mind, and to maintain the watch as the business proceeds, we believe they will often be sensible of the prevalence of Christian love, be assisted to keep their own wills in due subjection, and manifest to others that they have no desire that their sentiments may be adopted, rather than the solid judgment of the meeting. 1821.

The true nature and spirit of Christian discipline are thus instructively unfolded by the Apostle Paul: "Brethren, if a man be overtaken in a fault, ye which are spiritual restore such an one in the spirit of meekness; considering thyself lest thou also be tempted." From this passage we may learn that the first object of our discipline ought to be, to restore offenders; and that it should ever be conducted in the spirit of humility, meekness and love.

While it is our steadfast endeavour, in the government of the Church, to maintain our integrity in the truth, a due sense of our own frailty will discourage all harsh judgment of our brethren; and the love of Christ, who came to seek and to save that which is lost, will lead his servants into earnest and patient endeavours to gather again those who are gone astray. Nor ought this Christian care to cease when disownment has taken place. It is the earnest desire of this meeting, that such individuals may not be overlooked in any part of the society; but that they may be the objects of the tender and watchful care of Friends, in order to their restoration. 1833.

We affectionately invite our friends upon whom the labours of our meetings for discipline may largely rest, to seek for ability to improve these occasions, by the expression of counsel or encouragement, or by the introduction of such subjects as may be profitably brought before their fellow-members and made the means of illustrating our religious principles.

And we would encourage representatives, in reporting their attendance to the duties of their appointment, to embrace in their report information, even if but brief, of such parts of the proceedings of the meeting to which they had been deputed, as may conduce to the interest and profit of their friends. 1861.

SECTION VIII.—ADVICES.

In order to bring the following important Advices before all the members of our religious society, as well as those who attend our meetings for worship, but are not in membership with us, it is concluded that they be read AFTER the close of a First-day morning meeting for worship once in the year. They are also to be read in the winter Quarterly Meetings for discipline; and in Monthly Meetings, either consecutively or in such portions, as well as at such times, as may be deemed the most desirable. 1861.

TAKE heed, dear friends, we entreat you, to the convictions of the Holy Spirit, who leads, through unfeigned repentance and living faith in the Son of God, to reconciliation with our Heavenly Father, and to the blessed hope of eternal life, purchased for us by the one offering of our Lord and Saviour Jesus Christ.

Be earnestly concerned in religious meetings reverently to present yourselves before the Lord, and seek, by the help of the Holy Spirit, to worship God through Jesus Christ.

Prize the privilege of access by Him unto the Father; continue "instant in prayer," and "watch in the same with thanksgiving."

Be in the frequent practice of waiting upon the Lord in private retirement, honestly examining yourselves as to your growth in grace, and your preparation for the life to come.

Be diligent in the private perusal of the Holy Scriptures; and let it be your earnest endeavour that the daily reading of them in your families be devoutly conducted.

Be careful to make a profitable and religious use of those portions of time, on the first day of the week, which are not occupied by our meetings for worship.

Live in love as Christian brethren, ready to be helpful one to another, sympathizing with each other in the trials and afflictions of life, and manifesting an earnest desire that each may possess a well grounded hope in Christ.

Watch over one another for good: when occasions of uneasiness first appear in any, let them be treated with in privacy and tenderness before the matter is communicated to another. Should differences arise, be willing early to avail yourselves of the advice and judgment of your brethren; and may friends be ready to undertake, and be prudent in executing, the blessed office of peacemaker.

Cherish a Christian interest on behalf of such attenders of your meetings as are not in membership; evincing a lively concern for their religious welfare and growth in the truth.

Follow peace with all men, desiring the true happiness of all; be kind and liberal to the poor, and endeavour to promote the temporal, moral, and religious well-being of your fellow-men.

With a tender conscience, and in accordance with the precepts of the Gospel, take heed to the limitations of the Spirit of Truth in the pursuit of the things of this life.

Maintain strict integrity in your transactions in trade, and in all your outward concerns. Guard against a spirit of speculation, and the snare of accumulating wealth. Remember that you will have to account for the mode of acquiring, as well as for the manner of using, your possessions; and, in the final disposition of them, be careful to make a judicious and equitable appropriation.

In contemplating the engagement of marriage, look principally to that which will help you on your heavenward journey. Pay filial-regard to the judgment of your parents. Bear in mind the vast importance, in such a union, of an accordance in religious principles and practice. Ask counsel of God; desiring, above all temporal considerations, that your union may be owned and blessed of the Lord.

Watch with Christian tenderness over the opening minds of your children; inure them to habits of self-restraint and filial obedience; carefully instruct them in the knowledge of the Holy Scriptures; and seek for ability to imbue their hearts with the love of their Heavenly Father, their Redeemer, and their Sanctifier.

Be careful to maintain in your own conduct, and to encourage in your families, that simplicity in deportment and attire, that avoidance of flattery and insincerity in language, and that nonconformity to the world, which become the disciples of the Lord Jesus.

Guard watchfully against the introduction into your households of publications of a hurtful tendency. Observe simplicity and moderation in the furniture of your houses, and in your style and manner of living.

Avoid vain sports and places of diversion, all kinds of gaming, the unnecessary frequenting of taverns and other public-houses, and the improper use of intoxicating liquors; and guard against such companionships, indulgences, and recreations as by their influence may interfere with your growth in grace.

Finally, dear friends, let your conversation be as it becometh the Gospel. Exercise yourselves to have always a conscience void of offence toward God and toward men; endeavouring to maintain the unity of the spirit in the bond of peace. 1791.—1801.—1833.—1861.

SECTION IX.—QUERIES.

This meeting feels a lively concern to remind our members, that the intention of directing sundry queries to be answered, relative to the conduct of individuals in the several branches of our Christian profession, is not only to be informed of the state of our meetings, but also to impress on the minds of friends a profitable examination of themselves, how far they act consistently with their religious principles. We would therefore earnestly recommend to every one of our members, more especially when the answers are drawn up, to examine whether he himself is coming up in that life of self-denial and devotedness unto God, which so highly becomes all who make profession of the name of Christ.

Yet it is not to arrangements, however perfect, but to individual faithfulness to Christ, in daily dependence upon the help of the Holy Spirit, that we must look for growth in the truth, and vitality in the Church. As this faithfulness and dependence are maintained, we believe these queries will tend to promote the religious welfare of our members, and the upholding of our

Christian discipline in a lively and healthy condition.* 1731.—1833.—1861.

General Directions.
The answers to the queries are to be drawn up in writing in the respective meetings, under a serious consideration of the state of the meeting. Those from the men's meeting are intended to refer to the state and conduct of the whole body of men and women Friends. 1787.—1819.—1833.

In framing the answers, vague and general terms should, as far as practicable, be avoided. Where deficiency is acknowledged, report is to be made in the answer whether due admonition and care have been extended. In no case whatever is a friend to consider himself at liberty to bring forward an exception on suspicion only, the actual existence of which has not been certainly ascertained. 1861.

A copy, duly signed, of the answers to the queries agreed upon in each Quarterly Meeting of men Friends in the spring, is to be forwarded to the Recording Clerk in London, within one week after such meeting, with a view to the preparation of a general summary of all the answers from the Quarterly Meetings, under the direction of the Meeting for Sufferings. This summary is to be read in the Yearly Meeting, after the general answers to the queries have been gone through, and previously to the meeting entering upon the consideration of the state of the Society. 1861.

Men's Queries.
In the Spring the first seven queries are to be answered by Monthly to Quarterly Meetings, and from thence to this meeting, and the first six by Preparative to Monthly Meetings.

In the Autumn, the 8th, 9th, and 10th are to be answered by Monthly Meetings to Quarterly Meetings, and the 8th and 9th by Preparative to Monthly Meetings. The last clause of the 7th query is also to be read and considered, in the Autumn, both in Quarterly and Monthly Meetings.

1. Are your meetings for worship regularly held? Do Friends attend them duly, and at the time appointed?

---

* This paragraph to be read in the Spring Quarter in all our meetings previously to answering the queries.

2. Are friends preserved in love one towards another; and do they avoid and discourage tale-bearing and detraction?

3. Are friends frequent in reading the Holy Scriptures; and do those who have children, servants, and others under their care, encourage them in the practice of this religious duty?

4. Are friends careful to maintain a religious life and conversation, consistent with our Christian profession? and do those who have children or others under their care endeavour, by example and precept, to train them up in accordance therewith?

5. Are friends faithful in bearing our Christian testimony against all ecclesiastical demands?

6. Are friends faithful in maintaining our Christian testimony against all war?

7. Are your meetings for transacting the affairs of the Church regularly held and duly attended? Is the discipline administered timely, impartially, and in a Christian spirit? And are Quarterly and Monthly Meetings careful to give to their subordinate meetings such assistance as may, from time to time, be required?

8. Are friends just in their dealings, punctual in fulfilling their engagements, and clear of defrauding the public revenue?

9. Are the necessities of the poor among you properly inspected and relieved; and is good care taken of the education of their offspring?

10. Is the advice to friends on the subject of their outward affairs, and the timely making of their wills, annually given?* Are the rules respecting removals, the revision of the lists of members, and the recording of births, marriages, and burials, observed? Are the titles of your meeting-houses, burial-grounds, &c., duly preserved and recorded: and is all other trust-property under your care rightly secured and applied?

In order to realize the benefit of serious self-examination, and to induce an earnest concern for the good of others, the four following queries are to be read in our meetings for discipline; to be then seriously and deliberately considered, but not answered. In Quarterly Meetings, No. 1 in the Summer; Nos. 2 and 4 in the Unanswered Queries.

* See page 154.

Autumn; No. 3 in the Winter. And in Monthly and Preparative Meetings, each of the four queries once in the year, at such times as by these meetings may be deemed the most desirable.

1. What is the religious state of your meeting; and is there among you evidence of a growth in the truth?

2. Are you individually giving evidence of true conversion of heart; of love to Christ, and self-denying devotedness to Him; and of a growing preparation for the life to come?

3. Do you maintain a watchful care against conformity to the world; against the love of ease and self-indulgence, or being unduly absorbed by your outward concerns to the hindrance of your religious progress; bearing in mind that "here have we no continuing city"?

4. Do you exercise a judicious religious care over your younger members, manifesting an earnest concern that, through the power of Divine grace, they may all become established in the faith and hope of the Gospel?

Women's Queries.

In the Spring the first six of the Queries are to be answered by Preparative to Monthly Meetings, by Monthly to Quarterly Meetings, and by the latter to the Yearly Meeting.

In the Autumn, the 7th and 8th are to be answered by Preparative to Monthly Meetings, and by Monthly to Quarterly Meetings.

1. Do friends attend meetings for worship and discipline duly, and at the time appointed?

2. Are friends preserved in love one towards another; and do they avoid and discourage tale-bearing and detraction?

3. Are friends frequent in reading the Holy Scriptures; and do those who have children, servants and others under their care, encourage them in the practice of this religious duty?

4. Are friends careful to maintain a religious life and conversation, consistent with our Christian profession; and do those who have children or others under their care endeavour, by example and precept, to train them up in accordance therewith?

5. Are friends faithful in bearing our Christian testimony against all ecclesiastical demands?

6. Are friends faithful in maintaining our Christian testimony against all war?

7. Are friends just in their dealings, punctual in fulfilling their engagements, and clear of defrauding the public revenue?

8. Are the necessities of the poor among you properly inspected and relieved; and is good care taken of the education of their offspring?

In order to realize the benefit of serious self-examination, and to induce an earnest concern for the good of others, the four following queries are to be read in meetings for discipline; to be then seriously and deliberately considered, but not answered. In Quarterly Meetings,—No. 1 in the Summer; Nos. 2 and 4 in the Autumn; No. 3 in the Winter. And in Monthly and Preparative Meetings, each of the four queries once in the year, at such times as by these meetings may be deemed the most desirable.

1. What is the religious state of your meeting; and is there among you evidence of a growth in the truth?

2. Are you individually giving evidence of true conversion of heart; of love to Christ, and self-denying devotedness to Him; and of a growing preparation for the life to come?

3. Do you maintain a watchful care against conformity to the world; against the love of ease and self-indulgence, or being unduly absorbed by your outward concerns to the hindrance of your religious progress; bearing in mind that "here have we no continuing city"?

4. Do you exercise a judicious religious care over your younger members; manifesting an earnest concern that, through the power of Divine grace, they may all become established in the faith and hope of the Gospel?

SECTION X.—OVERSIGHT.

General Counsel — If any weakness, shortness, failure, or unfaithfulness appear in any professing the same truth with us, we hope faithful friends and brethren will continue their Christian care for their

General Counsel.

help, instruction and admonition, in the love and power of the Lord, as in his wisdom they shall see cause, still aiming at their good, their inward peace of conscience, and salvation in Christ Jesus. 1701. P. E.

Beware of that wisdom which descendeth not from above, but is earthly, sensual, and puffeth up the mind; but be ye, like our great pattern the Lord Jesus, meek and lowly in heart, not seeking your own glory, but the honour of Him that hath called you. Be ready to every good office of love, even to the least of Christ's disciples, and He will esteem it as done to Himself: delight to encourage those who are honest and sincere in heart, and to strengthen the feeble-minded under their trials and conflicts; so shall ye become as nursing-fathers and nursing-mothers in the church of God, and be qualified with wisdom from above to administer suitably to the conditions of others, to the comforting of their souls, that they may have cause to bless the Lord on your behalf. 1743. P. E.

You that are elders and overseers in the church, and concerned in the maintenance of good order and the preservation of the discipline, keep your own hands clean, and garments unspotted; that you may rebuke with authority, and, being clothed with the meekness and gentleness of the Lamb, may steadfastly persevere in the discharge of the duty committed to you; that when the great Shepherd shall appear, you may receive the reward of "Well done, good and faithful servant;"—"enter thou into the joy of thy Lord." 1753.

We especially intreat those appointed as elders and overseers to be diligent in the discharge of their important duties; that the ignorant may be informed, the weak strengthened, the tender encouraged, the scattered sought out, the unwary cautioned, the unruly warned. If private labour be faithfully and early administered when necessary, the hands of those concerned in the further exercise of the discipline will not be weakened by a consciousness of their having themselves departed from the true order of the Gospel. 1780.—1801.—1833.—1861.

We find, at this as at other times, that several persons have been added to us by convincement. We desire it may also have been by conversion. Such, truly convinced and converted, are a strength to us. They know the sacrifice which they have made for their present condition, and value it accordingly. But we are sometimes grieved that persons finding their way, and probably through self-denial, into our society, do not always retain their ground; the salt doth not always retain its savour. In tenderness therefore we intreat the newly-convinced not to esteem their admission as a period of rest from conflict. It rather requires a deeper exercise. And we beseech friends among whom such may dwell, to treat them with great circumspection as well as kindness. Beware of hurting them by any ill example. They may be offended, and, if they are sincere, they are in the number of those whom we are cautioned not to offend. On the other hand, they are tender and inexperienced, and they may be laden with the concerns of our discipline faster than their strength will bear. Thus, friends, on every occasion we see that sound judgment and sound practice require depth and solidity. Let us then keep in view, and earnestly desire to be endued with, that discernment which is one means, under the direction of the Holy Head, of edifying the body of Christ. 1807. P. E.

We have in this meeting been led to the reflection, that one of the great benefits of religious society is, that it places us under the care one of another, and that we are called upon to watch over each other for good. When we see any of our brethren or sisters overtaken with a fault, or neglecting an important duty, we ought to cherish a solicitude for their improvement; and, in that love which would lead them to Christ, to offer such counsel or encouragement as we may think best calculated to help them. Much depends on the manner in which advice is offered, and on our embracing the right opportunity to convey it. If it should not immediately have a salutary effect, we are not to be too much discouraged; we ought to take heed that we become not impatient or discomposed, but repeat our efforts in a spirit of love and forbearance. The result of this Christian concern for our friends is often greater than is at the time apparent.

In the exercise of this duty, it becomes those who have the earliest opportunity of knowing the faults of others, seriously to consider on all occasions, whether they ought not to endeavour to reclaim them before they disclose the matter to another. At the same time we believe it has often happened, that the lengthened concealment of the errors of our friends from those

General Counsel.

who were best qualified to advise them, has been productive of serious injury, which might have been prevented by an early, yet prudent, disclosure to those of greater experience. 1827. P. E.

We are afresh engaged to encourage all Friends to watch over one another for good. We greatly desire the increase of true overseers amongst us, under whatever name they may stand in the church. We exhort ministers, elders and overseers, to take the oversight of the flock, not by constraint, but willingly, and of a ready mind. May those who are called to minister in word and doctrine, be diligent in the exercise of their gifts in the fear of the Lord, and in humble dependence on the ability which He giveth. And may the elders not consider themselves solely appointed to the care of the ministry; but maintain a lively concern that all the members of their respective meetings may walk in the paths of safety, and be led into the pastures of life. We earnestly desire that every appearance of good may be cherished; that counsel and encouragement may be extended to the young and inexperienced, and a parental care exercised over those who appear to be in danger of wandering from the fold of Christ. May the body be thus edified in love, and the fellowship of the Gospel increase amongst us. 1833.

This meeting has been brought under concern in reference to a practice, into which some members of our religious Society have been drawn, of frequenting public worship, conducted in a manner at variance with our Christian profession, where modes and forms are made use of, from which we are religiously restrained, and by which our ancient testimony to the call and qualification of gospel ministry is infringed upon. We are therefore engaged to recommend overseers and other concerned friends in their respective meetings, where such cases may occur, in tenderness and love, faithfully to labour with such individuals for the removal of this cause of uneasiness. 1840.

Non-members.

We esteem it very necessary that young convinced and well inclined persons and friends be early visited, in the love of God, by faithful friends; for their encouragement, help and furtherance in the truth. 1710. P. E.

This meeting has been again introduced into a feeling of

religious interest on behalf of those children, who, though not members of our society, are connected with it in a greater degree than with any other religious community. It is grateful to find that the attention of Friends in various parts has been increasingly turned to the right education of this class, and to the provision of schools for this purpose; and we desire to encourage the friends who have formed such establishments, and who have the charge of them, as well as those who have the care of our public schools in which a limited number of children not members are admitted, to take measures by which the children of this description may, on their quitting these schools, be introduced to the kind notice of some well concerned friend or friends in the places where they may be settled as apprentices or otherwise; so that the religious care which has been bestowed upon them in their education may not be lost, for the want of the exercise of a friendly oversight in the succeeding and often dangerous steps of their youth. 1841.

It appears, from information received by this meeting, that young men, members of our society, who have removed to London from various parts of the country, are frequently, from the want of proper superintendence and suitable employment, placed in circumstances of great difficulty and danger. This meeting has been painfully affected on this subject; and whilst we feel a tender sympathy with such individuals, we believe it right earnestly to impress on the attention of Friends, in our several Quarterly and Monthly Meetings, the very great peril which young men cannot fail to incur, who come to this great metropolis, or other large places, without any definite prospect of protection or employment: it is but too evident that such a proceeding may lead even to their ruin. We believe that much may be effected by the kind endeavours of friends, in procuring for our young men situations in the country; and if these endeavours were diligently used immediately on the return of lads from school, it would often be the means of preventing future difficulties. It is also of great importance to forward certificates on behalf of such young persons, as early as possible after their removal; and to place them, even before the sending of their certificates, under the kind notice of Friends.

_{Junior members.}

Junior Members.

In reference to this subject, which has thus engaged our attention, we are again concerned earnestly to advise Friends, in their choice of servants, apprentices, and assistants, to prefer the members of our Society: a preference which seems to form an essential part of the care which we owe to our religious body. 1821.

This meeting earnestly recommends to all friends who are concerned for the prosperity of the truth, to exercise a tender care over the younger members of our society, bearing in mind the exposed situation of many of them and their critical period of life. We would encourage friends to cultivate an acquaintance with such, to call upon them at their places of abode, and to manifest, by the general tenor of their conduct towards them, a kind interest in their welfare and preservation from harm, and a solicitude that they may be established on the right foundation,—in the faith and hope of the Gospel. We believe this feeling of regard, if cherished, will induce friends, when any are not diligent in attending our religious meetings, to press upon them the advantage and importance of this primary duty. It will lead them also to encourage our young people to read the Holy Scriptures daily, with desires that the Lord may bless these invaluable writings to their spiritual instruction. And we intreat friends to promote, especially among the younger part of our body, an acquaintance with the writings of our approved authors; in which are set forth the grounds of our religious testimonies, the persecutions suffered by our faithful predecessors in the support of them, and many instances of the visitations of divine love, so often mercifully granted in early life. 1833.

Religious education is not confined to the nurture of early childhood, nor to the training of youth during the period generally passed at school. The circumstances of young people from the time of their leaving school, and as they pass onwards to early manhood, have awakened our tender solicitude. Their inexperience, their temptations, and the disadvantages under which some of them are placed, give them a strong claim upon the kind consideration and watchful care of friends: those especially, in whose families they are placed, whether as apprentices or otherwise, have the opportunity of contributing largely to the comfort, and help, and good of those in their employ, by protecting them from harm, and strengthening their best resolutions. We believe that many of our friends are honestly engaged rightly to discharge these duties; we are well aware that they cannot do so without personal sacrifice, but we would have them to consider that, in such acts of fatherly kindness, they may be the means of doing much towards keeping from evil this interesting portion of their household. As there is joy in Heaven over the repentance of one transgressor, surely those who are made instrumental in sheltering their younger brethren from evil, must be employed in a service acceptable to their Lord; and they will not lose their reward. 1844. P. E.

The offices of Elder and Overseer amongst us are of great importance, and, when rightly filled, of great value. We feel much for our friends who are appointed to these stations. In the right performance of their service much humiliation may prevail; but, whilst it is well that they should be sensible of their own infirmity, this consideration ought not to be allowed to interfere with the right discharge of their duty. We encourage them to cherish an interest in the spiritual welfare of all their fellow-members, to exercise a watchful care and affectionate oversight, and more especially to manifest their sympathy with their younger friends, in the peculiar circumstances in which some of them may be placed. We invite them to be diligent in warning and counselling the young, in privacy, faithfulness and love; endeavouring to attract them to the paths of virtue and self-denial, and to a living, experimental faith in Christ, as their Shepherd, their Saviour, and their King. Nor would we limit the performance of these duties to those who occupy such stations: we are all to watch over one another for good, and to be mutually interested one for another, being united together as lively stones in the spiritual building of which the Lord Jesus Christ is the chief corner-stone. 1851. P. E.

SECTION XI.—MINISTERS AND ELDERS AND THEIR MEETINGS.

Local Meetings.

It is agreed that, as far as can suitably be done, there be held in each Monthly Meeting a meeting of ministers and elders once in three months, some time previous to those Monthly Meetings which immediately precede the Quarterly Meeting; in which meetings, after some time spent in solid retirement, the queries addressed to ministers and elders are to be read and considered, and, at the specified times, answered in writing, according to the directions of this meeting in that behalf. Opportunity also may here be given for tender advice and assistance, as the nature of any case may require: and representatives, taken from the members in either station, are to be appointed to attend the Quarterly Meeting of Ministers and Elders, constituted of such representatives, and of the other approved ministers and elders of the Quarterly Meeting. A list of the names of all the ministers and elders of the several Monthly Meetings, is to be kept by the Quarterly Meeting of Ministers and Elders, and annually revised. 1757.—1801.—1833.—1861.

Quarterly Meetings.

At each Quarterly Meeting of Ministers and Elders, the queries are to be read; and, in Spring and Autumn, the answers thereto from its subordinate meetings: to which latter meetings such advice is to be extended as circumstances may require. At the Quarterly Meeting of Ministers and Elders next preceding the Yearly Meeting, a general answer is to be drawn up, to be sent by representatives to the Yearly Meeting of Ministers and Elders. The Quarterly Meeting is to be furnished with the names of these representatives, together with a report in writing of the regular holding of the Quarterly Meeting of Ministers and Elders during the year. The answers to the queries prepared by that meeting are to be in readiness to be produced if called for. 1757.—1801.—1833.—1861.

This meeting recommends to ministers and elders, when they deem it proper to submit to the Monthly Meetings to which they belong, the propriety of acknowledging a friend as a minister, that, previously to doing so, they should apply to, and have the advice of, the Quarterly Meeting of Ministers and Elders, of which they form a part. No record of such cases is to be made in any meeting of ministers and elders. 1830.

It is the sense and judgment of this meeting, that it is of advantage to the Society to hold a Yearly Meeting of Ministers and Elders, in London, preceding the Yearly Meeting; to be continued by adjournments, so that such adjournments do not interfere with the sittings of this meeting : and that such meeting do not in any wise take upon it, or interfere with, any part of the discipline of the church, belonging either to this meeting, or to any subordinate meeting. _{Yearly Meeting.}

The several Quarterly Meetings of Ministers and Elders in Great Britain are to appoint at least two of their members as representatives. The Yearly Meeting of Ministers and Elders of Ireland is also to appoint some of its members, as may be convenient; and the whole are to form, together with such recorded ministers and appointed elders as may be in London, the said Yearly Meeting of Ministers and Elders.

That meeting is to receive and read the answers to the queries from the Quarterly Meetings of Ministers and Elders, by which an opportunity will be given of imparting such advice as shall be necessary; and, after having informed itself, by means of the answers received, of the state of the ministers and elders in the several Quarterly Meetings, it is to lay annually before this meeting a summary yet clear account thereof. The said meeting is also to desire all friends in the station of elder then in London, to meet at the close of the different meetings for worship in the city and its vicinity, which they may attend during the time of holding this meeting. And it is to be considered the proper business of the friends thus met to communicate such advice and in such manner as they, in the wisdom of truth, may find needful, and to make a general report to some adjournment of the said meeting. 1753.—1757.—1801—1833.—1861.

It is the sense and judgment of this meeting, that ministers who believe it to be their religious duty to travel in the service of the Gospel in foreign parts, do submit the same, not only to the Monthly Meeting to which they belong, but also to their Quarterly Meeting, and, unless the service be confined to those professing with Friends in the south of France or at Minden and Pyrmont, to the Yearly Meeting of Ministers and Elders, or to the Morning Meeting, in order to be favoured with the concurrent testimonies of the said meetings, to strengthen them in so great and weighty engagements.

When either of these meetings shall have confirmed the liberation of a minister to travel in foreign parts, in the service of the Gospel, the same shall be reported to this meeting. 1763.—1861.

Morning Meeting.

The meeting which is held in London under the denomination of the Morning Meeting, first established in the year 1672, is considered by this meeting as constituted of the acknowledged ministers and appointed elders of the Quarterly Meetings of London and Middlesex, Bedfordshire and Hertfordshire, Berkshire and Oxfordshire, Buckinghamshire and Northamptonshire, Essex, Kent, and that of Sussex, Surrey and Hants. It is to meet once in three months, subject to being convened, in the intervals, at the call of any three of its members. 1833.—1861.

This meeting considers that, agreeably to the established usage of the Society, it is the duty of the Morning Meeting to exercise a tender Christian care over those ministers from foreign parts who may from time to time visit the city of London and its vicinity.

It is also the office of that meeting to judge of the religious concerns of such ministers as may have been liberated by their Monthly and Quarterly Meetings, to travel in the service of the Gospel in foreign parts, when great inconvenience would ensue from their waiting for the occurrence of the Yearly Meeting of Ministers and Elders: the said meeting is also left at liberty to grant certificates to ministering friends returning to America under similar circumstances. On all such occasions the Morning Meeting is to inform the Yearly Meeting of Ministers and Elders of its proceedings. 1833.—1861.

The circumstances of our friends, who come from America to this country in the work of the ministry, have engaged our brotherly consideration. Whilst feeling the importance of in nowise interfering with the blessed guidance of the Spirit of truth in their religious movements, this meeting is of the judgment, that advantage would arise from our dear friends proceeding to London as soon as may be after their arrival in this country, whenever they can conveniently do so, and feel it not incompatible with the pointings of duty. This course is recommended in order that, in accordance with the regulations of this meeting, their certificates may be verified by the Meeting for Sufferings, and an opportunity be at the same time afforded them for attending the Morning Meeting of Ministers and Elders, and thus early partaking of the sympathy and aid of the members of that meeting. But, in offering this suggestion, we desire that our brethren and sisters from a distant land, travelling amongst us in the service of the Gospel, may continue to receive from Friends everywhere a large measure of kind assistance and Christian sympathy. 1855.

Counsel. Let the elders, when they see occasion, advise ministers to be very prudent in their conduct, not as busy-bodies, nor meddling with family or personal affairs, in which they are not concerned, or required to be assisting; and to be very tender of one another's reputation, and of that of friends among whom they travel; neither giving ear to, nor spreading, reports tending to raise in the minds of others a lessening or disesteem of any of the brotherhood; and, as soon as their service in the ministry is over, to return to their habitations, and there take a reasonable and prudent care of their own business, household and family. And we advise ministers to have it much at heart to maintain a perfect harmony and good understanding with the Monthly Meetings to which they belong, and that they show themselves ready to hear and receive advice, as well as teach and instruct. 1731.

Every meeting of Ministers and Elders may, as it shall seem meet in the wisdom of truth, advise, exhort, and rebuke, in Christian tenderness and faithfulness, any of its members, or any who may be travelling in the work of the ministry within the compass of such meeting. But if the Monthly Meeting to which such ministers belong shall take the case under its own care, then, on notice being given of the same, the proceedings of the Meeting of Ministers and Elders shall cease. 1735.—1833.—1861.

This meeting, feeling the importance of extending care and counsel, as well as manifesting due sympathy, towards those who are liberated to travel in the work of the ministry, wishes to encourage friends under the appointment of elder, to be willing, as way may open, to accompany ministers when thus travelling; believing that their cordial union in such service may be a strength to the minister. And it is the judgment of this meeting, that, when such companions, or other friends who may travel in a similar character, are likely to go far from home, or to be absent for a length of time, they be furnished with a minute of the approbation of the Monthly Meeting to which they belong, when the same can suitably be obtained. 1833.

Advices.
Advices to be read in the Summer and Winter Quarterly Meetings of Ministers and Elders; to be read also once a year in their subordinate meetings.

Let ministers and elders be constant in their endeavours, through the power of the Holy Spirit, to live under the government of Christ.

Let them be frequent in reading, and diligent in meditating upon, the Holy Scriptures, and be careful not to misquote or misapply them. In preaching, writing, or conversing about the things of God, let them keep to the use of sound words or Scripture terms.

Let them be careful to adorn the doctrine of God our Saviour in all things: keeping themselves unspotted from the world, and being examples of meekness, temperance, patience and charity.

Whilst diligent when engaged in business, let ministers and elders be watchful not to become entangled with the cares of this world; and let them guard against the snare of accumulating wealth; manifesting Christian moderation and contentment in all things.

May they cherish a deep religious interest on behalf of those who are called to the ministry; watching over the young and inexperienced with tender Christian concern, and encouraging all in the right way of the Lord.

Let ministers wait for the renewed putting forth of the Holy Spirit; and be careful, in the exercise of their ministry, not to exceed the measure of their gift, but to proceed and conclude in the life and authority of the Gospel.

Let ministers be concerned to preach, not themselves, but Christ Jesus the Lord; reverently asking wisdom of God, that they may be enabled rightly to divide the word of truth. May nothing be done or offered with a view to popularity, but all in humility and the fear of the Lord.

Bearing in mind that the treasure is in earthern vessels, let them beware of laying stress on the authority of their ministry; the baptizing power of the Spirit of Truth accompanying the words being the true evidence.

Let ministers, at all times, be tender of each other's reputation, and watchful lest they hurt each other's service in religious meetings. As servants of the same Lord, with diversities of gifts, but the same Spirit, may ministers and elders maintain a lively exercise harmoniously to labour for the spreading and advancement of the truth.

Let ministers guard against all tones and gestures inconsistent with Christian simplicity, and endeavour to express themselves audibly and distinctly. And let them beware of using unnecessary preambles, and of making additions towards the conclusion of a meeting, when it was left well before.

When travelling in the service of the Gospel, let them be concerned to move under heavenly guidance, so that their visits may be neither unprofitably short and hurried, nor burdensome or unnecessarily expensive; giving no offence in anything, that the ministry be not blamed.

And lastly, as prayer and thanksgiving are an important part of worship, may they be offered in spirit and in truth, with a right understanding seasoned with grace. When engaged herein, let ministers avoid many words and repetitions, and be cautious of too often repeating the high and holy name of God or his attributes; neither let prayer be in a formal and customary way, nor without a reverent sense of Divine influence. 1775.—1792.—1833.—1861.

Queries.

The two introductory Queries are to be read and weightily considered, but not answered; the first in Summer, the second in Winter.

The four last are to be answered in writing to the Quarterly Meetings of Ministers and Elders, in the Spring and Autumn; and from thence, in the Spring, to the Yearly Meeting of Ministers and Elders.

Are ministers and elders engaged to watch unto prayer; that they may themselves be preserved in humble dependence upon Christ, and in an earnest religious exercise for the conversion of sinners, and for the edifying of the body in the faith and love of the Gospel?

Are ministers and elders concerned faithfully to occupy the spiritual gifts entrusted to them, to the honour of God?

1. Are ministers and elders diligent in attending their meetings for worship and discipline, and careful to promote the attendance of their families?

2. Do any overcharge themselves with trade or other outward engagements, to the hindrance of their service?

3. Are they careful to rule their own houses well; and do they endeavour, by example and precept, to train up their families in a religious life and conversation, consistent with our Christian profession?

4. Are they preserved in love; administering encouragement or counsel, as occasion may require, in reference to ministry or conduct?   1757.—1801.—1833.—1861.

⁎⁎ For ministers and elders—see also pp. 63 to 66, and pp. 150 to 152.

SECTION XII.—MEETING FOR SUFFERINGS.

AGREED that certain friends of this city be nominated to keep a constant meeting about sufferings four times in a year, with the day and time of each meeting here fixed and settled.* That

* It appears by the records of the Meeting for Sufferings, that the mode of meeting every week was commenced in the year 1676, and continued until the year 1794.

at least one friend of each county be appointed by the Quarterly Meeting thereof, to be in readiness to repair to any of the said meetings at this city, at such times as their urgent occasions or sufferings shall require. 1675.

It is agreed to be sufficient that the Meeting for Sufferings be held in course, on the first Sixth-day in each month; subject nevertheless, on any emergency, to the call of any five of the members thereof. 1794.—1798.

---

1. The Meeting for Sufferings consists of friends appointed in accordance with the following regulations, (2, 3, and 4,) and approved by this meeting; of those in foreign parts appointed by meetings corresponding with this meeting; and likewise of men friends in the stations of approved ministers and appointed elders. *Constitution.*

2. Each Quarterly Meeting is to appoint any number of friends not exceeding four, to be its London correspondents, and, as such, members of the Meeting for Sufferings. The London correspondents are however, in all cases, to be selected from a list prepared in the following manner. The several Monthly Meetings in the Quarterly Meeting of London and Middlesex are annually to appoint small committees of judicious friends, who are directed to take particular notice of those friends in their respective meetings whose conduct and conversation appear to be agreeable to the description given in the eighth regulation. These committees are to meet unitedly in the Second Month, and, after deliberate consideration, nominate friends suitable to be appointed to this service.

A list of the friends who have been so nominated, and of such London correspondents as do not already stand for more than two Quarterly Meetings, is to be transmitted annually by the Recording Clerk, before the end of the second month, to those Quarterly Meetings whose number of London correspondents is not full; in order that they may either make a selection themselves, or commission their representatives to the Yearly Meeting to do so. In making such selection, Quarterly Meetings are recommended, where they have no special reason to the contrary, to give a preference to the names of those friends who have not

Constitution. yet been chosen correspondents. No friend is in any case to be appointed London correspondent for more than three Quarterly Meetings.

When a friend, who has been a London correspondent of the Meeting for Sufferings, removes from the Quarterly Meeting of London and Middlesex into any one of the six adjoining Quarterly Meetings, he is still to be a member of the Meeting for Sufferings, and to continue to act in the capacity of London correspondent for the Quarterly or other meeting for which he so acted previously to his removal.

3. The several Quarterly Meetings are also to appoint, from amongst their own members, suitable friends to be their correspondents in the country, and, as such, members of the Meeting for Sufferings. Nominations for this appointment are to be made, not in the meetings at large, but by committees of either the Quarterly or Monthly Meetings, as may be deemed best. Such nominations are in all cases to be submitted for the approval and confirmation of the Quarterly, and subsequently of the Yearly Meeting. In every Quarterly Meeting, the list of its London and Country correspondents, and of any friends appointed under Rule 4, is to be read over annually.

4. Each of the six Quarterly Meetings adjoining that of London and Middlesex, viz., Bedfordshire and Hertfordshire,—Berkshire and Oxfordshire,—Buckinghamshire and Northamptonshire,—Essex,—Kent,—and Sussex, Surrey and Hants, is, from time to time, as there may be occasion, to appoint a committee to consider whether there be one or more friends within its Quarterly Meeting so circumstanced, as to be able to perform the duties connected with the Meeting for Sufferings, in the same manner as the London correspondents. The other Quarterly Meetings are left at liberty to make a similar appointment, where any suitable friends are found willing in like manner to devote themselves to the service. The names proposed are to be submitted to the respective Quarterly Meetings, and, if approved, to be offered to the Yearly Meeting for its acceptance and confirmation. In no Quarterly Meeting are more than four riends to be so appointed, and they are in each case to be either among its existing country correspondents, or such friends as the Quarterly Meeting deems eligible for the appointment.

5. The correspondents for Ireland, for the colonies, for foreign parts, and for the Yearly Meetings in North America, are to be proposed by the Meeting for Sufferings from among its own members, and confirmed by the Yearly Meeting.

6. The Meeting for Sufferings is, at its discretion, to report to this meeting the names of such of the London correspondents, and of friends appointed under the fourth regulation, as do not attend it six times in the year; in order to their being discharged by this meeting, unless sufficient reason be rendered for their absence.

7. With a view of diffusing more generally, among friends in different parts of the country, an interest in the various important matters which come under the consideration of the Meeting for Sufferings, all the country correspondents are encouraged to attend it as often as circumstances will admit of their so doing.

8. This meeting, having considered the nature and importance of the affairs transacted by the Meeting for Sufferings, is impressed with the necessity of their being managed by men who are of clean hands, and who adorn the doctrine they profess, in their lives and conversation. And it is the earnest desire of this meeting, that friends be particularly careful in their choice of such as are to act as members of that meeting, informing themselves, as much as may be, of the qualifications of those who are intended for such service; and that such only may be nominated as are faithful in the several branches of our Christian testimonies, and exemplary in their conduct and conversation amongst men. 1747.—1759.—1857.—1861.

Duties entrusted to it. The Meeting for Sufferings (so called from the nature of its original object) is a standing committee of this meeting, and is entrusted with a general care of whatever may arise during the intervals of this meeting, affecting our religious Society, and requiring immediate attention; particularly of such matters as may occasion an application to the legislature for the relief of the Society in regard to its Christian testimonies. 1833.

This meeting desires that friends in the several counties will be diligent in acquainting the Meeting for Sufferings with any applications that are likely to be made to Parliament, in cases

Duties entrusted to it. that may affect Friends; such as enclosing lands, building or repairing steeple-houses, or other local occasions, which may be known in the country much sooner than to the Meeting for Sufferings; for want of which intelligence, opportunities may be lost for soliciting relief, that by timely application might have been obtained. 1765.

Upon consideration of sufferings in general, it is advised that, in cases of difficulty, and where friends who are sufferers stand in need of advice in any particular case, they send up their respective cases to the Meeting for Sufferings in London. 1682. P. E.

Immediately after the Spring Quarterly Meetings, the accounts of distraints are to be sent to the Recording Clerk in London, in order to their being examined by the Meeting for Sufferings, or a committee of that meeting; by whom a report is to be made to the Yearly Meeting, specifying the aggregate number of cases, and amount of distraints and returns under each separate head, as well as the total amount of net distraints reported by each Quarterly Meeting, together with any information of a special character which may be suggested by such examination. 1861.

This meeting is of the judgment, that the Yearly Meeting of Ministers and Elders, or the Morning Meeting, when it sees right to liberate a friend to travel in the work of the ministry in foreign parts, out of the acknowledged limits of any Monthly Meeting, should inform the Meeting for Sufferings of such conclusion. The last-mentioned meeting is desired to extend such Christian care as it may deem necessary, in aiding friends thus liberated in the prosecution of their concern, and also from time to time during the said engagement, particularly as it relates to their being suitably accompanied. And it is further left to the said meeting to exercise its discretion in regard to the companions of such travelling friends; care being taken that, when convenient, a minute of the approbation of the Monthly Meeting of which any such companion is a member, has been obtained.

In the case of any friend, from America or elsewhere, liberated to travel on similar service, the foregoing provision is also to apply, after such friend shall have laid his concern before our Yearly Meeting of Ministers and Elders, when it can conveniently be done, or otherwise before the Morning Meeting, which meeting is to inform the Meeting for Sufferings of the circumstance. 1827.—1833.

It is the judgment of this meeting that, when any friend from America arrives within the compass of this meeting, on religious service, he should produce his certificates to the friends of the meeting within the compass of which he may land; and that the said certificates or copies of them be forwarded to the Meeting for Sufferings in London, which meeting is without delay to proceed to an examination of them, and inform the friend, by a minute duly attested by the signature of its clerk, of the result of such examination. And it is further the judgment of this meeting, that the said friend do abstain from travelling on religious service, until such minute shall have been received by him. Our correspondents in America are requested to inform their correspondents in London, as soon as any friend has obtained certificates for religious service in this country. 1829.

It is agreed that the Meeting for Sufferings be at liberty to print or purchase, and distribute in such manner as it may deem proper, such works as that meeting may think desirable; it being distinctly understood that the Society of Friends is not thereby committed to everything contained in such books. 1732.—1833.—1861.

SECTION XIII.—NATIONAL STOCK.

AGREED, that a collection be occasionally made in the several counties and places for defraying the expenses of the Society, as printing and distributing books for the service of truth, the passage of ministering friends who are called into the service of the Lord beyond sea, the salary of a clerk, and house-rent for keeping records, with other incidental charges; to be sent up to the correspondents of the several counties and places, and paid to the cashiers. 1672.—1676.

Disbursements out of the national stock to be such only as shall be agreed to, and directed by, the Meeting for Sufferings in London. 1679.

It is agreed, that in future the cash of this meeting be kept at the bankers' in the names of six friends, under the denomination of trustees, to be appointed by the Meeting for Sufferings, and renewed from time to time, whenever, by death, a desire to be excused, or any other reasonable cause, the trustees shall be reduced to three; for which purpose, the names of the trustees shall be called over in the Meeting for Sufferings previous to the Yearly Meeting; and that the drafts be in future signed in the meeting by three of the members present, and afterwards countersigned by one or more of the trustees. 1793.

Special objects.

This meeting agrees that the national stock may be employed in defraying the expenses of ministering friends from other countries, who may be returning from visits to any part of Great Britain, although such visits may not have been general; such expenses having been examined and allowed by the Quarterly Meeting in which the same shall have been incurred. The said fund may also be expended in defraying the charges of ministers who may be called to travel in any foreign country, in which there are not any Friends, or none suitable to bear such charges. 1793.

The expenses of friends from America, engaged in this country in the work of the ministry, whilst travelling within the compass of a Quarterly Meeting, and also when passing from any Quarterly Meeting to an adjoining one, are to be defrayed as heretofore; but, when those friends shall pass from one Quarterly Meeting to another, which is not adjoining, and without having any public religious service or engagement within the compass of an intermediate Quarterly Meeting, the Quarterly Meeting from which they may have passed shall be at liberty to apply to the Meeting for Sufferings, which meeting may, in its discretion, reimburse the whole or any part thereof out of the national stock. 1846.

This meeting agrees that the expenses of ministering friends, and of such companions as may be needful, in visiting any of the islands adjacent to Great Britain, including those of Guernsey and Jersey, also such parts of Scotland and Wales as are out of the acknowledged limits of any Monthly Meeting, may, at the discretion of the Meeting for Sufferings, be paid out of the national stock.* 1799.—1800.—1833.—1861.

This meeting further agrees that any expenses incurred by the Quarterly Meeting of Sussex, Surrey and Hants, in its care of the members of our Society in the islands of Guernsey and Jersey, may be applied for by that Quarterly Meeting, and paid at the discretion of the Meeting for Sufferings. The expenses referred to in this and the preceding paragraph are to be previously examined and allowed by the respective Monthly and Quarterly Meetings. 1817.—1833.—1861.

The original objects of the national stock appear to have been the defraying of the necessary expenses of friends called to labour in the Gospel in foreign parts, and the charge for books for distribution on our religious principles, both in our own and in foreign languages. General objects.

The printing of epistles and other papers issued on behalf of the Society, as well as the providing of birth and burial notes, have long formed part of the expenditure.

A considerable charge is necessarily incurred in keeping in repair the meeting-houses in London, and the various offices connected with them, which are the property of the Society.

The chief part of the salary of the Recording Clerk in London is also paid out of the national stock.

In addition to the before-mentioned objects, numerous incidental expenses are constantly incurred, as well as some other charges, which the Meeting for Sufferings has been authorized by this meeting to pay. 1833.—1861.

SECTION XIV.—CARE OF THE POOR.

ADVISED that, where friends want ability in the world, their Monthly and Quarterly Meetings assist them; that the children of the poor may have due help of education, instruction, and necessary learning; and that the children both of the rich and

* See also p. 152.

the poor may be early provided with useful employments, that that they may not grow up in idleness, looseness and vice; but that, being seasoned with the truth, taught our holy self-denying way, and sanctified of God, they may become a reputation to our holy profession, the comfort of their honest parents, and instrumental to the glory of God, and to the good of the succeeding generations.   1709. P. E.

With respect to the poor among us, it ought to be considered that the poor, both parents and children, are of our family; and although some may think the poor a burthen, yet be it remembered, when our poor are well provided for, and walk orderly, they are an ornament to our Society; and the rich should consider, "It is more blessed to give than to receive." "He that hath pity upon the poor lendeth unto the Lord; and that which he hath given will he pay him again." 1718. P. E.—1833.—1860.

As mercy, compassion and charity, are eminently required in this new-covenant dispensation which we are under, so, respecting the poor and indigent among us, it is the advice of this meeting that all poor friends be taken due care of, and that nothing be wanting for their necessary supply; according to our ancient practice and testimony. 1720. P. E.—1860.

We have ever esteemed the duty of ministering to the wants of the poor as one of primary obligation. This duty ought to be exercised cheerfully and without grudging; and, in assisting our poorer brethren, care should be taken not to wound their feelings. It highly becomes a people professing to be united in the faith and hope of the Gospel, to provide for the relief of their own poor. The care of the poor was one of the earliest evidences which Christianity afforded to the Gentiles of the superiority and divine character of its principles; and a similar provision for those who are united with us in religious fellowship appears to have been one of the earliest occasions of our Meetings for Discipline.

The provision made for its poor by our Society is, however, it should be remembered, entirely a voluntary one; and its only ground is Christian charity. Whilst enjoining the duty of charity on those who are of ability to extend it, we would remind our poor friends, that it is their duty, by frugality and industry, to use their strenuous endeavours to maintain themselves and their families, and, by small savings in time of health, to provide for sickness and old age, so as not to be dependent on others.

We would also observe, that the provision of the Society was never designed to contract the duty of charity between individual Friends; or to lessen the claims which near relations, in times of necessity, have upon each other. In an especial manner, we esteem it the privilege and the duty of the children of persons who are destitute to minister to the wants and comforts of their parents with an affectionate cheerfulness, and not to throw the care of them on others. 1833.

The last Yearly Meeting, after deliberate consideration, came to the conclusion to rescind all those Rules of Settlement applicable to the maintenance of the poor, which, with various modifications, had existed for upwards of a century. Henceforth, on the acceptance of a certificate of removal by inference or otherwise, the care of friends in necessitous circumstances ceases to devolve on the recommending Monthly Meeting.

The importance of simplicity in administration, and of personal intercourse between the giver and receiver, in connexion with the voluntary and Christian character of all our relief, has had considerable influence with this meeting in coming to such a conclusion. And the hope is strongly entertained that the exercise of that brotherly love which is the foundation of our whole system of relief, will not less abound between meetings than between individuals, and will tend to harmonious co-operation in carrying out this part of our Christian economy. 1861.

SECTION XV.—MARRIAGE REGULATIONS.

SUCH friends as have, with serious advice, due deliberation, and free and mutual consent, absolutely agreed, espoused, or contracted upon the account of marriage, shall not be allowed or owned amongst us, in any unfaithfulness or injustice one to another, to break or violate any such contract or engagement. 1675.—1833.

This meeting, having deliberately considered the great exercise brought upon our Society by divers in profession with us, who, contrary to our known principles, and the wholesome discipline established among us, are joined in marriage by the priest with persons either of our own or other persuasions, doth earnestly advise, that all friends use their utmost endeavours to prevent such marriages, when the parties' inclinations may come to their knowledge.

And it is the sense and judgment of this meeting, that, when any marry by the priest, or in any other manner contrary to the established rules of the society, they shall be dealt with by the Monthly Meeting in the spirit of Christian love and tenderness. 1768.

This meeting, having taken into consideration the Yearly Meeting minute of 1675,* made against the marriage of first cousins, declares it to be its sense and judgment, that no Monthly Meeting should pass first cousins in order for marriage; and it earnestly desires all friends, whenever they know or hear of any first cousins designing or intending to marry, that they immediately advise them against it. 1747.—1801.

The modifying or rescinding of the rules which disallow the marriage of first cousins amongst us, has been at this time deliberately considered, and this meeting does not deem it right to make any alteration in the said rules. 1833.

This meeting is of the judgment that, as compliance with the laws of the land, in cases wherein conscience is not violated, is an acknowledged principle of Friends, the Society cannot consistently with this principle allow, in our meetings, the passing of marriages which are not authorized by the law on this subject, and which are included in the degrees of consanguinity or affinity prohibited thereby. 1811.

ORDER OF PROCEDURE.

When the parties are members of the same Monthly Meeting.
I. The man is first, in person, to declare his intention to the men's Monthly Meeting, in terms to the following effect, viz., *that he intends to take* D. E. *to be his wife, if the Lord permit.*

* See p. 83.

He is at the same time to produce the written declaration of the woman, signed by her, and attested by two witnesses; which declaration is to be in words to the following effect:—

To *Monthly Meeting of Friends.*
Dear Friends,
I hereby inform you that I intend to take A. B. to be my husband, if the Lord permit; and that it is with my consent that he lays before you his intention of marriage with me.

Witnesses, D. E.
    F. G.,
    H. I. *Date*

II. A certificate or certificates are to be produced from the parents or guardians (if any) of both parties, signifying *that it is with their consent that the parties proceed to accomplish their intended marriage;* such certificates to be signed by the parents or guardians, and attested by two witnesses.

III. Information of the intended marriage is then to be sent to the women's meeting, which may be done in the following form :—

The *Monthly Meeting of women friends is hereby informed that* A. B., *of* N., *has this day declared his intention of marriage with* D. E., *of* P., *and has produced a written declaration, signed by her, to the like effect* [*together with the proper testimonials of the consent of all other parties concerned.**]

    Signed in and on behalf of   *Monthly Meeting, held* this   day of   *month*, 18   S. T., *Clerk*.

IV. If there appear no sufficient objection, the said meetings are respectively to appoint two men and two women friends to inquire into the clearness of the parties from any other marriage engagement. Those appointed by the men's Monthly Meeting are also to see, in case there be children by a former marriage or marriages, that their rights are legally secured; and to take care that public notice of such intended marriage be given at the close of a First-day Morning Meeting, to which the parties respectively belong. This is to be done as early as convenient after the appointment, and in the following form, or to the same

---

* The words within brackets to be omitted or varied, if there be no parent or guardian, or only one.

effect : — *Friends, there is an intention of marriage between A. B., of N., and D. E., of P.; if any person have anything to object, let timely notice be given.* The same friends are also to exercise care in timely advising the parties concerned to take those proceedings which the law now requires (see pp. 201 to 204), as, unless those regulations be complied with, the meeting cannot liberate the parties for the accomplishment of the marriage.

V. The friends appointed are to make report, at a subsequent Monthly Meeting, of the day and place of publication of the intended marriage, as well as on the other subjects of their appointment. The particulars of this report are to be recorded. If no sufficient obstruction appear to the meeting, liberty is then to be granted to the parties to solemnize the marriage; and the women's meeting is to be informed of this conclusion.

When members of different Monthly Meetings.

VI. The man is in person to declare his intention to the men's Monthly Meeting to which he belongs, and there to produce the written declaration of the woman, and the certificates of consent of the parents or guardians (if any) of both parties, as prescribed in Rules I. and II. If there appear no sufficient objection, two men friends are to be appointed, who are to proceed as directed in Rule IV.; and a notification in the following form, signed by the clerk, is to be forwarded to the Monthly Meeting to which the woman belongs, viz. :—

   To   Monthly Meeting of Friends.
  Dear Friends,
  We hereby inform you that A. B., *a member of this meeting, has this day declared to us his intention of marriage with* D. E., *a member of your Monthly Meeting, and has produced a written declaration, signed by her, to the like effect* [*as well as certificates of the consent of all other parties concerned.**] *An appointment is made agreeably to the direction of the Yearly Meeting; and if no obstruction arise, a certificate will be forwarded to you in due course.*
  Signed on behalf of Monthly Meeting, held at the of the month, 18   S. T., Clerk.

* See Note to Rule III., p. 195.

VII. On receipt of this notification,* the Monthly Meeting of men friends to which it is addressed is to proceed in the manner prescribed in Rule IV., and is then to forward the notification to the women's meeting, which is also to make an appointment of two friends to inquire into the clearness of the woman from any other marriage engagement. A certificate of clearness on behalf of the man, from the Monthly Meeting of which he is a member, must, however be produced to the Monthly Meeting to which the woman belongs, before liberty to solemnize the marriage is granted; which certificate may be in the following form:—

   To   *Monthly Meeting of Friends.*

Dear Friends,

A. B., *a member of this meeting, has communicated to us his intention of marriage with* D. E., *a member of your Monthly Meeting. We hereby certify on his behalf, that due attention has been paid to the rules of the Yearly Meeting which are to be observed by us on such occasions; and, no objection arising, we leave him at liberty for further proceedings in regard to his intended marriage. Requesting to be informed by you, in usual course, when the same is accomplished, we remain, with love,*

        Your Friends.

   Signed in and on behalf of   Monthly Meeting, held at   this   day of the   month, 18

            S. T., *Clerk*.

VIII. The friends appointed are to make report at a subsequent Monthly Meeting, as directed by Rule V., the particulars of which, and also the production of the above certificate of clearness, are to be recorded. If no sufficient obstruction appear to the Monthly Meeting, liberty is then to be granted to the parties to solemnize the marriage, and the women's meeting is to be informed of this conclusion.

IX. Monthly Meetings are to make a suitable appointment of friends, to take the needful care that good order be observed on the day of marriage, and that the certificates and the registers of

General regulations.

---

* The production of this notification is not in any case to be dispensed with, even although the certificate of clearness may be already issued.

the marriage be properly filled up, and duly signed and witnessed: they are to make a report to the next Monthly Meeting.

General regulations.

X. Marriages are to be solemnized at the usual week-day meeting, or at a meeting appointed at some seasonable hour in the forenoon, on some other convenient week-day (previous notice in the latter case having been given); and at the meeting-house to which the woman belongs, unless leave be obtained of the woman's Monthly Meeting to solemnize the marriage in some other meeting-house, with the consent of the friends of such other meeting.

XI. After the meeting has been held a seasonable time, the parties are to stand up, and, taking each other by the hand, to declare in an audible and solemn manner to the following effect: the man first, viz., *Friends, I take this my friend D. E. to be my wife, promising, through Divine assistance, to be unto her a loving and faithful husband, until it shall please the Lord by death to separate us;* and then the woman in like manner, *Friends, I take this my friend, A. B., to be my husband, promising, through Divine assistance, to be unto him a loving and faithful wife, until it shall please the Lord by death to separate us.*

XII. A certificate (with a five shilling stamp affixed) in the following form of words, is to be audibly read at the close of the meeting by some proper person, the express names and descriptions of the parties being first inserted: they are then to sign the same; the man first; then the woman with her maiden or widow name; the relations next; and such others present at the solemnity as think proper.

A. B. of   [grocer], *Son of* D. B. *of   in the   of   , [yeoman], and E. his wife, and D. E. daughter of* M. E. *of   in the   of   , [draper], and M. his wife, having duly made known their intention of taking each other in marriage to the Monthly Meeting of Friends, commonly called Quakers, of* *   *in the   of   , the proceedings of the said A. B. and D. E., after due inquiry, were allowed by the said meeting, they appearing clear of all others, and having*

---

* Where the parties belong to different Monthly Meetings, this blank is to be filled up with the name of the Monthly Meeting to which the woman belongs.

consent of parents [or *guardians*, as the case may be]. *Now these are to certify, that, for the accomplishing of their said marriage, this   day of the   month in the year one thousand eight hundred and   , they, the said* A. B. *and* D. E., *appeared at a public assembly of the aforesaid people, in their meeting-house in* [or *at*, as the case may be]   ; *and he the said* A. B. *taking the said* D. E. *by the hand, declared as followeth :—*

And the said D. E. *did then and there, in the said assembly, declare as followeth :—*

And the said A. B. *and* D. E., *as a further confirmation thereof, and in testimony thereunto, did then and there to these presents set their hands.*

A. B.
D. E.

<small>We, being present at the above said marriage, have also subscribed our names as witnesses thereunto, the day and year above written.</small>

XIII. If the man be a member of a different Monthly Meeting from that to which the woman belongs, when report is made to the Monthly Meeting of which the latter was a member, that the said marriage has been solemnized, a notification in the following form is to be sent to the Monthly Meeting to which the man belongs; and the said meeting, on receiving such notification, is desired in every case to enter on its minutes a copy thereof, and to record the woman as its member.

The Monthly Meeting of   is hereby informed that the Marriage between A. B. *and* D. E. *was solemnized in Friends' meeting-house at   in the County of   on the   day of the   month, 18 Signed in and on behalf of   Monthly Meeting held at   E. F., Clerk, the   of   month, 18   .*

1833.—1856.—1861.

When one or both of the parties are not in membership.

It is concluded by this meeting, after very full consideration of the subject, to extend to Monthly Meetings the liberty of allowing marriages to be solemnized in our meetings, and according to our usages, *by persons not in membership, but professing with us and attending our Meetings for Worship;* such marriages having been legalized by the Legislature.

It is at the same time the earnest concern of this meeting, that the testimony of our Society as to the inexpediency of marriages between persons not of the same religious views should remain unimpaired.

The following regulations are to be observed in reference to such marriages.

1. In all cases of intended marriage, where either or both of the parties shall not be in membership, but shall profess with Friends and attend our Meetings for Worship, the man shall produce or forward to the Monthly Meeting to which, if a member, he shall belong, or within the limits of which, if not a member, he shall reside, a certificate on behalf of the party, or of each of the parties (as the case may be) not in membership, in the following form, signed by two friends, both of whom shall be members of, and one of them, either an Elder or Overseer in the Monthly Meeting within the limits of which the person to whom the certificate relates shall reside, or Clerk of the same Monthly Meeting. Where the person to whom the certificate relates shall be a woman, one of the persons signing the same may be a woman friend in any of the stations above specified.

We, the undersigned A. B. *and* C. D., *hereby certify that we are acquainted with*   *of*   *who is desirous of being married according to the usages of the Society of Friends; and that*   *is a person professing with Friends, an attender of our Meetings for Worship, and, it is believed, of orderly life and conversation.*

    A. B. *Elder or Overseer in* [*or Clerk of*]   *Monthly Meeting,*

    C. D. *member of*   *Monthly Meeting.*

Witness to the signature of A. B.
              G. H.
Witness to the signature of C. D.
              I. K.

2. Subject to the production of such certificate or certificates (as the case may be), the proceedings in relation to all marriages coming within the present Regulations shall be conducted throughout according to the existing Rules,* in the same manner as if the person or persons so professing with us were a member or members of the Monthly Meeting or respective Monthly Meetings within the limits of which he, she, or they, respectively shall reside. Where, however, the parties reside within the same Monthly Meeting, the certificate or certificates produced under the preceding Rule is or are to be sent, together with the usual information of the intended marriage, to the women's Monthly Meeting; and where the parties reside within different Monthly Meetings, the allusion to membership, in the notification and certificate to be sent from one of such Monthly Meetings to the other, [see Rule VI., p. 196] will of course be altered, the expression "*a person professing with us and an attender of our Meetings for Worship, residing within the limits of Monthly Meeting,*" being introduced in lieu of such allusion to membership, wherever the case shall require it. The notification should also be accompanied by the certificate or certificates, entitling the party or parties not in membership to be married according to our usages.

3. Marriages under these circumstances are not to confer on the contracting parties, or on their children, any rights of membership.

4. A woman who is a member marrying a man not in membership, who resides within the limits of another Monthly Meeting, is not to become a member of such other Monthly Meeting, without the usual certificate of removal. 1860.—1861.

ARRANGEMENTS CONSEQUENT ON THE MARRIAGE AND REGISTRATION ACTS.

The Marriage Act† (6 & 7 Wm. IV., c. 85) expressly provides "that the Society of Friends, commonly called Quakers, may

* This includes a personal declaration of intention to the Monthly Meeting by the man, although he may not be a member of our Society.

† This Act has no application to marriages solemnized in Scotland, and, even in the case of both or either of the parties to a marriage in Scotland being resident in England, the notice to the Superintendent Registrar, and certificate by him referred to in these regulations, are not necessary.

Registration. continue to contract and solemnize marriage, according to the usages of the said society; and every such marriage is hereby declared and confirmed good in law,* provided that the parties to such marriage be both of the said Society;† provided also that notice to the Superintendent Registrar shall have been given, and the [said] Registrar's certificate shall have issued in manner provided by this Act."

1. "One of the parties" is to "give notice" of the intended marriage, "under his or her hand," "to the Superintendent Registrar‡ of the district within which the parties shall have dwelt for not less than seven days then next preceding; or, if the parties dwell in the districts of different Superintendent Registrars, shall give *the like notice* to the Superintendent Registrar of *each* district."§ It will be proper that the notice or notices should be given *at least* twenty-one days before the Monthly Meeting at which the parties are likely to be cleared for marriage, so as to allow time for the issuing of the certificate, and for its production at the Monthly Meeting, as hereinafter directed. And every such notice must be accompanied with the payment of a fee of one shilling to the Superintendent Registrar for entering the same. The notice is in a printed form to the following effect:—

To the Superintendent Registrar of the District of *Stepney*, in the *County* of *Middlesex*.

I hereby give thee notice that a marriage is intended to be had

---

* By the Act (10 & 11 Vict. c. 58) the marriages of Friends, solemnized according to their usages in England before the Act of 6 & 7 Wm. IV., are declared to have been and to be valid.

† By the Act (23 & 24 Vict. c. 18), by which marriages are authorized, according to our usages, between persons, both or one of whom, although not in membership, shall profess with or be of the persuasion of our Society, this proviso is practically repealed so far as regards such marriages.

‡ In districts under the Registration Act (6 & 7 Wm. IV. c. 86) there are sometimes appointed Deputy Registrars, as well as Registrars and a Superintendent Registrar; care must be taken to give the notice to the Superintendent Registrar.

§ By the statute 3 & 4 Vict. c. 72, Sec. 1, the building in which the marriage is to be solemnized must be within the district wherein one of the parties shall have dwelt for the time required by the Marriage Act. But by Sec. 5, Friends are exempted from this provision, so that the building wherein the marriage is to be solemnized need not be situate within either of the districts in which the parties respectively dwell.

within three calendar months from the date hereof, between me and the other party herein named and described (that is to say;)

Name.	Condition.	Rank or Profession.	Age.	Dwelling Place.	Length of Residence.	Meeting House in which the Marriage is intended to be solemnized.	District and County in which the other party resides, when the parties dwell in different Districts.
James Smith.	*Widower* [or] *Bachelor*	*Carpenter*	*of full age* [or] *minor*	*No. 46, High Street, Middlesex*	* *more than a month*	*Friends' Meeting House, Maidstone*	*Maidstone, Kent*
Martha Green.	*Spinster* [or] *Widow*		*Minor* [or] *of full age*	*Grove Farm, near Maidstone*	* *more than a month*		

Witness my hand this *sixth* day of the *Seventh* Month, *1837*.

        (Signed)   *JAMES SMITH.*

[The words and figures in italics to be filled up as the case may be.]

2. After the expiration of twenty-one days after the entry of the foregoing notice, the Superintendent Registrar, upon being requested by or on behalf of the party by whom the notice was given, is to issue a certificate in the form provided by the Act, which should certify the date of the notice given, and the several particulars thereof. Where the parties reside within different districts (as before stated), a separate certificate of notice must be obtained from each Superintendent Registrar. The Superindent Registrar is entitled to a fee of one shilling for every such certificate. The said officer is required to preserve all such notices, and to enter them in a book kept by him; which notice-book is to be open to inspection without charge. If the marriage should not take place within three calendar months after the entry of the notice, or notices, such notice or notices become void; and all the proceedings above described, namely, the notice or notices, entry and issue of the certificate or certificates, must be gone through again. The certificate or certificates, thus obtained, must be delivered, previously to the marriage, to the Registering Officer† of the Monthly Meeting within the limits of which the marriage is to be solemnized.

  * Or if more than seven days, and not more than one calendar month, state the number of days.

  † The designation given by the Act to the friend who acts as Registrar to the Monthly Meeting. See No. 7, p. 205.

Registration.

3. In order to ensure due compliance with the foregoing legislative provisions (without the observance of which the marriage will be void in law) this meeting directs that the Monthly Meeting, of which the woman is a member, or within the limits of which, if not a member, she shall reside, be not at liberty to clear the parties for marriage, unless the certificate of the Superintendent Registrar, or certificates (as the case may be) shall have been produced to it: a record of their having been so produced and examined is to be made.* The said meeting is also to take due care that such certificate or certificates be delivered (as above directed) previously to the marriage, to the Registering Officer of the Monthly Meeting within the limits of which the marriage is intended to be solemnized; accompanied by a notice or minute, signed by the Clerk, informing him that the parties are cleared accordingly. It is recommended that timely notice be given to the Registering Officer of the day and place intended for the solemnization of the marriage; in order that, as he is the person to register the marriage, he may, if practicable, be present thereat.

4. It is not necessary that our meeting-houses should be registered for the solemnization of marriages. But, having regard to our position under the Act in this respect, and to the tenor of our rules, [see especially No. X., p. 198), this meeting directs that no marriage shall take place at a meeting-house in which a meeting for worship is not regularly held.

5. The Act (19 & 20 Vict. c. 119) authorizes marriages by license between members of our Society, under the restrictions specified in the Act, and slightly modifies or explains the provisions of the former Acts, where one of the parties is resident in Ireland.

With regard to the license, upon notice of the intended marriage being given to the Superintendent Registrar of the district where either of the parties resides, such Superintendent Registrar may grant a certificate and license on the next day but one after the entry in his book of the notice; and the granting of such license to one of the parties, where they reside in different dis-

---

* It is not necessary, where the parties are members of or reside within the limits of different meetings, that they be produced to the Monthly Meeting to which the man belongs, or within the limits of which he resides.

tricts, supersedes the necessity of giving notice of the marriage to the Superintendent Registrar of the district where the other party resides. Where a license is taken out, the parties are made liable, under the Act, to the observance of certain formalities, and to the payment of an additional fee and stamp, as therein specified. Friends adopting this mode of procedure must of course produce the license to the Monthly Meeting, before they can be set at liberty for the accomplishment of their marriage.

6. The same Act also provides that where a marriage is about to take place without license, and one of the parties resides in Ireland, a notice, in the form *there used*, in that behalf, and a certificate issued in pursuance thereof, shall be as valid and effectual for authorizing the solemnization of a marriage in this country as the usual notice to, and certificate from, a Superintendent Registrar in England would be.

7. In every Monthly Meeting a suitable friend is to be appointed to register all marriages that may be solemnized within the limits of such meeting. The importance of the duties of this office renders it necessary that it should be kept constantly filled by a person fully competent to act therein, according to the provisions of the law, and who may not be likely to be interrupted in the performance of his duties, by absence from home or other causes. On every fresh appointment of such friend (who, according to the Registration Act, 6 and 7 William IV., c. 86, is designated *a Registering Officer of the Society of Friends*), Monthly Meetings are to take care to report, without delay, by minute signed by the Clerk, his name and address, to the Recording Clerk of the society, No. 86, Houndsditch, London; who is required by the act to certify the same in writing to the Registrar-General in London.* The requisite marriage

---

* Each Registering Officer acts only within the district or Monthly Meeting for which he has been certified as above. An account of our several Monthly Meeting districts has been rendered to the Registrar-General. If a marriage be solemnized at a meeting-house out of the limits of the woman's Monthly Meeting, (see Rule X., page 198,) the marriage is to be registered by the Registering Officer of the Monthly Meeting wherein the said meeting-house is situated; in which case, the certificates of notice and the minute of the woman's Monthly Meeting clearing the parties (see Rule 3, p. 204,) must be delivered to the said officer previously to the marriage.

Registration.

register-books, and printed forms for certified copies thereof, are furnished from the office of the Registrar-General.

8. The Act directs that, as soon as may be after the solemnization of a marriage, the Registering Officer [of the Monthly Meeting] within the limits of which it has been solemnized, "shall register, or cause to be registered," in duplicate books supplied to him, "the several particulars relating to the marriage;" and "such Registering Officer, whether he shall or shall not be present at such marriage, shall satisfy himself, that the proceedings in relation thereto have been conformable to the usages of the society;" and "every such entry shall be signed by the said Registering Officer, and by the parties married, and by two witnesses."

In order to fulfil these requisitions of the Act, this meeting recommends that the register-books be filled up, signed and witnessed at the time of the marriage, or immediately after.* The Registering Officer, having received the certificates of notice, as well as the minute of the woman's Monthly Meeting, informing him that the parties are cleared for marriage, [as directed by Rule 3, p. 204,] is, after the solemnization of the marriage, to register, or cause to be registered, the several particulars in his duplicate register-books according to the following form:—

MARRIAGE REGISTER.

No.	When Married.	Name and Surname.	Age.	Condition.	Rank or Profession.	Residence at the time of Marriage.	Father's name and surname.	Rank or Profession of Father.
1	*6th of 8th mo. 1837.*	*James Smith.*	*Of full age*	*Bachelor.*	*Carpenter*	*No. 46, High Street, Stepney, Middlesex.*	*John Smith.*	*Carpenter*
		Martha Green.	*Minor.*	*Spinster.*		*Grove Farm, near Maidstone, Kent.*	*James Green.*	*Farmer.*

Married in the Friends' Meeting-house, *Maidstone*, according to the usages of the Society of Friends.

This marriage was solemnized between us } *James Smith, Martha Green,* } in the presence of us } *A. B.* Registering Officer. *C. D. Miller, Maidstone. E. F. Druggist, Rochester.*

[The words and figures in italics to be filled up as the case may be.]

* The arrangements necessary to accomplish the object of the due registration of a marriage, under the various circumstances which may occur, must be left to the care and discretion of Monthly Meetings, and of the friends

9. In filling up the registers great care must be used that no error be committed.* On the discovery of any error in an entry, the Registering Officer is required by the Act, within one calendar month after such discovery, in the presence of the parties married, or, in their absence, then in the presence of the Superintendent Registrar of the district, and of two other witnesses, (who are respectively to attest the same,) to correct the error " by entry in the margin, without any alteration of the original entry;" and he is to sign the marginal entry, and add thereto the date when the correction was made. (See section 44 of the Registration Act.) In general, the several particulars of a marriage register should correspond with those of the certificate of notice. Penalties are imposed by the Act for wilful injury or loss of registers.†

10. Every Registering Officer is required to make a quarterly return in the First, Fourth, Seventh, and Tenth Months, of copies of the entries of marriages which have been registered by him in the three calendar months preceding; or, if no marriage has been registered by him in that period, a certificate that such is the case.‡ Blank forms for these certified copies are supplied from the register-office. This return must be delivered to the Superintendent Registrar of the district within which the Registering Officer resides, notwithstanding that the marriages regis-

---

appointed to attend the marriage under Rule IX., [page 197,] as well as of the other parties concerned. Should the Registering Officer be unavoidably prevented from being present at the solemnization of the marriage, care must be taken that the entries be, notwithstanding, duly made and signed by the parties and witnesses; and the Registering Officer, having satisfied himself of the regularity of the proceedings, is afterwards to add his signature.

It will be proper that the friends appointed to attend the marriage, should include in their report to the Monthly Meeting, information of the due registration of the marriage.

* It is recommended that the several names and particulars to be registered, be written down distinctly on a separate paper, previously to their being entered in the registers, in order to ensure greater accuracy.

† The Act directs that, when the duplicate register-books are filled, one of them is to be delivered to the Superintendent Registrar of the district; the other is to remain under the care of Friends, and be kept with their other records.

‡ A penalty, not exceeding £10, is imposed for neglecting to make this return regularly.

tered by him, or some of them, may have been solemnized at meeting-houses situated out of that district, but within the limits of the Monthly Meeting of which he is Registering Officer.

11. As soon as may be after the close of every year, Monthly Meetings are to make a return to the Recording Clerk, No. 86, Houndsditch, London, of all marriages which have taken place, within their compass, during the year. 1833.—1861.

₊ For Counsel in Relation to Marriage see pages 83 to 86.

SECTION XVI.—REGULATIONS FOR RECORDING BIRTHS AND DEATHS.

The Registration Act having established a public civil registry of all births and deaths in England and Wales, in a mode free from objection in reference to our religious testimonies, which registry came into operation on the 1st of the 7th month, 1837, the registry of births and deaths amongst Friends, from that time, has become incorporated with, and forms part of, such public civil registry. The registers of births and burials formerly in use by Monthly and Quarterly Meetings have therefore been discontinued; but, in order that our lists of members may be correctly kept, and that evidence may be preserved of all interments which take place in our burial grounds, one or more suitable friends are to be appointed, in every Monthly Meeting, to issue birth and burial notes. The persons so appointed, on filling up such notes, are to enter, in a check-margin, the requisite particulars, and the name of the person to whom the notes are delivered. After passing the Monthly Meeting, and, where necessary, being entered in the list of members, the birth and burial notes are to be delivered to the friend who issued them, and affixed to the check-margins from which they were taken;* and when such books, after having been filled up, are no longer required for reference, they are to be delivered up to the Monthly Meeting, to be deposited with its records. 1846.—1861.

* In the case of burial-notes, the Registrar's certificate should also be affixed, when practicable.

SECT. XVI.] RECORDING OF BIRTHS AND DEATHS.

Births.

1. In the case of a birth, notice should be given thereof by the parent or occupier of the house, within forty-two days after the birth, to the Registrar of the district within which it took place; who is required, without fee, to make an entry of the name of the child, and other particulars to be registered.* It is important that the entry should be made within the time prescribed, and that the informant should see that it is correctly made.†

2. In order to secure the evidence of the right of membership in our Society to those children who are entitled thereto according to its rules, and to bring them regularly under the notice of the respective Monthly Meetings to which they belong, in addition to giving notice of the birth of any such child to the Registrar of the district, there is to be prepared forthwith a note in the form hereto subjoined, to be signed by the parent or some other friend of the child; and such note is to be produced to the Monthly Meeting in which the child is entitled to membership, and a minute is to be made thereat, noticing the production of such note, the date of the birth, the names of the parents and of the child, and the place and date of public registry; after which, the friend who has the care of the list of members is to enter the particulars thereof in such list. It is recommended that Monthly Meetings exercise a watchful care, either through their overseers, or by the friends appointed to issue birth-notes, or in such other way as may be judged best, to ensure the early and regular production of these notes, as above directed.

The Monthly Meeting of   is hereby informed that
on the   day of the   month, one thousand
eight hundred and   , was born at
in the Parish of   in the   of
unto   of   in the Parish of
            in the   of   (a)
and   his wife   who was named

(a) Here add the description, as "Grocer," "Merchant," &c.

* Day of birth, name, sex, name and surname of father, name and maiden name of mother, rank or profession of father, date of registry, signature and address of informant, and signature of Registrar.

† A certified copy of the entry may be had, either at the time of the registration of the birth or afterwards; for which a fee of two shillings and sixpence is payable, and which certified copy is legal evidence of the birth.

*and whose birth was registered at the public reg[ister]
district of   on the
                    month, 18*

Read and entered at   Monthl[y]
Society of Friends, held the   day [of]
Month, 18

(b) To be signed here by the parent or other friend[.]

₊ This note is to be produced without delay to the [Monthly Meeting] which the child is entitled to membersh[ip].

Deaths.   3. In the case of a death, some person pres[ent]
or in attendance during the last illness, or the [other]
inmate of the house in which such death occurre[d, within]
five days* of such death, give information to [the Registrar of]
the district, of the name of the deceased, and [the particulars]
to be registered.†

4. The Act further provides that the " Regis[trar]
upon registering any death, or as soon thereaft[er as]
required so to do, shall, without fee, deliver t[o the undertaker]
or other person having charge of the funeral, [a certificate that]
such death has been duly registered;" "and i[f any body]
shall be buried, for which no such certificate sh[all have been]
delivered, the person" burying "shall forthw[ith give notice]
thereof to the Registrar;" "and every perso[n burying]
any dead body, for which no certificate shall [have been]
made and delivered, as aforesaid," "and who [shall not within]
seven days give notice thereof to the Registr[ar, shall forfeit a]
fine of £10.

5. In order to insure attention to the forego[ing provisions of]
the Act, this meeting directs, that care be tak[en that a cer-]
tificate of the Registrar of the district within [five days]

---

* The Act states *eight* days: but the earlier registrat[ion is]
obviously desirable.

† Day of death, name and surname, residence, age, rank [or profession]
of the deceased, cause of death; to which are also to be [added the name]
and address of informant, the date of registry, and the si[gnature of the Registrar.]
A certified copy of the entry, which is legal evidence o[f the death, may be]
had on payment of a fee of two shillings and sixpence.

took place, be obtained by the person having charge of the funeral, previously to any interment taking place. Care is also to be taken that no grave be made in any of our burial grounds without an order from the friend appointed to issue burial-notes, which order is to be in the following form:—

To the Grave-maker at Friends' Burial-ground at
in the Parish of   in the   of
    Make a grave for the interment of the body of
which is appointed to take place on the   day of the
    month, 18   at   o'clock in the   noon.
                        (a)
      The   day of the   month, 18

(a) To be signed here by the friend appointed to issue burial-notes.

All orders for burial are to be preserved by the grave-maker, but not to be produced to the Monthly Meeting.

6. In every case of the burial of a member of our Society, whether in one of our burial-grounds or in a public cemetery, and also in every case of the burial of any person, not a member, in one of our burial-grounds, a burial-note is to be filled up and signed immediately after the interment, and is to be produced without delay to the Monthly Meeting within the compass of which the burial-ground or cemetery is situated.* Burial-notes are to be in the following form:—

This is to certify that the body of   of
in the parish of   in the   of
                 (a)
who died the   day of the   month, one
thousand eight hundred and   aged about
and whose death was registered at the public registry-office for the
district of   on the   day of the
month, 18   was buried in the (b)   in the parish
of   in the   of   on the

(a) Here insert description, including, in the case of a wife, widow, or child, the name or names of the husband or parents.

(b) "Friends' burial-ground" or "cemetery," as the case may be.

* In the case of the burial-grounds of London, the burial-note is to be produced to the Monthly Meeting whose officer shall have given it out.

Deaths.   day of the   month, 18
                               Witness (c)
       Read and entered at   Monthly Meeting of the
    Society of Friends, held the   of   month, 18
                                                            Clerk.

(c) To be signed here by the undertaker, grave-maker, or superintendent of cemetery, stating which of these capacities the person signing fills.

7. If the deceased were a member of another Monthly Meeting, a notification of the name, age, description, residence, date of death, and places and dates of public registry and interment, is to be transmitted from the former to the latter Monthly Meeting, in the following form :—

            To   Monthly Meeting of Friends.
    We hereby inform you that   of   in the
parish of   in the   of
aged about   died the   day of the
month, one thousand eight hundred and   and that
h   death was registered at the public registry office for the district
of   on the   day of the
month, 18   The body of the aforesaid friend was interred in
the   in the parish of   in the
of   on the   day of the
month, 18 .
    Signed in and on behalf of   Monthly Meeting, held
at   the   of the   month, 18
                                                            Clerk.

8. On the production of a burial-note, or of such notification as aforesaid, (as the case may be) to the Monthly Meeting of which the deceased was a member, a minute is to be made recording the name and the date of death, and the place and date of public registry; after which the friend who has the care of the list of members is to enter the particulars thereof in such list. The same course is to be pursued in regard to the burial-note of a member of another Monthly Meeting, or of a person not a member of our Society; except that no entry thereof is to be made in the list of members, and that a record is to be made on the burial-note and in the Monthly Meeting minute-book, specifying the Monthly Meeting of which the deceased was a member, or that the deceased was not a member (as the case may be).

9. Notwithstanding the establishment of the public civil registry of deaths, the Bank of England and many other public bodies, by way of precaution, insist on the production of a certificate of burial. The friend in whose custody, for the time being, is the book containing the burial-notes, is the person to give this certificate. With the view of promoting accuracy and uniformity in these certificates, blank forms will be supplied by the Meeting for Sufferings to the different Monthly Meetings for the purpose.

10. As soon as may be after the close of every year, Monthly Meetings are to make a return to the Recording Clerk, No. 86, Houndsditch, London, of all births and deaths which have taken place within their compass during the year.

SECTION XVII.—REMOVALS.

WE feel it our concern to caution Friends to be very circumspect how they remove themselves and their families from the places of their residence: it having been observed that the dissolving of old, and the forming of new, connexions, have, in many instances, been attended with effects prejudicial to a growth in the truth and the service thereof, both in the heads and younger branches of families; especially where the inclination to such removals hath originated in worldly motives. And, as the growth and establishment of children in a religious life and conversation, being the most interesting, ought to be the principal, engagement of the minds of parents, we desire that, in putting them forward in a way of life, the probable effect it may have on their minds may be the chief object in view. We recommend Friends, both young and old, in these cases, to give close attention to the pointings of divine wisdom, and also timely to consult experienced friends, previously to their resolving to change their situation. 1784. P. E.—1833.—1861.   *Counsel*

Regulations.

1. All friends removing from one Monthly Meeting to another are to have certificates from the Monthly Meeting of which they are members, recommending them to that into the compass of which they are removed; and it is considered, as obviously of importance, that such recommendation should take place without any unnecessary delay, in order that the individuals may come under the early notice and oversight of the meeting, within the district of which they are residing. If, on removal, any friend does not himself apply for a certificate, the Monthly Meeting from which he is removed is to recommend him without such application. In case this should be omitted for the space of three months, the Monthly Meeting into which such friend is removed, is at liberty to apply for a certificate; and any Monthly Meeting to which an application of this kind shall be made, is to comply therewith, or assign sufficient reasons for not doing so.

2. Before issuing a certificate of removal, Monthly Meetings are, except in the case of a young person under, or about, the age of sixteen years, to make a suitable appointment of friends, for the purpose of inquiry respecting the conduct of the person removing. Such inquiry is also to extend to the situation of the party with respect to pecuniary circumstances, so that care may be effectually taken not to proceed to a recommendation, if the individual removing has disreputably omitted to discharge, or to make proper arrangements relative to, his just debts.

3. After inquiry made, agreeably to the last preceding rule, and report thereon, the Monthly Meeting shall, unless anything appear in the conduct (including that which relates to pecuniary engagements) of the party removing, to require its notice of him as a delinquent, proceed to issue a certificate of removal on his behalf. Such certificates are to be in one or other of the following forms:—

    To   *Monthly Meeting of Friends.*
Dear Friends,
    A.B., *a member of this meeting, has removed to* (a) *in the compass of yours, and, upon inquiry made relative to his conduct and respecting debts, nothing appears to prevent the issuing of a certificate on his behalf; we therefore re-*

(a) Here insert the residence of the party removed.

commend him to your Christian care, and remain with love,
Your Friends.

Signed in and on behalf of   Monthly Meeting, held
at   the   of   mo, 18
J. K., Clerk.

If the certificate respects a female, add :—
Signed in and on behalf of the Women's Monthly Meeting.
L. M., Clerk.

A wife is to be included in the same certificate as her husband : children under the age of sixteen years (or about that age at the discretion of Monthly Meetings) are, on removal with their parents, to be also recommended without separate certificates. In the case of a wife, and of children as thus pointed out, a certificate is to assume this form :—

A. B., *and* C. *his Wife, members of this meeting, have removed to   in the compass of yours, and, upon inquiry made relative to their conduct and respecting debts, nothing appears to prevent the issuing of a certificate on their behalf; we therefore recommend them to your Christian care, with their children,* D., E., F., *&c., and remain, &c.*

For a young person under the age of sixteen years (or about that age at the discretion of Monthly Meetings) who, in consequence of separately removing, or from any other cause, is the sole subject of a certificate, the following form may suffice :—

A. B., *a minor, a member of this meeting, has removed to   in the compass of yours, and nothing appears to prevent the issuing of a certificate on his behalf; we therefore recommend him to your Christian care, and remain, &c.*

If a friend, on whose behalf a certificate is issued, is an acknowledged minister, information thereof is to be included in the certificate ; and, in the case of a woman friend in the station of a minister removed by marriage, information of her being in that station is to be communicated by minute. The same course is to be pursued in the case of an elder, if the removal be into another Monthly Meeting within the limits of the same Quarterly Meeting.

The signature of the Clerk or Clerks is to be considered as

⁎⁎* In all cases, certificates are to be accompanied with the address of a friend to whom the acknowledgment of its acceptance may be addressed.

Regulations.

sufficiently authenticating a certificate. If the certificate be addressed to any Monthly Meeting in America, it is to be countersigned by one of our correspondents in London for the Yearly Meeting of which the said Monthly Meeting forms a part.

4. On receiving certificates, Monthly Meetings are to appoint a few friends to visit the persons recommended. This, it should be borne in mind, will furnish occasion for encouraging the appearances of good, as well as of advising against those of a contrary tendency; and may be the introduction to an acquaintance fruitful of future advantage; an advantage which may, in an especial manner, prove a blessing to such of the younger part of our Society as are placed in exposed situations, if they should thus obtain the kind and watchful care and counsel of judicious friends.

5. On accepting a certificate, either upon receiving the report of such a visit or previously, an acknowledgment is to be transmitted to the Monthly Meeting which issued it, in the following form:—

To the Monthly Meeting of
We hereby inform you of our acceptance, this day, of your certificate on behalf of   , dated the   of   month, 18
Signed in and on behalf of   Monthly Meeting,
held at   the   of   month, 18
                                                A. B., Clerk.

6. If a Monthly Meeting, to which a certificate is delivered, shall find that the party is not resident within its district, it may forward the certificate to any other Monthly Meeting, within the compass of which he does reside, informing the recommending Monthly Meeting thereof. But, if this be not done, or if, on any ground, the Monthly Meeting to which a certificate is delivered, shall deem the same improper to be accepted, it shall return such certificate to the Monthly Meeting issuing it, and state the reason. Such return and statement are to be made, at the latest, from the second Monthly Meeting after that at which the certificate has been delivered; or acceptance at such second Monthly Meeting is to be inferred.

7. Upon the acceptance of a certificate, either by acknowledgment or inference, as aforesaid, a friend becomes a member of the accepting Monthly Meeting in all respects. 1833.—1860.

SECTION XVIII.—ARBITRATION.

It is advised that, in all cases of controversy and difference, the persons concerned therein either speedily compose the difference between themselves, or make choice of some faithful, unconcerned, impartial friends to determine the same; and that all Friends take heed of being parties with one another. 1692. P. E.—1833. *(Counsel.)*

Let Friends everywhere be careful that all differences about outward things be speedily composed, either between themselves, or by arbitrators: and it would be well that Friends were at all times ready to submit their differences, even with persons not of our religious persuasion, to arbitration, rather than to contend at law. "Hear the causes between your brethren, and judge righteously between every man and his brother, and the stranger that is with him." 1737.—1833.

It is the advice of this meeting, that persons differing about outward things do, as little as may be, trouble ministering friends with being arbitrators in such cases. 1697.

---

1. If any Friend shall refuse speedily to end a difference in which he is a party concerned, or to refer it as before advised, or shall fail to appoint an arbitrator within the period of one month after notice in writing so to do has been given him by the overseers or other friends who have given advice on the subject, they being of opinion that such case of difference should be referred to arbitration and having unavailingly endeavoured to effect the same, the case should then be reported to the Monthly Meeting to which the friend belongs; and, if such meeting is also of the judgment that the case ought to be so referred, and the friend shall still refuse to refer it, or fail to appoint an arbitrator without further delay, the Monthly Meeting, after the exercise of due care, and with a just regard to the interests of all parties, is to express its disunity with his conduct, and may proceed to disown him as a member of our Society. *(General Regulations.)*

2. When cases of difference are referred, and judgment and award are made, signed, and given thereupon, the parties con-

General Regulations.

cerned are to stand to and perform the said award; and, if any one shall refuse so to do, the Monthly Meeting to which such person belongs, upon notice thereof to them given, shall admonish him thereunto; and if, after admonition, he persist to refuse, the meeting may then proceed to disownment.

3. If any friends that shall be chosen to hear and determine any difference (after they have accepted thereof, and the parties differing have become bound to stand to their determination) shall decline and refuse to stand and act as arbitrators, the person or persons so refusing are to be required to give the reasons of their refusal unto the Monthly Meeting to which they belong; and, if that meeting shall not esteem those reasons sufficient justly to excuse them, the meeting is to press them to stand to what they have accepted; and if, after such admonition, they shall continue to refuse to stand as arbitrators, the meeting may proceed to disown them, or either of them, as members of our Society.

4. This meeting concludes, with respect to the appointing of arbitrators in cases of differences between Friends, that a person, or persons, not of our religious Society may be chosen to the office, if both parties unite in agreeing thereto. The concurrence of the overseers, or of the Monthly Meeting, is also to be had, if the case is under their or its notice. It is, however, the judgment of this meeting, that the long-established practice of confining the choice to Friends should, as much as circumstances will admit, be still observed.

5. Whereas cases may arise, in which it may be needful for proceedings at law to be taken, each Quarterly Meeting is desired to appoint a committee, with power to grant, in its discretion, permission to proceed at law or in equity, as the case may appear to require. If all the parties are members of the same Quarterly Meeting, the committee of that meeting is to be the approving one; if not, the approbation is to be obtained at a joint conference of all the committees of the respective Quarterly Meetings of which any one individual on either side is a member. Any such committee or conference is to be summoned, in the cases under this regulation, at the instance of either party, by any one of its members; and not less than three are to be competent to act. In the case of a joint conference, at least one

friend from each Quarterly Meeting's committee is to be present. Quarterly Meetings are directed annually to read over the names of the friends on the committee, and to transmit them to their Monthly Meetings, and also to furnish the Recording Clerk in London with a list of them.

6. If, however, any members of our Society, after having contracted debts or otherwise become legally responsible, should prove so unworthy as to remove themselves, or to remove or appropriate property or effects, or to act in any other way inconsistent with justice and fair dealing, permission in writing to take legal proceedings may be granted by any two members of one of the before-mentioned committees, after having together heard the circumstances of the case, and being unitedly satisfied that it is one which does not admit of delay.

7. It is the sense and judgment of this meeting that, if any member of our Society shall arrest, sue, or implead at law any other member thereof, except under permission granted as provided in the two preceding regulations, such person ought to be dealt with for the same by the meeting to which he belongs; and, if he shall not give satisfaction to the meeting for such his disorderly proceeding, that then he may be disowned by the meeting. Or, if the party so sued or arrested, taking with him, or, if under confinement, sending, one or two friends to the person who goes to law, shall complain thereof, the said person shall be required immediately to stay proceedings; and, if he does not comply with such requisition, the Monthly Meeting to which he belongs may disown him, if the case require it.

8. This meeting is of the judgment, that the rules for the settlement of differences about property are not to be considered as binding upon trustees or executors acting for others, in the performance of their duties as such; nor upon any Friends acting on behalf of, and so as to incur a legal responsibility to, persons not of our religious Society.

9. Matters of defamation are not subjects to be arbitrated, until the defamation is proved, as well as the fact that some injury is sustained by the defamed in his trade or property; and in that case the damage should be submitted to arbitration. 1697.—1782.—1828.—1833.—1860.

Mode of conducting Arbitration.

I. Each party having chosen one or two indifferent, impartial and judicious friends, those so chosen are to agree upon a third, or a fifth friend (unless the parties first agree in the nomination) whose name is to be inserted with the others in the bonds of arbitration, or other written agreement.

II. The arbitrators so appointed, or the majority of them, are to fix the time and place of their meeting.

III. The arbitrators are not to consider themselves as advocates for the party by whom they are chosen, but men whose incumbent duty it is to judge righteously, fearing the Lord. They are to shun all previous information respecting the case, that they may not become biassed in their judgments before they hear both parties together.

IV. The parties are to enter into written engagements, or bonds in the usual form, if either of them require it, to abide by the award of the arbitrators, or a majority of them, to be made in a limited time.

V. Every meeting of the arbitrators is to be made known to the parties concerned, until they have been fully heard; nor are there to be any separate, private meetings, between some of the arbitrators, or with one party separate from the other, on the business referred to them; and no representation of the case of one party, either by writing or otherwise, is to be admitted, without its being fully made known to the other, and, if required, a copy is to be delivered to the other party.

VI. The arbitrators are to hear both parties fully, in the presence of each other, whilst either hath any fresh matter to offer, until a certain time to be limited by the arbitrators. Let no evidence or witness be withheld or rejected.

VII. If there should appear to the arbitrators, or to one or more of them, to be any doubtful point of law, the majority of them are to agree upon a case, and consult counsel thereupon. The arbitrators are not required to express in the award the reasons for their decision. One writing of the award is to be delivered to each party.

VIII. Arbitrators are to propose to the parties that they should give an acknowledgment in writing, before the award be made, that they have been candidly and fully heard. 1782.—1833.

SECTION XIX.—APPEALS.

DEAR friends, in the spirit of the Gospel, which is peace on earth and good will to all men, labour to maintain the discipline of the church; wherein you will be favoured with wisdom, prudently to determine the affairs that may come before you, and be instrumental to prevent appeals from coming to this meeting, which tend to prolong it, and give uneasiness to Friends. 1736.

RULES FOR THE CONDUCTING OF APPEALS.

1. If any person shall, after a final decision in his case by any Monthly Meeting, (which final decision, where disownment takes place, is the issuing of a minute or testimony against him) think himself* injured or aggrieved by its proceedings in the case, he may appeal to the Quarterly Meeting of which such Monthly Meeting forms a part. Notice of such intended appeal is to be given, in writing, to the Monthly Meeting within three months after such decision is communicated, by or on behalf of such meeting, to the party concerned; or if, because the party could not be found, or by reason of his having left the kingdom, the decision has not been so communicated, then within two years, at the furthest, after the issuing of it. *Appeals to Quarterly Meetings.*

2. The appeal is to be brought to the first or second Quarterly Meeting which occurs after the Monthly Meeting immediately succeeding that at which the notice above-mentioned has been given. In the notice, the appellant shall specify to which of the two he means to present his appeal. If he has made choice of the first, and circumstances should arise to prevent him from pursuing his intention, he is to be at liberty to bring the appeal to the second Quarterly Meeting, provided that previously thereto he renew his notice to the Monthly Meeting. The Monthly Meeting receiving notice of appeal, as first mentioned, shall appoint respondents to act on its behalf, and shall inform the appellant that an appointment has been made. If, in the

---

* [*or herself, &c.*]; persons of both sexes having equal right of appeal.

Appeals to Quarterly Meetings judgment of the Monthly Meeting, such notice of appeal be given before a final decision in the case, the Monthly Meeting, instead of appointing respondents, is to send forward to the Quarterly Meeting a minute, stating that a final decision has not been given in the case, and that consequently the appellant has no right of appeal, which minute the Quarterly Meeting shall, without entering into the case, record as its judgment. But, after the final decision of the case, the Monthly Meeting shall not be at liberty to omit or delay the appointment of respondents, either because it does not deem the case one that admits of appeal, or on any other ground.

3. The appeal, in writing and sealed up, is to be delivered to the clerk for the time being, soon after the representatives are called over, with an endorsement simply specifying the appellant, his assistant, or assistants, (if any are intended) the meeting appealed against, and that appealed to. The indorsement shall be read, and also the minute of the Monthly Meeting appointing respondents to act on its behalf. But, if no respondents have been appointed, nor any minute produced from the Monthly Meeting informing the Quarterly Meeting that a final decision has not been given in the case, the Quarterly Meeting, without appointing any committee or otherwise entering into the case, shall direct the Monthly Meeting to make the necessary appointment, in order to the appeal being heard at the ensuing Quarterly Meeting. If, at the ensuing Quarterly Meeting, no appointment of respondents is reported, the Quarterly Meeting, without entering into the case, is at once to record a reversal of the decision appealed against.

4. Unless an appeal relate to matter of faith and doctrine, and unless the Quarterly Meeting is satisfied thereof, and also inclines that, without any previous reference, it should be heard in the meeting itself, such meeting shall, when any appeal is so brought as above, proceed to nominate a committee of twelve disinterested Friends, to hear the same and judge thereof; the appellant, and the assistant or assistants of an appellant, and the respondents having withdrawn previously to such nomination. No member of a Monthly Meeting appealed against is to be at liberty to take any part in nominating the committee of the Quarterly Meeting.

5. After the nomination has taken place the appellant and respondents shall be called in, the names of the proposed committee are to be read in their presence, and each party is to be allowed (after having had the opportunity, if desired, of withdrawing a short time for consultation) to object to any of the committee, not exceeding three. In objecting, no cause shall be assigned. The places of the friends who have been thus objected to shall be supplied by a fresh nomination; which nomination shall be final.

6. The appointment of the committee being completed, a time and place shall be fixed for their meeting, of which due notice is to be given to the parties concerned. On the principle of the importance of promoting the speedy settlement of differences, the time shall be as early an one as can with convenience be chosen.

7. The committee, not less than ten of whom are to be a quorum, shall, when met, proceed upon the business referred to them, by opening and reading the appeal in the presence of the appellant and respondents. In case an appeal referred to a committee be found by them to relate to faith and doctrine, the committee shall, without proceeding further, report accordingly to the Quarterly Meeting, that the said meeting may decide whether the appeal shall be heard in the meeting itself, or be again referred to the committee.

8. In all appeals heard by a committee of a Quarterly Meeting, the appellant shall, after the appeal has been read, be heard in support thereof, and afterwards the respondents in reply, in the presence of each other, until both parties have been fully and fairly heard; after which the parties are to withdraw previously to the committee's deliberation on the case.

9. When, in the committee, the whole or the greater part of the members present (such members present not being less than the quorum) have agreed in a judgment on the case, a report in writing shall be prepared, which is to be signed, as the report of the committee, by those so uniting in judgment. If the members so present as above are equally divided in judgment, the report shall be in favour of the appealing party. The committee shall not be expected to assign any reasons for the judgment expressed in their report; and it is recommended,

Appeals to Quarterly Meetings. that the purport of it be simply the confirming or annulling of the decision of the Monthly Meeting.

10. The committee shall give notice in writing to both parties, of the time when it is intended to deliver in the report; which is to be at an adjournment of the Quarterly Meeting, or at the next Quarterly Meeting in course.

11. The report of the committee shall be read in the Quarterly Meeting, in the presence of both parties, if they incline to attend; and, except when the circumstance occurs which forms the subject of the next succeeding rule, and with the exception also of such appeals relating to faith and doctrine as may come to be opened in the Quarterly Meeting itself, according to the liberty hereafter given (see Rule 13), the judgment expressed in any such report shall be recorded as the decision of the Quarterly Meeting in the case.

12. If, in the case of an appeal not relating to faith and doctrine brought by an individual in consequence of his disownment, the report of the committee, confirmatory of the judgment of the Monthly Meeting, be signed by less than eight of its number, such judgment is to be reversed.

13. The report of any committee, expressing a judgment on the merits of an appeal relating to faith and doctrine, may be objected to by the party against whom it is given, and such party may require the case to be heard by the meeting itself.

14. Whenever an appeal relating to faith and doctrine comes to be heard in the Quarterly Meeting itself, the following regulations are to be observed:—

First—The appeal is to be read in the presence of both parties, and the appellant shall then be heard in support of the same, and afterwards the respondents in reply, in the presence of each other, until both parties have been fully and fairly heard.

Second—In stating and replying, no persons are to be permitted to speak on the case but those who, as or for the appellant and as respondents, are immediately concerned in the appeal; except that any friend (not being a member of a Monthly Meeting concerned in the appeal, or of a committee that may have heard it and reported a judgment on the merits thereof) who may apprehend it proper for a question to be put to either party, shall have the liberty of requesting that it may be done through the clerk.

Third.—The parties immediately concerned in the appeal shall withdraw, previously to the meeting's deliberation on the case; and, after they have so withdrawn, or during their absence in consequence of any prior withdrawing, no member of a meeting concerned in the appeal, or of a committee that may have heard it and reported a judgment on the merits thereof, is to be allowed to speak on the subject before the meeting.

Fourth.—When the meeting has come to a conclusion in the case, its decision shall be entered on minute, and then the parties are to be at liberty to come in again and hear it read.

15. In all cases, a copy of the minute of the Quarterly Meeting recording its decision in the case, shall be sent to each party.

16. Should any Quarterly Meeting be unable to appoint, on an appeal, a committee of disinterested friends to the number of twelve, such Quarterly Meeting shall, after making its own appointment, apply to some neighbouring Quarterly Meeting, for such an addition as may be necessary to complete the number: in which case notice is to be given to the appellant and respondents of the intended application, that they may have the opportunity of attending such neighbouring Quarterly Meeting, and exercising (according to Rule 5) their right of objection, if such right has not been before exhausted. And such meeting is to be informed by the applying Quarterly Meeting, whether any and what right of objection remains to the respective parties.

⁎⁎ See also General Rules relating to Appeals, p. 230.

---

17. If any person shall think himself injured or aggrieved by the judgment of any Quarterly Meeting given against him, he may appeal from such judgment to the Yearly Meeting; in which case, notice, in writing, of his intention to appeal, is to be given by him, not later than to the second Quarterly Meeting after that at which such judgment has been recorded. *Appeals to the Yearly Meeting.*

Appeals to the Yearly Meeting.

18. A Quarterly Meeting receiving such notice shall appoint respondents to act on its behalf, and shall inform the appellant that an appointment has been made. But, if notice of appeal be given to a Quarterly Meeting relating to a case in which the said meeting has been informed, by minute of the Monthly Meeting concerned, that a final decision has not been given, the Quarterly Meeting, instead of appointing respondents, is to send forward to the Yearly Meeting a minute, stating that a final decision has not been given in the case, and that consequently the appellant has, at that time, no right of appeal; which minute the Yearly Meeting shall, without entering into the case, record as its judgment. But no Quarterly Meeting shall be at liberty to omit the appointment of respondents on any other ground.

19. If any person, having given notice of his intention of appealing, is prevented from bringing his appeal to the Yearly Meeting immediately succeeding such notice, he may continue his appeal to the next following Yearly Meeting, on renewing his notice in writing to the meeting appealed against, at any time preceding the second Yearly Meeting. In this case, however, the appeal shall not be received, unless satisfactory reasons for the delay be stated to the Yearly Meeting, or to its committee on the appeal.

20. The appeal, in writing and sealed up, is to be delivered to the clerk for the time being, before the close of the first sitting of the Yearly Meeting, with an indorsement simply specifying the appellant, his assistant or assistants, (if any are intended) the meeting appealed against, and that appealed to. The indorsement shall be read, and also the minute of the Quarterly Meeting appointing respondents to act on its behalf.

21. An appeal having been delivered in, the representatives are to meet at the close of the first sitting of the Yearly Meeting, and a committee shall be by them nominated to hear and judge of the appeal, agreeably to the following regulations.

22. The committee shall consist of one representative from each meeting in Great Britain represented in the Yearly Meeting, with the exception of the meeting against which the appeal is brought, and of any meeting appealing, or to which belongs a subordinate meeting appealing; the representatives of which

excepted meeting or meetings shall withdraw previously to the nomination.*

23. After the nomination has taken place, the appellant and respondents in each case of appeal are to be called in, the names of the proposed committee shall be read in their presence, and each party is to be allowed (after having had the opportunity, if desired, of withdrawing a short time for consultation) to object to any of the committee, not exceeding six respectively, but shall not assign any cause for such objection; after which they are to withdraw. If any of the committee be so objected to, they shall be set aside, but only as to that particular appeal. Their places are to be supplied from the other representatives of the Quarterly Meetings to which they respectively belong; but in case of there being no representative left from any such Quarterly Meeting, the deficiency shall be made up by nominating one friend out of each such meeting in alphabetical order, that has not fewer than four representatives present, beginning, at any future time, with the next meeting in rotation. And any or all of those nominated in the stead of others first selected and set aside, as above mentioned, shall themselves be liable to be objected to by either party; in which case a further nomination to supply their places shall be made in like manner as before: but this third is to be a final nomination.

24. The committee or committees thus nominated shall be reported to the Yearly Meeting at its second or third sitting, when all appeals are to be delivered to the committee or committees, in order to be immediately proceeded on; not less than three-fourths of the number appointed for a particular appeal being at any time present thereon.

25. All appeals are to be opened and read in the presence of the respective appellants and respondents. In case an appeal shall be found to relate to matter of faith and doctrine, the committee shall, without proceeding further, report accordingly to the Yearly Meeting; that the said meeting may decide whether

---

* If there be two appeals, the committee thus selected shall be considered as also nominated to hear the second, with similar exception as is provided with regard to the first; and with the addition of a representative from the meeting, or each of the meetings, before excepted: and so on for any number of appeals.

Appeals to the Yearly Meeting. to proceed to hear the appeal in the meeting itself, or to refer it again to the committee.

26. In all appeals heard by a committee of the Yearly Meeting, the appellant shall, after the appeal has been read, be heard in support thereof, and afterwards the respondents in reply, in the presence of each other, until both parties have been fully and fairly heard; after which the parties are to withdraw previously to the committee's deliberation on the case.

27. When, in the committee, the whole or the greater part of the members present (such members present not being less than the quorum) have agreed in a judgment on the case, a report in writing is to be prepared, which is to be signed, as the report of the committee, by those so uniting in judgment. If the members so present as above are equally divided in judgment, the report shall be in favour of the party originally appealing. The committee shall not be expected to assign any reasons for the judgment expressed in their report, and it is recommended that the purport of it be simply the confirming or annulling of the decision of the Quarterly Meeting.

28. The committee shall give notice in writing, to both parties, of the time when it is intended to deliver in their report.

29. The report of the committee shall be read in the Yearly Meeting, in the presence of both parties, if they incline to attend; and, except when the circumstance occurs which forms the subject of the next succeeding rule (Rule 30), and with the exception also of such appeals relating to faith and doctrine as may come to be opened in the Yearly Meeting itself, according to the liberty hereafter given (Rule 31), the judgment expressed in any such report is to be recorded as the decision of the Yearly Meeting in the case.

30. If, in the case of an appeal not relating to faith and doctrine, in which the disownment of an individual is involved, the report of the committee, confirmatory of the disownment, be signed by less than two-thirds of its number, the individual is to be reinstated in membership.

31. The report of any committee expressing a judgment on the merits of an appeal relating to faith and doctrine, may be objected to by the party against whom it is given, and such party may require the case to be heard by the meeting itself.

32. Whenever an appeal relating to faith and doctrine comes to be heard in the Yearly Meeting itself, the following regulations are to be observed:—

First.—The appeal is to be read in the presence of both parties, and the appellant shall then be heard in support of the same, and afterwards the respondents in reply, in the presence of each other, until both parties have been fully and fairly heard.

Second.—In stating and replying, no persons are to be permitted to speak on the case, but those who, as or for the appellant, and as respondents, or as original appellant, are immediately concerned in the appeal; except that any friend (not being a member of a Quarterly Meeting concerned in the appeal, or of a committee that may have heard it, and reported a judgment on the merits thereof) who may apprehend it proper for a question to be put to either party, shall have the liberty of requesting that it may be done through the clerk.

Third.—The parties immediately concerned in the appeal shall withdraw previously to the meeting's deliberation on the case, and, after they have so withdrawn, or during their absence in consequence of any prior withdrawing, no member of a meeting concerned in the appeal, or of a committee that may have heard it and reported a judgment on the merits thereof, is to be allowed to speak on the subject before the meeting.

Fourth.—When the meeting has come to a conclusion in the case its decision shall be entered on minute, and then the parties are to be at liberty to come in again and hear it read.

33. The respondents on behalf of a Quarterly Meeting, in any case of appeal from a Monthly Meeting in which an individual is concerned as original appellant, shall be accompanied by such individual, if he incline to attend; who, so attending, is to have an equal right with them of being heard. If, in the committee of the Yearly Meeting, the decision should be against such respondents, and they should be willing to submit to such decision, the original appellant shall, nevertheless, in appeals relating to faith and doctrine, have such right as appellants possess under

Rule 31, of requiring that the matter be opened in the meeting itself; in which case such person is to appear in the character of appellant, and the friends appointed by the Monthly Meeting in that of respondents.

34. In every case, a copy of the minute of the Yearly Meeting recording its decision thereon, shall be sent to each party.

35. No appeal that has once been determined by the Yearly Meeting shall be received a second time.

₊ See also the following General Rules.

<small>General Rules relating to Appeals.</small>

36. The notice to be given to any Monthly or Quarterly Meeting of an intended appeal shall be according to the following form, or in words to the like effect:—

To the Monthly [or *Quarterly*] *Meeting of   to be held at   the   day of   month, 18   .*

I hereby give notice that I intend to appeal to the Quarterly Meeting of   [or to the Yearly Meeting] to be held at [or in]   the   day of   month, 18   , against your decision in my case.

A. B.

37. In all cases of appeal, whether to a Quarterly or to the Yearly Meeting, in which notice and renewed notice shall be given by the appellant, such appellant shall, three weeks at least previously to the time of holding the meeting specified in the first notice, apprise the clerk of the Monthly or Quarterly Meeting appealed against, that the appeal is not about to be then brought.

38. If either of the parties concerned in an appeal, when stating or replying to the case, shall digress into irrelevant matter, it is recommended that the committee or meeting before which the appeal is brought, do, through the medium of the clerk, stop such proceeding, and require that the subject of the appeal be kept to. And no member of a committee or meeting, by which any appeal is heard, is to express, in the presence of the parties, any opinion on the subject or subjects at issue.

39. If any member of a committee on an appeal be prevented attending during any part of the time in which the case is pro-

ceeded in by the appellant and respondents, he cannot afterwards unite with the rest, either in the further hearing of the case, or in the deliberation upon it, unless with the previous consent of the appellant and respondents.

40. All committees appointed to hear and judge of an appeal, shall, after having had the case duly laid before them, require the parties to sign an acknowledgment that they have been fully and fairly heard; such acknowledgment to be brought, with the report of the committee, to the meeting appointing it. If either party refuse to sign an acknowledgment of this tenor, the committee in making their report shall give in a statement that the parties have been fully and fairly heard, according to the judgment of at least four-fifths of the members present at the decision; which statement shall, as to any further procedure in the case, have the same effect as an acknowledgment.

41. If an appellant shall print his appeal, or any matter relating thereto, or cause to be printed, or be in any way accessary to the printing of the same, such appeal shall not be received by the Quarterly or Yearly Meeting. And if any Monthly or Quarterly Meeting appealed against, or the respondents appointed on its behalf, shall print, or cause to be printed, or be in any way accessary to the printing of, any matter respecting an appeal, such respondents and their constituent meeting are to be precluded from being heard in defence of the judgment appealed against; the effect of which (provided the appellant has proceeded regularly) shall be a reversal of such judgment.

42. The foregoing rules and regulations are to apply to any meeting which shall consider itself injured or aggrieved by the decision of any other meeting.

43. An appellant shall be allowed to avail himself, throughout the course of prosecuting his appeal, of the aid of one or two members of our Society, in speaking on the case on his behalf, or in otherwise assisting him, or in conducting the appeal in his stead: but the appellant is not to be himself absent, unless from some reasonable cause, approved by the committee or meeting hearing the appeal.

44. Informalities in procedure which, in the judgment of at least four-fifths of the members of the committee appointed to hear and judge of the appeal, and present on the occasion, do

not affect the merits of the case, shall not necessarily operate to influence the decision of the committee. 1806.—1813.—1815.—1821.—1822.—1833.—1861.

Appeals from Ireland. The Friends of Ireland, by a letter from their last National Meeting, and also by their representatives present, have earnestly requested to be excused from attending appeals against them to this meeting, except in matters of faith and principle, wherein they desire not to be excused; but, having urged many hardships and inconveniences which they apprehend must attend their following appeals in other cases, this meeting, upon solid and deliberate consideration of their request, in·much brotherly condescension agrees thereto, until some manifest inconvenience shall be found to arise from such exemption. 1760.

Scotland. In consequence of the local circumstances of Friends in Scotland, several variations in the foregoing rules have been adopted, as applicable to appeals within the General Meeting for Scotland, and from thence to this meeting. The rules thus varied are to be found in the last or third edition of this work, (pp. 16 to 21) except that the first sentence in Rule 12 (p. 20) is now omitted, and that Rule 44 (in present edition) is made applicable to such appeals. 1833.—1861.

SECTION XX.—TRUST PROPERTY.

Registry of places of worship. THE registration of places of religious worship in England is now regulated by the Act 18 and 19 Vict., c. 81; and forms of certificate, for the purpose of effecting the registration of our meeting-houses under this Act, may be obtained (without payment) upon application to the Superintendent Registrar of births, deaths and marriages for the district in which the meeting-house is situated.

Such certificate, when properly filled up, is to be delivered in duplicate (accompanied by the payment of a fee of 2s. 6d.) to the Superintendent Registrar, for transmission to the Registrar-General, who, after recording the same, will return one copy to be delivered to the certifying party. A certificate of registry under the seal of the General Register Office, may be afterwards obtained from the Registrar-General, on payment of a fee of 2s. 6d. And such certificate is to be received in any Court as evidence of the facts therein mentioned.

Whenever any freehold, copyhold, or leasehold property is newly acquired for meeting-houses or burial-grounds, or for the benefit of Quarterly, Monthly, Preparative, or other Meetings, or for any other charitable purpose under the care of Friends, the trusts should be declared, either in the deed or instrument of conveyance,* or in a contemporaneous separate deed or instrument; and on every such new acquisition, *whether by purchase or gift,* either the conveyance or such separate deed or instrument should be sealed and delivered by the conveying party in the presence of two credible witnesses, and enrolled in Chancery within six calendar months after the making of the conveyance. If these formalities are not complied with, the conveyance will be void. See 9 Geo. II., c. 36; 24 Vic., c. 9. Conveyance of Trust Property.

Whenever an appointment of new trustees of any real or personal property belonging to, or under the direction or care of, a Quarterly, Monthly, Preparative or other Meeting, may become desirable, either from reduction of the existing trustees, who are solvent members of our Society and resident within the United Kingdom, to two, or from other circumstances, it is recommended that such appointment be speedily made, and the trust property legally transferred accordingly. Of course, this recommendation is not to interfere with any special provision for appointing trustees, made at the original creation of the trust. Change of Trustees.

* Forms applicable to the conveyance of freehold, copyhold, and leasehold property respectively, were printed in the third edition of the "Rules or Discipline, &c.," pp. 280 to 283; and are now printed separately, and kept by the Recording Clerk in London, for the use of Friends.

In transfers to new trustees, the forms referred to in the note (p. 233) may, in general be used. But where there has been any previous declaration of trust, *especial* care should be taken not in any way to alter the trust. In these cases the forms must only be followed as far as the circumstances will properly admit.

The formalities of enrolment and attestation, above pointed out, are not considered necessary on transfers to new trustees.

Custody of Deeds and Records of Trusts. Care is to be particularly taken that all title-deeds and writings relating to meeting-houses, burial-grounds and trust property of any kind, held for the use of any part of the Society, as well as all deeds and records relative to donations and legacies, be deposited in a place of security, free from damp, and from danger by fire; and that the custody of them be entrusted to two or more friends appointed for the purpose. It is suggested that, where practicable or convenient, the title-deeds of such property situate within the limits of any one Quarterly Meeting, be deposited (under the direction of the said Meeting) in the most suitable and, as far as practicable, central place, combined with security; that it may be more generally known where they are to be met with.

Monthly Meetings are to take care that a correct account of the nature of all trusts, with the names of the trustees of such real or personal property as they are entrusted with or entitled to, be recorded in a book kept for that purpose; in which should be inserted the place of deposit of the title-deeds of such property. In all cases of legacies or donations, copies of the wills, or of the clauses of the wills, with the date of probate, and of the deeds of gift, are, as far as practicable, to be procured, and carefully recorded in the said book.

Accounts. Monthly Meetings are to exercise due care that all legacies and donations be properly secured and duly applied, according to the directions of the testators and donors: and, in order that the appropriation of these, as well as of all other trust funds under the care of Monthly Meetings, may be duly attended to, distinct accounts are to be regularly kept of the receipts and expenditure thereof; which accounts are to be annually examined by the Monthly Meeting, or a committee appointed by it, when the list of trustees is to be read over with reference to the advice given (in page 233) as to the appointment of new trustees.

Monthly Meetings are to furnish the Quarterly Meetings, of which they form parts, with a brief account of the nature of the trusts and the names of the trustees of the real and personal property possessed by them; and also to transmit from time to time accounts of any additions thereto or alterations therein. Quarterly Meetings are to record such accounts in a proper book, with an index; and the names of the trustees are to be annually examined by or on behalf of the Quarterly Meeting. *Reports to superior meetings.*

Where the trust property belongs to, or is under the care of, Preparative or Particular meetings, the Monthly Meeting is to exercise a general superintendence over them, in conformity with the spirit of the foregoing provisions.

Where the trust property belongs to, or is under the care of, Quarterly Meetings, they are to conform to the foregoing regulations, so far as applicable to their case. But it is not expected that they should furnish to this meeting any account of the trusts, or trustees, unless specially required.

Where the trust property belongs to, or is under the care of, any distinct body or committee of friends, as in the case of schools and other charitable foundations, it is recommended that the spirit of the above rules should be attended to, and the provisions complied with, as far as the circumstances will permit.

Should any meeting be dissolved or cease to retain its distinct character, care should be taken that a minute be previously entered on its books, for regularly transferring the property under its direction to the superintendence of the meeting which may succeed it in authority, in all instances where the nature of the trust admits of this being done. This will be the case with every trust created agreeably to any of the forms referred to in the note (p. 233). 1794.—1832. *Case of a meeting dissolved.*

Scotland.   The statute of charitable uses, 9 Geo. II., c. 36, does not extend to Scotland; but the foregoing recommendations, which relate to the general care and oversight of trusts by Quarterly, Monthly, and other Meetings, are to be considered applicable to the General Meeting of Friends in Scotland and its subordinate meetings.

Charitable Trusts Acts.   All estates and property held by or under the care of any of our meetings, in trust for any charitable or public purpose, including property, the capital or income of which is held as part of the general funds of any meeting, are subject to the operation of the Charitable Trusts Acts,* which contain provisions to the following effect, viz. :—

1. The Trustees of every charity are required, on or before the 25th of Third Month, in every year, to transmit to the Charity Commissioners for England and Wales, in London, an account of the income and expenditure of the charity.†

2. The Charity Commissioners are authorized, upon application by the trustees of any charity, to sanction the leasing, sale, or exchange of any landed property belonging to such charity, upon such terms as the Commissioners may think fit, although no power of leasing, sale, or exchange may be vested in the Trustees.

3. The Charity Commissioners have also power, under certain restrictions, upon the application of the trustees, to make an effectual order for the establishment of a new scheme for the application or management of any charity.

> *₊* All places for religious worship duly certified, whilst they continue to be used as such, are exempted from the operation of the Charitable Trusts Acts. See 18 and 19 Vict. cap. 81, sec. 9.

* Statutes 16 and 17 Vict. cap. 137; 18 and 19 Vict. cap. 124; 23 and 24 Vict. cap. 136.

† Printed forms for making out these accounts, so far as regards charities under the care of any of our meetings, may be obtained from the Recording Clerk, at 86 Houndsditch, London. And it is advised that the same, when filled up, be sent to him for transmission to the commissioners, on or before the 1st of Third Month, in every year.

FINALLY, friends, collectively and individually, farewell! May all our meetings be held as in the immediate presence of the Heavenly President. May the aged in Christ be encouraged to keep the word of his patience, maintaining their watch, as servants in waiting; knowing Him, amidst the infirmities of their declining years, to lift them above every wave of discouragement, with the sweet assurance that their redemption draweth nigh. May the middle-aged be stirred up to continued diligence. calling often to remembrance the days of their early visitations and the vows of their espousals; and especially guarding against the benumbing, deadening influence of the earthly mind. Now is your time, dear friends, to labour, and to prove your faithfulness to your Lord; let not the sun go down upon you before your work is done. And for you, beloved younger friends, who have enjoyed many privileges both in your training and in your education, greatly do we desire that you may be encouraged to devote yourselves with all earnestness to the service of your Lord and Redeemer, and that all that you have, and all that you are, may be sanctified to his use. And in the end, in the Lord's unmerited mercy, may it be given to all, of every age and condition, through heartfelt subjection to the powerful work of redeeming love, to have their part in the unspeakable blessedness of them that enter in through the gates into the city of God, to go no more out for ever. 1799. P. E.—1857. P. E.

INDEX.

₊ *The large capitals denote the headings of chapters, the smaller capitals the headings of sections.*

Acceptance of Certificates of Removal............................... 216
Accounts, Advice on keeping clear 90, 92, 154
ADVICES, GENERAL 165
Advices to Ministers and Elders 182
AFFAIRS OF LIFE, ADVICE RELATING TO...................... 86
Affairs, Advice on the frequent inspection of, &c. 90, 154
AFFIRMATIONS 118, 119
AMUSEMENTS AND RECREATIONS 97
APPEALS 221
 to Quarterly Meetings 221
 to Yearly Meeting............ 225
 from Ireland 232
 from Scotland 232
 General Regulations......... 230
ARBITRATION 217
 General Regulations......... 217
 Mode of conducting 220
AUSTRALIAN MEETINGS FOR DISCIPLINE 153

BIRTHS AND DEATHS RECORDING OF 208
Births, Notice of, to Registrar . 209
Birth-notes, Form of................ 209
BOOKS AND READING 101
Books, Printing and Distribution of 189
BURIALS AND MOURNING HABITS 127

Burial-orders, Form of............. 211
 notes, Form of 211
Burials, Notification of............ 212
 of non-members 127

CARE OF THE POOR 191
Certificates of removal............ 214
 of marriage 198
Children, Scriptural Instruction of 31, 32, 33, 69, 75
CHRISTIAN DOCTRINE 1
 PRACTICE 22
 DISCIPLINE ... 129
CIVIL GOVERNMENT................ 120
Commercial travellers 68, 79
Correspondence with members abroad 155
COUNSEL, GENERAL CHRISTIAN 42

Days and Months, names of...... 48
Death, Punishment of 123, 124
Delinquencies, Mode of dealing with 146
Detraction......................... 55, 56
DISCIPLINE, HISTORICAL SKETCH OF 129
DISCIPLINE, COUNSEL IN RELATION TO MEETINGS FOR 160
Distraints, Accounts of, to be applied for annually............ 154
Doctrine, unsound, how to be dealt with 147

ECCLESIASTICAL DEMANDS 104
Efforts for the spiritual benefit
 of others......... 38, 39, 40, 41, 62
Elders, duties, appointment and
 displacement of.................. 153
Elections, public 120
EMIGRANTS, ADVICE TO 96
EMPLOYERS, COUNSEL TO......... 76
Executors and Administrators . 88

Families visiting, by appoint-
 ment 142, 154
FASTS AND REJOICINGS, NA-
 TIONAL 125
Field Sports 97
FIRST DAYS, RIGHT OCCUPA-
 TION OF............................ 103
Forgiveness of Injuries......... 56, 57

GENERAL CHRISTIAN COUNSEL . 42
GIFTS AND SERVICES FOR BENE-
 FIT OF OTHERS 37
Gravestones 127
Guernsey and Jersey, Expenses
 relating to 191

HEADS OF FAMILIES, COUNSEL
 TO 66
Heathen, Condition of 38
HISTORICAL SKETCH OF DISCI-
 PLINE............................. 129

Insolvency, Advices and Rules
 relating to......... 89, 90, 148, 149
Intemperance 49, 50, 53

LIBERALITY AND BENEVOLENCE,
 EXHORTATIONS TO 61
Libraries, Care of 154
Lists of Members 145
  Non-members 145
LOVE AND UNITY, EXHORTA-
 TIONS TO 55

Magistrate, Office of......... 122, 123
MARRIAGE, ADVICE RELATING
 TO 83

MARRIAGE REGULATIONS 193
 when parties are members
  of same Monthly Meeting 194
 when members of different
  Monthly Meetings......... 196
 General Regulations......... 197
 when one or both parties not
  members 200
 Registration 201
Marriages contrary to rules...... 194
MEETINGS FOR PUBLIC WORSHIP 22
Meetings for Worship, establish-
 ment or discontinuance of ... 142
  attending small, 142,
    144, 162
  habitual neglect of, 148
MEETINGS FOR DISCIPLINE,
 COUNSEL RELATING TO 160
MEETING FOR SUFFERINGS ... 184
 Constitution of 185
 Duties entrusted to 187
Meeting-houses, Lending of...... 144
  Registry of...... 232
Membership 144
Ministers, Acknowledgment of.. 150
  Disunity with 151
  Certificates for Travel-
   ling............... 143, 151
  Companions to... 182, 188
  Travelling expenses
    152, 190
  from America ...180, 189
MINISTERS AND ELDERS AND
 THEIR MEETINGS 178
  Local Meetings............... 178
  Quarterly Meetings 178
  Yearly Meeting............... 179
  Morning Meeting 180
  Counsel 181
  Advices 182
  Queries 184
MINISTRY, ADVICE RELATING TO 63
MODERATION AND SELF-DENIAL,
 EXHORTATIONS TO 47
MONTHLY MEETINGS 143
 Division and junction 143
 Care of small meetings...... 144

MONTHLY MEETINGS—(contd.)
   Lending Meeting-houses ... 144
   Membership 144
   Non-members 145
   Delinquencies 146
   Overseers 149
   Ministers 150
   Testimonies 152
   Elders 153
   Appointments, various 154
   Libraries 154
   Correspondence with members abroad 155
Morning Meeting of Ministers and Elders..................... 180
Mourning habits 127
Municipal offices 122
Music, Study and Practice of
                    98, 99, 100

NATIONAL STOCK................... 189
   Special objects 190
   General objects............... 191
   Audit 141
Non-members..................145, 174

OATHS 118
Offices, Civil 121
Overseers 149
OVERSIGHT 171
   General counsel relating to 171
   Non-members 174
   Junior members 175

Parliament, Applications to, affecting Friends................. 187
PARENTS AND HEADS OF FAMILIES, COUNSEL TO............ 66
Plainness in apparel, &c.
              47, 48, 50, 51, 52
POOR, CARE OF THE............... 191
PRAYER AND PRIVATE RETIREMENT 28
PREPARATIVE MEETINGS.......... 155
Punishment of death 123, 124

QUARTERLY MEETINGS........... 142
   Care of subordinate meetings 142
   Concerns of Ministers 143
QUERIES 167
   General Directions 168
   Men's........................... 168
   Women's 170
   Ministers and Elders' 184

READING THE HOLY SCRIPTURES 31
READING AND BOOKS............ 101
RECORDING OF BIRTHS AND DEATHS 208
   Births........................... 209
   Deaths 210
RECREATIONS AND AMUSEMENTS 97
Registration of Marriages 201
   Births 209
   Deaths........................... 210
Registering Officer for Marriages 205
REJOICINGS AND FASTS, NATIONAL 125
REMOVALS.......................... 213
   Counsel 213
   Regulations 214
   Certificates 214
RETIREMENT AND PRAYER...... 28

SCRIPTURES, ON READING THE 31
SIMPLICITY, MODERATION, AND SELF-DENIAL..................... 47
SLAVERY AND SLAVE-TRADE ... 113
Spirituous liquors, Dealing in ... 92

Testimonies concerning deceased Friends 152
Travelling in foreign countries... 99
TRUST PROPERTY................. 232
   Registry of places of worship 232
   Conveyance of trust property 233
   Change of trustees 233
   Custody of deeds and records 234
   Accounts 234

TRUST PROPERTY—(contd.)
    Reports to superior meetings 235
    Case of a meeting dissolved 235
    Scotland........................ 236
    Charitable Trusts Acts...... 236
Typical observances.........14, 16, 45

WAR 108
    Obtaining profit by 109
    Hiring substitutes............ 109
    Rifle and Volunteer Corps... 112

Wills, Counsel relating to...... 87, 88
WOMEN'S MEETINGS 156
    Establishment of 156
    Duties devolving on......... 157
    Queries 170
WORSHIP, MEETINGS FOR 22

YEARLY MEETING.................. 139
    Object and character 139
    Constitution 140
    Regulations 140
YOUNG, COUNSEL TO THE 77

RICHARD BARRETT, Printer, 13, Mark Lane, London.

www.ingramcontent.com/pod-product-compliance
Lightning Source LLC
Chambersburg PA
CBHW020800230426
43666CB00007B/779